The Failure of the Word

The Protagonist as
Lawyer in
Modern Fiction

The Failure of the Word

RICHARD H. WEISBERG

Yale University Press
New Haven and London

Designed by James J. Johnson
and set in Goudy Old Style type.
Printed in the United States of America by
BookCrafters, Inc., Chelsea, Michigan.

---

*The paper in this book meets the guidelines for permanence
and durability of the Committee on Production Guidelines
for Book Longevity of the Council on Library Resources.*

Library of Congress Cataloging in Publication Data

Weisberg, Richard H., 1944–
    The failure of the word.

    Includes index.
    1. Lawyers in literature. 2. Fiction—19th century—
History and criticism. 3. Fiction—20th century—
History and criticism. I. Title.
PN3426.L37W44   1984   809.3′ 9352344   84–2309
ISBN 0–300–03211–0

10 9 8 7 6 5 4 3 2 1

For the Joyful Scientists,
Cheryl,
Danny, Benno, and Sam

Ye shall do no unrighteousness in judgment. . . . Thou shalt not avenge nor bear any grudge against the children of thy people, but thou shalt love thy neighbor as thyself.

—Leviticus 19:15, 18

Contents

Preface

The following chapters deal intensively with eight major works of
modern fiction. In each of these texts, a central figure—usually the
protagonist—employs complex narrative structures to avoid relatively simple central realities. These protagonists prefer the safety of
wordiness to the risks of spontaneous human interaction. Highly
formalized language mediates between them and the exigencies of
life, protecting but also gradually distancing them from the sources
of positive and creative action. They cannot accept love, because of
its unpredictability and its nonverbal essence; nor can they fulfill
the expectations of social responsibility thrust upon them by internal or external factors.

One of the oldest literary paradigms, that of insult and revenge, structures all of these highly modern texts. But, beginning
with *Notes from Underground*, the "insult" has been reduced to a figment of the protagonist's overheated verbal imagination. Harking
back to Hamlet, but lacking the need for vengeance revealed to that
protagonist, these seminal characters use words not only to avoid
disturbing realities but also to create them. Schahabarim, Flaubert's
articulate priest, nurtures and tantalizes Salammbô through language; when she fulfills his verbal imaginings through action, he
feels insulted and resents her bitterly. Indeed, within that exotic
novel generally, inactive, wordy characters come to dominate and
control warriors and princesses. Yet, even in their subservient state,
the less articulate beings threaten the verbalizer's formalistic world

view and, like the Underground Man regarding the soldiers and pretty women of St. Petersburg, he envies and despises them at one and the same time.

As the modern novel developed from these texts of the early 1860s, authors explicitly set the values of the verbalizer into the framework of courts and lawyers. Recognizing that heroism and religious faith were dying absolutes, writers sensed that legality was emerging as the controlling principle in modern society. But law, being no more than a relativistic *method* of ordering reality through language, exhibited the same stance toward spontaneous life as had the philosophical or priestly forms of earlier texts. The protagonist as lawyer surfaced, talking, writing, and ultimately reorganizing realities which would otherwise be both fascinating and threatening. Flaubert's great novel *L'Education sentimentale* (1869) is given over to lawyers. And *Crime and Punishment* (1866), Dostoevski's next long narrative after *Notes from Underground*, pits against each other—and the world—the complementary perspectives of a law student and a lawyer. The youthful Raskolnikov takes his article on crime one step beyond the "new word" he is proposing; he actually commits murder. This incursion upon the usual structure of these legalistic texts was never to be repeated by Dostoevski. Never again does the protagonist as lawyer act (however "wrongly"); he only generates, through language, resentful ideas in others. The lawyer, Porfiry Petrovich, initiates this progression in *Crime and Punishment* by eventually coercing Raskolnikov into confession and moral conformity.

In *The Brothers Karamazov* and *Billy Budd, Sailor*, texts written or completed during the 1880s, the now fully developed verbal character uses the language of the law to control a less articulate, more popular, and basically well-adjusted criminal defendant. The earlier, private "revenge" against the imagined "insult" of such positive beings has developed into a public, communal vengeance against threatening, nonconforming types. The complexities of the legal outlook, now institutionalized in the courts of law, distort reality and result in the avoidance of justice.

In the twentieth century, history tragically confirmed the literary vision of philosophical, priestly, and legal formalism in the service of resentful values. Innocent victims paid the price. The theme reached its pinnacle in two works about law by Camus, *The Stranger*

(1942) and *The Fall* (1956). In the former, lawyers interfere with the reality of a character whose moral system dramatically differs from their own (particularly in his preferring history and materiality to wordiness and metaphysics). In *The Fall*, a Parisian lawyer, whose verbal trickiness threatens his attempt at self-understanding, comes to represent French culture itself. Twelve years after Vichy, Camus' barely penitent attorney admits the cosmic consequences of a society's empty elegance. The word had failed not because of any intrinsic unworthiness but rather its incapacity to support, purely on its own, either an individual or a culture. The legalistic, verbal reorganization of reality may have helped to resolve disputes in courtrooms; but as a means of organizing society, it could never hope to replace the moribund substantive values of Christianity or individual heroism. When European Fascism introduced actual (as opposed to imagined) insults, the Hamlet paradigm of structured speech as a replacement for legitimate action took on new meanings in the mouths of fictional lawyers.

This book situates the source of modern literature's holocaustic predictions and postmortems in the futile wordiness of legalistic protagonists. Lacking spiritual substance, these figures exhibit all the characteristics of modern Western culture's own deepest malaise: perpetual rancor, or *ressentiment*. As within the culture itself, however, the gloss of articulate speech and formalistic elegance protects these resentful verbalizers from the careful scrutiny of others. In this way, they manage to gain influence and thus to expand their disguised rage outward until finally nothing of substance is permitted to survive.

The centrality of legalistic ressentiment to modern fiction becomes clear as we move through the lives and works of the four writers treated here. After exploring, in part 1, the relationship of resentment to art and law in the nineteenth and twentieth centuries, I analyze the graphic descriptions of the malaise in the great intellectual protagonists of Dostoevski and Flaubert. Parts 2 and 3 suggest that the wordy characters' spiritual problems devolve immediately from those of their prolix creators. For Dostoevski, the act of narrative writing totally contradicted the Christian values of self-lessness and simplicity in which he purported to believe. For Flaubert, the exigencies of literary art directly conflicted with his desires to be heroic, spontaneous, and politically and sexually forceful.

Their narrative predilections gave little peace to either, nor any sense of a life well lived. No wonder they produced articulate characters who reflect and convey their own ambivalent approach to organized speech, and whose narrative abilities, divorced from any positive ethic, wreak havoc on the lives of others. But Dostoevski and Flaubert wished to expand their observations about language beyond self-critique; thus they increasingly placed resentful words in the mouths of legalistic figures in roles of public responsibility.

Albert Camus, whose first and last great novellas about law are examined in chapter 7, lived to see France wallow in words and nearly destroy itself through long-suppressed rancor. His task was to convey, always through the legal thematic he inherited from Dostoevski and Flaubert, the awful disjunction of ethics and language which had infected large parts of the Continent. However contemporary Camus' beliefs, his narrative art resonates with the nineteenth-century European theme of legalized ressentiment, and it is fitting that his law-related works be treated in this context.

In part 4, the book takes a half-step back in time and a giant leap westward to approach its central text, *Billy Budd, Sailor.* All the threads of this study meet in that American masterpiece. As Captain Vere, combining roles of witness, prosecutor, judge, and executioner, contrives to hang the heroic Billy, he also projects into power the false use of words and destroys for subjective reasons all that had been sacred on his ship. Ressentiment, through the joint creative deed of Vere and his implied ally Claggart, manages to prevail and to become law. But glimmerings of the ethical and the heroic survive in Melville's tale, as they do in history, and a restoration of meaningful language may accompany their emergence.

This text does not avoid making connections, where merited, between narrative and real violence. And it suggests, finally, the necessity of recognizing that verbal formalism and reactive hatred are the principal legacy of the old value system, which had always implicitly been corrupted by them. The resented "others," those practicing a less evasive approach to self and history, have survived the unprecedented hysteria of that moribund system; their alternative is commended to us by the courageous self-chastisement of these eight novels.

Acknowledgments

The intellectual and emotional roots of this book run far and deep, and many who have nurtured its growth deserve to be mentioned. During my graduate studies at Cornell University in the mid-sixties, I was fortunate to be taught, there and in Zurich, by Geoffrey Hartman, whose influence is indelible. The revered Paul de Man was my advisor for a master's thesis on Mallarmé. That work in turn grew out of an undergraduate paper I had written at Brandeis University for Professor W. Wolfgang Holdheim, and, when he arrived at Cornell in 1969, it was natural to begin work with him again, this time on the prose subjects treated here. He was instrumental in setting me on the path to this book. Other teachers at Cornell whose guidance was invaluable were Professors Eric A. Blackall, George Gibian, David I. Grossvogel, and Neil Hertz.

The collegiality on the faculty of the University of Chicago of people like Bruce Morrissette, Clayton Koelb, and Edward Wasiolek further inspired me, and it was a difficult decision to leave those environs for the practice of law. But eventually that choice lent flavor to my approach to modern fiction, so much of which is bound up in law, justice, and investigatory narrative. As I worked through the cross-disciplinary aspects of my project, I received sustenance from wonderful teachers and friends in the field of law: David Haber, Fowler Hamilton, John Hazard, Benno Schmidt, Jr., J. Allen Smith, and Irving Younger, and the late Harry Kalven and Max Rheinstein.

As the manuscript grew into its final form, two colleagues who had followed its progress for a half dozen years played a central role: Professor Robert Cover of the Yale Law School and Professor Arthur J. Jacobson of the Cardozo Law School. These men patiently helped me through a number of wrong turns; while they may not agree with everything in this book, they kept me true to my own vision.

To my research assistants and students through the years goes my very special gratitude. As I learned from them and received a salary at the same time, I fully came to realize the privileged position of the professor. At the risk of omitting many who helped me with this book, I must especially mention Michael Braff, Bruce Cohen, S. Deon Henson, Bobbi Hurwitz, Robert S. Mulvey, and Daniel F. Tritter, law students at Cardozo; and Marguerite Allen, Diane Ignashev, T. C. Ayers, and Sue Ann Weinberg, graduate scholars at the University of Chicago and at Columbia. The technical assistance of Helene Gross and her team of secretaries at Cardozo was (as we say in law) a cause-in-fact of this book, and I thank them warmly.

To friends and relatives who have seen me through the ups and downs of this process and also have provided specific substantive and stylistic suggestions, I can only try to indicate the extent of my feelings: to my wife, Cheryl, my brother, David, and my good friends Peter Alscher and Richard Neugebauer goes much more than my thanks.

Two full-year grants gave me the time to develop the major lines of this project: a research fellowship from the National Endowment for the Humanities and a fellowship from the Society for the Humanities of Cornell University.

Finally, I would like to thank the editors of the journals in which parts of this book were originally published: *American Imago, Columbia Law Review, Modern Fiction Studies, New York University Law Review, Northwestern Law Review,* and *Rutgers Law Review.* Special thanks goes to my colleague Professor Jean-Pierre Barricelli, with whom I had the great pleasure of coauthoring the chapter "Literature and the Law" in *The Interrelations of Literature* (New York: Modern Language Association, 1982).

The Failure of the Word

Introduction

In 1943, several months after the French police had rounded up tens of thousands of Jews for deportation to the East, a Parisian lawyer named Joseph Haennig published a learned treatise on the definition of a Jew. Citing favorably to several Nazi judicial decisions, Haennig skillfully argued that the burden of proof on Jewishness should rest with the state in the equivocal case of an individual with only two Jewish grandparents. Some French courts under Vichy had already exceeded the Germans in their vigorous application of the racial laws; Haennig used his lawyerlike talents not to challenge the existence of those laws, but rather to have them "humanely" interpreted.

Joseph Haennig was clearly not a villain. He was one of literally scores of lawyers soberly debating the fateful legalisms of "racial definition." Earlier in the Occupation, he had defended a Jew who was facing incarceration and death for a "political" crime. Now he was hoping to lighten the burden of "persons of mixed blood" who sought to avoid the legal status of Jew. Yet Haennig's behavior, taken as a paradigm, raises dreadful questions, more potentially catastrophic in their resolution than those posed by the leaders of European repression and racism. For in Joseph Haennig's avoidance of central realities, in his willingness to create language in the service of a legal superstructure that he knew had just swept thousands of Frenchmen into the camps, he exhibited the same fatal evasiveness that marked the larger culture and its main institutions. Good people and bad had accepted the unacceptable. Words, once strident and propagandistic, now gently advanced the monstrous cause by making it debatable. The basic premise of racism implicitly accepted, the casuistry of legal rhetoric could be employed as easily as if the issue involved a real estate transaction or an auto accident.

A century or so earlier, American lawyers and legislators had also failed to address directly a rotten structure of racism. The curious aspect of the Haennig syndrome, however, was its willingness to accept such a structure without any overt historical or economic reason. France reveled in the racial possibilities brought onto its territory by the foreign conquerors. The reaction of French culture under the Occupation crystallized the matter as a pan-European dilemma; Western egalitarianism and liberality embraced racial ostracism and ultimate genocide more effusively than had the still seemingly neobarbarous and deeply romantic Germanic states. The implications for all Western culture, including America, were undeniable.

For the French literary community, too, the presence of the Hun liberated volumes of words, published and spoken. Again, too, its virulent anti-Semites, such as Céline and Brasillach, would never be seen as representative of French culture once the madness ended. But the day-to-day collaboration of less strident authors and publishers, largely undisturbed by the spectacle of the 1942 round-ups or the ostracism of non-Aryan artists, created ambiguities more puzzling still than those within the texts they were generating. Simone de Beauvoir, her career flourishing, had a popular program (politically neutral, she would say) on Vichy radio. The terror in the streets was unfelt by those fortunate enough to attend the acclaimed Paris openings of Sartre's Les Mouches and Huis clos.

Law and literature, the mainstays of modern, standardized European language, bent and ultimately broke under the Fascist boot. Endless and serious debate poured forth on issues that mainstream European culture would earlier have declared eccentric and odious. Many careers in law and the arts continued unchanged; quite a few thrived.

What Friedrich Nietzsche had foreseen, a Europe peopled by the violently resentful and sick unto death, came to pass under the eyes and ears, and with the assistance, of men and women of the highest verbal talent. Their participation, passive or active, has implicated for generations to come the very languages and organizing structures of their various pursuits. Haennig's piece, published in the traditional reporter of French law and jurisprudence (see appendix), renders problematical the everyday rhetoric of his profession. And Sartre's postwar philosophy (like Heidegger's prewar *Sein und Zeit*) seems tarnished by his Occupational career comforts.

Quite beyond the individuals and even the specific institutions lies the problematic of European values—their overturning through holocaust and what will replace them. Dostoevski, like his admirer Nietzsche, was asking these questions two generations before the fall. He, too, recognized a Christendom in severe distress, though from the perspective of a culture that still hoped to find its own, non-Western values. Through his intellectual and legal characters, Dostoevski predicted the violent power of misdirected words, the cruelty of language and forms generated by spiritually empty individuals.

Indeed, across several national cultures, and within the writings of otherwise quite varied novelists, modern literature during the years prior to and including the Second World War reveals a strongly self-critical interest in verbal falsification. Protagonists with otherwise impeccable intellectual credentials strive to endow reality with narrative meaning, but with remarkable consistency their attempts end in failure. Whatever their personal fates in these works, the wordy protagonists, or evocations of them in less central characters, leave behind them a series of obfuscating or even mendacious verbal structures.

Ivan Karamazov, like the Underground Man who is his literary progenitor, espouses a philosophy of freedom from all forms while displaying a constraining inability to participate positively in the actual human situations with which he is faced. Nikolai Nelyudov, Ippolit Kirillovich, and Fetyukovich, the verbally gifted lawyers in *The Brothers Karamazov*, construct a theory of the murder of Fyodor Karamazov that is logically and artistically compelling but thoroughly false. In a similar manner, a refusal to grasp essential data ironically distorts the reasoning of examining magistrate and prosecutor in *The Stranger* as they face the unstructured, noncognitive and sensual reality of Meursault. More overtly, Jean Baptiste Clamence, Camus' most Dostoevskian character and an attorney, warns us not to believe anything he says; by training and by inclination he uses language and form to deceive his audience and himself. And Melville's Captain Vere, acting as a kind of prosecutor, adopts what he pretends are the "forms, measured forms" of the law and falls into a series of legal and moral errors which only his articulateness succeeds in hiding from his overawed listeners.

Yet almost all of these characters have won the admiration of those who contemplate their dilemmas. Sharing their literary sensitivities, even the most careful reader sometimes overlooks the fundamental negativity of these characters, or, where he perceives it, seeks to apologize for it. The reader may choose even to condone in such figures the same narrative predilection which attracts him to the act of reading itself; certainly the quality of articulateness almost always assures its possessor a sympathetic rather than a harsh critical reception.

The ability to speak and write well, however, often combines in the verbal protagonist with a tendency toward self-consciousness. The excessive awareness of the workings of his own cognitive apparatus in turn stems from a generalized urge to overanalyze all phenomena, usually beyond the limits necessary for accurate perception or action. In each of the representative texts under discussion the verbalizer's "legalistic proclivity," as I call it, comes into conflict with the reality that evolves around him, and he fails to deal truthfully with that reality. Were the failure merely a personal one, it would hardly be fatal to an ultimately sympathetic appraisal of the verbal mode. Lambert Strether, for example, although he alone among the characters in *The Ambassadors* substitutes the complexities of language for the comprehension of essentially simple realities, harms no one except himself and actually enriches the existence of many around him. But, as opposed to the Jamesian version of the narrative imagination, the novelistic mainstream perceives and emphasizes the harsh communal consequences of the verbal protagonist's failings. Such novels are structured so that prolix individuals assume positions of significant power over their essentially nonverbal opposites. The latter implicitly represent a variety of positive qualities inaccessible to the verbalizer and so inspire in the articulate character an often repressed bitterness which eventually finds expression through the indirect medium of a significant narrative structure.

Legal procedures or philosophical formulations satisfy the verbalizer's compulsions both to build a narrative structure around or against the spontaneous flow of reality and to take vengeance on those positive characters who have chosen to participate nonverbally in the magnificent formlessness of life. Legal, philosophical, and artistic ressentiment as a negative force in society and history becomes, coextensively with the depiction of the legalistic proclivity, a major concern of these novels.

Not surprisingly, then, many great writers have looked to the law as a fitting milieu in which to place their articulate characters. These writers indicate that the seemingly cool outward forms of legal procedures often mask the bitter subjective aims of those who employ them—aims which are, in Melville's words, "never declared," and which can only be discovered through careful analysis. Lawyers in general, however, both attract and repulse writers; targets of biting caricature and sarcasm on the one hand, they also metaphorize the thematic, formal, and even personal concerns of the literary artist who lashes out at them. When Hamlet chastises the skull of his hypothetical lawyer, he establishes the model for subsequent uses of legal figures by "literary men." He satirizes the lawyer's "quiddities and quillities," but his gruesome polemic's attack on clever language most convincingly applies to his own troubling case.

The legalistic campaign against a variety of criminal suspects, some totally innocent of the charges, others guilty of one transgression but actually tried for another, always results in a lengthy narrative statement by a prosecutorial protagonist. Since the fictional context of this statement has already provided—as real life rarely can—a "true" portrait of the anterior situation which the prosecutor is analyzing, the alert reader gradually detects the distortions and falsehoods which permit the prosecutor to fulfill certain self-interested ends. As when Ippolit Kirillovich brings all the force of his verbal talent to bear against Dmitri Karamazov (who is innocent of the parricide, but guilty of attracting Ippolit's wife), literary lawyers frequently seek to institutionalize their purely personal resentments.

In the same way, the "philosophers" in these books elevate to the status of narrative formulation an ethic of theoretical freedom from all structures, in order to disguise their inability to act positively in communal situations. Often the rest of the novel in which their philosophies are expounded reveals a specific insult to them which comes to dominate and determine the unreconciled verbalizer's every thought. Flaubert's highly articulate castrated Carthaginian priest, Schahabarim, faced with the noble appearance and unfettered sensuality of his pupil Salammbô, resentfully fills her ear with provocative notions to lead her astray. The Underground Man, having failed because of his overly self-conscious stance in every personal relationship he has encountered, attacks, through the medium of words, the essentially nonverbal approach to reality which brings fulfillment to others.

Thus, the confrontation of the reactive verbal formulator with specific examples of the active alternative mode most effectively dramatizes the self-critical problematic of modern literary procedures. The justice or injustice of the ordering agent's creative deed —the truth or falsehood of his narrative reaction to an already disclosed reality—emblematizes the efficacy or inefficacy of the novelistic mode itself. For whenever a lawyer's procedure or an intellectual's philosophy comes to center stage in a literary work, the writer at that precise point articulates an awareness of his own enterprise. Insofar as many verbal structures within modern novels distort the reality which they are supposedly grasping, those works take cognizance of the negative aspects of modern literary methods and meanings.

Were the novels discussed here atypical of the way the genre has developed over the past hundred years or so, their collective skepticism about the narrative mode could pass unremarked. But it seems fair to say that if comparative analysis lays bare a fundamental identity among such seminal individual works as these, then the revealed similarity probably strikes at the heart of novelistic meaning in the modern era.

Self-criticism, usually confined to private communication, becomes a public concern in the modern novel. It is as though the great literary artists of this troubled period in Western culture (whose works discussed here span a century of bloodletting and disruption, from 1862 to 1956) tacitly agreed that the complicity of narrative institutions in the trend toward communally condoned violence and injustice could only be exposed through the powerful medium of one of those very institutions. Law, philosophy, history, theology—conspirators in furthering the ascendancy of narrative structures over effective individual action—could not be counted upon to propagate a self-destructive dialectic.

Joseph Haennig's 1943 legal text, intended to "humanize" French law and Vichy by recommending the Nazi courts' interpretation of the anti-Jewish racial laws, leaves us gasping. But this text, generated by a verbally skillful and by no means evil man, would not have surprised those even more gifted creators of words whose works I am discussing. They knew that the chief spiritual underpinnings of Western culture had been rotting for centuries. Their greatest characters, intellectuals and lawyers, are also their most repressed and violent.

Unlike some of the wordy nihilists whose formulations fill their stories, however, these artists nonetheless direct their readers' vision to a positive model of existence. Arising from the ashes of the legalistic proclivity, the just individual makes an appearance in these works, if sometimes only by structural implication. Endowed with keen intelligence, this figure couples action with reason, a self-willed stance which also merits our present attention.

By the beginning of the nineteenth century, legal figures had already begun to populate the novel in significant numbers. Cooper, Scott, and Hawthorne rarely missed a chance to create an attorney, a trial scene, or a legalistic plot. Balzac's *Comédie humaine* reads like a French version of Martindale-Hubbel. And Dickens' lawyers captivated audiences, inspiring them alternately with laughter and fear. The prototype of the genre just prior to our period of concern, Mr. Jaggers (in *Great Expectations*), controls the lives of all the more central figures in the book.

But the true flowering of the protagonist as lawyer took place only after the generations of these great novelists. European culture settled into a reflective state. Capitalism, industry, and their fellow-servant law thrived and became more complex. The mimetic artist took a step back and began to perceive law and legalistic reasoning all around him. The time-honored absolutes of Christian religion on the one hand, and individual heroism on the other, retreated from his field of vision. Napoleon was gone, but his codes of law lived after him, spreading far and wide. Ecclesiastical tradition ceded to secular legality; one turned to an attorney for guidance, not a priest. Lawyers, or intellectuals employing lawyerlike modes of interaction and decision making, became more than catalysts for central characters' destinies; they became the "heroes" of late nineteenth-century fiction.

The characters were changing in these works. So, too, were the plots. More and more often, whole novels follow the paradigm of perceived insult, thwarted vengeance, and misdirected violence. Protagonists no longer respond simply and directly to real or imagined acts of injustice. Because of their nagging sense of futility, they make guiltless others the butt of their sometimes cool but nonetheless fatal eloquence. When the "nonlawyers" under their influence try to lead independent and harmonious lives, these resentful verbalizers bring their victims back under sway, perhaps even inspiring them to perpetrate physical violence upon themselves or others.

The protagonist as lawyer, with or without his *juris doctor*, became threatening precisely through his inability to take more than a formalized vengeance upon his perceived enemies. Given this interest in the paradigm of futile revenge seeking by verbally gifted protagonists, it is not surprising that late nineteenth-century fiction reacquainted itself with that first great literary lawyer, Hamlet. (Mallarmé, in the most hermetic and verbal contemporary climate, French symbolist poetry, made of Hamlet a virtual role model.) For the careful Danish prince's books and forms must inform any approach to more recent wordy protagonists faced with a puzzling and unjust world.

Hamlet's procedures are those of a lawyer, not an aristocrat or hero. Everything must be proven to him, even the self-evident. Whatever his intuitive response, however "prophetic" he knows his own soul to be, endless cross-examination and prolix argumentation become his mode. Urged to respond directly to the ghost's account of Claudius' villainy, he fatally dispels his impulse to do so. As the ghost departs in act 1, Hamlet moves from rhetorically noble will ("And thy commandment all alone shall live / within the book and volume of my brain, / Unmixed with baser matter") to equivocal legalizing ("meet it is I set it down. / That one may smile, and smile, and be a villain"). Throughout the play, however, Hamlet never forgets that in the face of known evil, only the first, "unmixed" response is correct. Thus, in act 4, he continues to soliloquize about the catastrophic baseness of "thinking too precisely on th' event." A noble thought (the ghost's "commandment" to avenge the regicidal injustice), once "quartered," not only loses its primal force but also leads to misdirected verbal violence, cowardice, and, paradoxically, needless destruction. Hamlet's imagery in the "How all occasions" soliloquy brilliantly evokes the play's innocent bloodletting. His legalistic delays result in the deaths of six relatively blameless bystanders. Thus at graveside Hamlet hypothesizes that the skull in which useless forms prevailed belonged to an equivocating, dissembling lawyer. His patient friend Horatio surely knows that the satiric thrust—always Hamlet's surrogate for the physical response the situation requires—rebounds upon the prince himself. Injustice has endured and even expanded through the verbal predilection of the protagonist as lawyer.

Like Mallarmé's, our thoughts must leap back to Hamlet to fathom the *moral* enterprise of modern literary art. In a context of clear injustice, the noble example of his sensitivity wars with the ignoble effects of his wordy investigations. The modern novel, emphasizing law, brings to fruition this essential dialectic.

Egoism belongs to the nature of a distinguished soul. . . . If we were to look for a name for its feeling, it would say, "This is justice itself."
—Friedrich Nietzsche, Beyond Good and Evil

PART I   The Conflict between Ressentiment and Justice

I   The Disappearance of the Just

RESSENTIMENT IN NINETEENTH-CENTURY CULTURE

When an individual perceives injustice, all that has defined him as a person is likely to emerge. By saying that we cannot predict how we would act in such a situation, we admit that we do not know ourselves, while at the same time we try to deny the likelihood of such a confrontation. The novelists studied here refused to avoid self-awareness; they knew what they were, and through their effort we may hope to approach ourselves. They foresaw that the tender refinements of advanced culture would give way, in the late nineteenth and twentieth centuries, to mass injustice against that culture's least powerful and least verbal segments.

For these writers, whose art involved them in the intricacies of language, the use and misuse of words often become the essential element in the confrontation. Characters with harmonious, positive makeups, coupling a seemingly naive acceptance of absolute values with a genuine affection for other people, almost always are depicted as responding quickly, nonverbally, and effectively to evil. Characters with complex intellects tend to be more repressed and relativistic; their response is verbal, indirect, and equivocal—more likely to increase than to dispel the potential for violence within a given situation.

Yet the verbally gifted character, at the maturing of the realistic novel in the Anglo-American and Continental writers of the 1860s and 1880s, had reached center stage, not to depart until well after World War II. Flaubert's mediocre law student, Frédéric Moreau, Melville's pedantic Captain Vere, and Dostoevski's brilliant magistrate Porfiry Petrovich are the main progenitors of Camus' postwar Clamence, Faulkner's Gavin Stevens, and Solzhenitsyn's Soviet prosecutors and their dreaded Article 58. It becomes harder and harder, in this fictional milieu, to find one of those seemingly simplistic seekers of justice, much less to admire him unabashedly if he were to be uncovered (think of Billy Budd).

In the arcane complexities of modern law and philosophy, novelists were finding a structure of negativity, and a phenomenon that Friedrich Nietzsche was calling ressentiment. Not by coincidence, Flaubert uses the word in his earliest "autobiographical" novellas, and Camus later places it in the mouth of his fallen lawyer Clamence. Dostoevski dwells on the similar Russian notion of *zlost'* (the Underground Man's chief characteristic, and the spiritual disease that Father Zossima calls the antithesis of true Christian love), and Melville fills several provocative paragraphs of his last masterpiece with a significant excursus into John Claggart's peculiar "envy-antipathy."

Modern fiction nowhere expresses better its unity with modern philosophy than in the novelistic interplay of rancor and law. For all our current emphasis on Marxist and Freudian elements in literature, we find a truer source for the novel as a form, and as a medium of ideas, in Nietzsche's brilliant aphorisms about ressentiment. No phenomenon in recent fiction is as pervasive, none as intricately bound to an understanding of law and language in modern Western culture. We need to recall and revivify the Nietzschean influence, to drink in his iconoclasm, but also to savor the moral absolutism behind his aphoristic offerings.

As a chronic condition of lingering, unwanted dependence upon a person or a situation somehow seen as insulting, ressentiment finds fertile ground among reactive types with no firm sense of personal values. Envious of the graceful and harmonious existence of just individuals around him, the man of ressentiment at his most creative uses his gifts of pervasive observation and complex intellect to insinuate himself into power. Nietzsche traces the *origins* of ressentiment to what he calls the "Jewish priestly class," and to its reaction against classical, pagan values. He stresses, however, the present association between ressentiment and European gentile culture.[1] Distinguishing the latter from Judaism in general, the moral genealogist's opening aphorisms on ressentiment imbue the phrase "Jewish priestly class" with a precise historical sense:

But how did the Jews, on their part, feel about Rome? A thousand indications point to the answer. It is enough to read once more the Revelations of St. John, the most rabid outburst of vindictiveness [Rache] in all recorded history. (We ought to acknowledge the profound consistency of the Christian instinct in assigning this book of hatred and the most extravagantly doting of the Gospels to the same disciple.[2] There is a piece of truth hidden here, no matter how much literary skulduggery may have gone on.) The Romans were the strongest and most noble people who ever lived. Every vestige of them, every least inscription, is a sheer delight, provided we are able to read the spirit behind the writing. The Jews, on the contrary, were the priestly, rancorous nation [priesterliche Volk des Ressentiment] *par excellence*, though possessed of an unequaled ethical genius; we need only compare with them nations of comparable endowments, such as the Chinese or the Germans, to sense which occupies the first rank. Has the victory so far been gained by the Romans or by the Jews? But this is really an idle question. Remember who it is before whom one bows down, in Rome itself, as before the essence of all supreme values—and not only in Rome but over half of the globe, wherever man has grown tame or desires to grow tame: before three Jews and one Jewess (Jesus of Nazareth, the fisherman Peter, the rug weaver Paul, and Maria, the mother of that Jesus). This is very curious: Rome, without a doubt, has capitulated.[3]

Nietzsche traces the ressentiment prevalent in nineteenth-century society, which manifested itself virulently in the creation of certain novelistic types, to a specific group of Jews, the earliest Christians, whose entire ethic derived from a negative reaction to Roman values. Nietzsche's perhaps unduly harsh judgment (due in part to his great, if somewhat romantic, admiration for classical culture) does not extend to the older religion itself. The essential values of Judaism remain, for Nietzsche, entirely opposed to ressentiment:

The Old Testament is another story. I have the highest respect for that book. I find in it great men, a heroic landscape, and one of the rarest things on earth, the naiveté of a strong heart. What is more, I find a *people*. In the New Testament, on the other hand, I find nothing but petty sectarianism, a rococo of the spirit, abounding in curious scrollwork and intricate geometries and breathing the air of the conventicle; to say nothing of that

occasional whiff of bucolic mawkishness which is characteristic of the epoch (and the locale) and which is not so much Jewish as Hellenistic. Here
humility and braggadocio [Wichtigtuerei] are bedfellows; here we find stu-
pendous volubility of feeling; the trappings of passion without real passion;
an embarrassing amount of gesturing; obviously there is a lack of good
breeding all the way through. (*Genealogy* 3.22:281–82)

In the Jewish "Old Testament," the book of divine justice [von der gött-
lichen Gerechtigkeit], there are men and things and speeches in such a
grand style that Greek and Indic literature has nothing to equal them. One
stands in awe and reverence before these enormous remains of what man
once had been, and one has sad thoughts about ancient Asia and its tiny
promontory Europe which insists on distinguishing itself by way of "human
progress" from Asia. On the other hand: whoever is only a scrawny, tame,
domestic animal with the needs of a domestic animal (like our "cultured"
men of today, including the Christians of cultured Christendom), has
nothing to surprise nor distress him when he views these ruins. One's taste
for the Old Testament is a touchstone as to "great" and "small." Perhaps
the cultured man of today will find the New Testament, the book of grace,
much more in accordance with his heart. (It has much of the regular,
tender-hearted, stuffy odor of the devotee and the small soul.) To have
pasted this New Testament (a rococo taste in every sense) together into
one book with the Old Testament, and to call this the "Bible," "The
Book," is possibly the greatest recklessness and "sin against the Holy
Ghost" that literary Europe has on its conscience.[4]

And the Jews are beyond any doubt the strongest, toughest and purest race
now living in Europe; they know how to assert themselves in the midst of
the worst possible conditions (better, in fact, than under more favorable
ones). That they can do this is due to certain virtues of theirs, virtues
which others would like to label as vices nowadays. Above all, due to their
resolute faith, which need not be ashamed before "modern ideas"; they
change, *when* they change, in much the same fashion in which the Russian
Empire makes its conquests (an Empire which has lots of time and is not of
yesterday): according to the principle "As slowly as possible." A thinker
with the future of Europe on his conscience will count on the Jews in all his
calculations for the future, just as he counts on the Russians.[5]

These remarkable aphorisms indicate Nietzsche's recognition
that Judaism, especially in its sacred texts, but even in the context
of growing European oppression, evinces a single-minded and heroic allegiance to unchanging and ultimately powerful ethical con-

cepts. This resolute ethos Nietzsche equates with not only meta-physical, but also historical, principles. Foremost among these is the quest for temporal justice through a unified system of just laws. So the Jewish people affirm, by their very presence, the possibility of positive temporal action. Together with his consistent admiration for the classical man's spontaneous perception of just behavior, Nietzsche's aphorisms on the Jews help to identify one of the few absolutes in his epistemology, a vibrant antithesis to the otherwise universal incursion of the resentful man. In his view of the heroic "book of divine justice," and in his belief that justice acts as a native force in the individual, Nietzsche categorically opposes other think-ers' more utilitarian approach to justice:[6]

The active man, the attacker and overreacher, is still a hundred steps closer to justice than the reactive one, and the reason is that he has no need to appraise his object falsely and prejudicially as the other must. It is an historical fact that the aggressive man, being stronger, bolder, and no-bler [Vornehmere], has at all times had the better view, the clearer con-science on his side. Conversely, one can readily guess who has the inven-tion of "bad conscience" on his conscience: the vindictive man [der Mensch des Ressentiment]. . . . Historically speaking, all law—be it said to the dismay of that agitator (Dühring), who once confessed: "The doc-trine of vengeance is the red thread that runs through my entire investiga-tion of justice"—is a battle waged against the reactive emotions by the ac-tive and aggressive, who have employed part of their strength to curb the excesses of reactive pathos and bring about a compromise. Wherever jus-tice is practiced and maintained, we see a stronger power intent on finding means to regulate the senseless raging of rancor [ressentiment] among its weaker subordinates . . . by the establishment of a code of laws which the superior power imposes upon the forces of hostility and resentment when-ever it is strong enough to do so; by a categorical declaration of what it considers to be legitimate and right, or else forbidden and wrong. Once such a body of law has been established, all acts of high-handedness on the part of individuals or groups are seen as infractions of the law, as rebellion against the supreme power. Thus the rulers deflect the attention of their subjects from the particular injury and, in the long run, achieve the oppo-site end from that sought by vengeance, which tries to make the viewpoint of the injured person prevail exclusively. Henceforth the eye is trained to view the deed ever more impersonally. . . . It follows that only after a cor-pus of laws has been established can there be any talk of "right" and "wrong." (Genealogy 2.11:207)

Nietzsche on justice is Nietzsche at his least "modern" and most Judeo-classical. In this marvelous aphorism, he reminds us that justice does exist. It exists because an objective notion of *textuality* also exists. Indeed, justice derives from an unchanging, impersonal text rather than from a private and idiosyncratic urge for revenge.[7]

Justice and ressentiment are in every sense antipathetic. Yet reactive emotion threatens to emerge in any legal environment. Thus each generation must define what justice means or—as is far more likely—certain exemplary generations must do so. From time to time, active and positively motivated individuals join together to codify their approach to existence into an enduring body of law. Whether we speak of the Mosaic generation or of the days of the constitutional conventions or the creation of the Napoleonic codes, the communal establishment of universal values precedes any possibility of social justice. Conversely, the programmatic abrogation of a system of laws (as in Christianity at its origins) can only lead to subjectivism and reactive violence. The code and its attendant procedures forever unbind the achievement of justice from intersubjective influence. Society no longer defines itself in terms of a victim seeking vengeance; instead, each transgression becomes merely one of many occasions for calm recommitment to the codified values. A material text has been produced, not to be subverted by the clever interpretations of leaders acting in a moral vacuum, but rather to be honored through a clearsighted communal allegiance.

Nietzsche knew that nineteenth-century Europe offered fertile soil to the reactive and the vengeful. In the narrative fiction of his contemporaries, words in the service of ressentient values predominated thematically and structurally. These writers anticipated in their works the actual rise to power of individuals who manipulated the private passions of a reactive populace; they feared that law itself would soon come to suppress the positive and the good.

RESSENTIMENT IN LEGALITY

Nietzsche's aphorisms on morals evince a philo-Semitic tendency in his thought[8] which derives in part from his admiration for the absolute notion of justice embodied in the sacred texts and the recent practice of the Jewish people. This inclination, in turn, contradicts

Nietzsche's otherwise ironic and iconoclastic approach to contemporary morality. Far from rejecting all absolutes, Nietzsche redeems the Judaic striving for temporal justice through a system of positive law. While the Jew sees this law as communicated by God, Nietzsche finds it emerging from a dialectical struggle between antithetical forces. For against the active sense of justice in the noble individual, the reactive cleverness of ressentiment rebels and, in the nineteenth century, prevails:

The ambition of these most abject invalids is to at least *mime* justice, love, wisdom, superiority. And how clever [geschickt] such an ambition makes them! For we cannot withhold a certain admiration for the counterfeiter's skill with which they imitate the coinage of virtue, even its golden ring. They have by now entirely monopolized virtue; "We alone," they say, "are the good, the just, we alone the men of good will." They walk among us as warnings and reprimands incarnate, as though to say that health, soundness, strength, and pride are vicious things for which we shall one day pay dearly; and how eager they are, at bottom, to be the ones to make us pay! How they long to be the executioners! Among them are vindictive characters aplenty, disguised as judges, who carry the word *justice* in their mouths like a poisonous spittle and go always with pursed lips, ready to spit on all who do not look discontent, on all who go cheerfully about their business. (*Genealogy* 3.14:259)

Why would the increasing influence of ressentiment in a society reflect itself first in a degradation of the notion of justice? Nietzsche's thought, as his student Max Scheler elaborates it, emphasizes the slow poisoning of the intellect characteristic of the ressentient man.[9] Ressentiment, unlike hatred, which can be resolved in a single decision or gesture, is a full-blown intellectual malaise, inclined to take institutional and formal, rather than personal and spontaneous, revenge. It emerges only subtly and gradually from an unresolved sense of insult. The "insult"—real, imagined, or provoked by the desire to possess an inaccessible object or trait—grates on the intellect as much as on the emotions. The wounded party may eventually find himself thinking of little else, even wallowing in an exaggerated sense of injury. Perversely, though, he elevates the perpetrator of the "insult," who dominates his thought, to the level of an idol. The rage which should theoretically be directed against this figure he venomously misapplies to innocent third parties. If unchecked by a major effort of will, this process continues to pollute the victim's relationships until his values are overturned utterly. Existential envy (*Existenzialneid*) of the perpetrator, which renders his presence a continuing necessity to the victim, and organic falsehood (*organische Verlogenheit*), which flows from the vicissitudes in his personal and intellectual perspective, culminate the insidious process.

In its frequent appearance among literary characters, ressentiment reveals its literal meaning, "resensing." The ressentient man lives through, again and again, the event that proves his passivity, resenses and reintellectualizes it to the point of creating a false ethic from it. If he, like Hamlet, already has what I have called a "legalistic proclivity,"[10] he may weave a verbal spell around those who observe him, convincing others and almost himself that he is freely and actively resolving his problem, while in fact he merely employs his verbosity to slip further into determinism and falsehood.

But, as in literature, where the writer once begrudged his ressentient Thersites thirty lines from his Achilles[11] but now subordinates a positive hero to an Underground Man or an Admiral Nelson to a Captain Vere, so in society the man of ressentiment has come into his own. Reactive envy, once raised to communal authority, contrives vindictively to overturn the absolute standards of justice of its life-directed enemy. Established in power, the clever representative of ressentiment transmits his illness to the passive populace.

For Nietzsche, and for the Jew, the prominent symptoms of modern cultural sickness were anti-Semitism,[12] mass hatreds, and a shift away from a universal, classical sense of earthly justice—applicable to oneself and hence to all one's fellows. These portents could not escape notice. The positively motivated individual was giving way. Social injustice was tolerated, and legalized violence became the periodic emblem of a civilization in distress.

RESSENTIMENT IN ART

Ressentiment arises, as we have seen, from a coexisting hatred of and dependence on some individual or group. Its morality is essentially reactive, a bitterly creative response to the positive forms of life around it:

The slave revolt in morals begins by rancor turning creative [dass das *Ressentiment* selbst schöpferisch wird] and giving birth to values—the rancor of beings who, deprived of the direct outlet of action, compensate by an imaginary vengeance. All truly noble morality grows out of triumphant self-affirmation. Slave ethics, on the other hand, begins by saying *no* to an "outsider," an "other," a non-self, and that *no* is its creative act. This reversal of direction of the evaluating look, this invariable looking outward instead of inward, is a fundamental feature of rancor. Slave ethics requires for its inception a sphere different from and hostile to its own. Psychologically speaking, it requires an outside stimulus in order to act at all; all its action is reaction. The opposite is true of aristocratic valuations: such values grow and act spontaneously, seeking out their contraries only in order to affirm themselves even more gratefully and delightedly. Here the negative concepts, *humble, base, bad,* are late, pallid counterparts of the positive, intense and passionate credo, "We noble, good, beautiful, happy ones." (*Genealogy* 1.10:170)

With prophetic awareness, Nietzsche consistently equates the reactive person with the mode of violence, and the noble individual with the calm peacefulness of self-assurance. For, as the literary treatment of ressentient verbalizers affirms, a nominal stance of docility can cover a torrent of abusive reactivity and, more often than a frank assertion of individual and communal rights, can lead to needless violence. The noble individual is the just one, in tune with his own existence and hence with that of others.

Modern artists, while they recognize a dichotomy between the just and the ressentient, appear to Nietzsche to adopt the reactive stance rather than the noble one. He contrasts mid and late nineteenth-century artists with the classical giants Goethe and Stendhal; he draws no line between "romantic" and "realist" artists, but rather perceives a general degradation in the contemporary milieu. While the word *ressentiment* is not used in Nietzsche's strongest statements on modern art, his attack upon elaborate, sickly, bourgeois decadence, and his honoring of antithetical Jewish and classical elements in art, unmistakably link these two areas of his later thought.

Richard Wagner stands, for Nietzsche, as the archetype of the ressentient artist. "Through Wagner," he states in *The Case of Wagner* (1888), "modernity speaks her most intimate language, one of decadence and sickness. . . . Wagner increases exhaustion: on that account he allures the weak and exhausted."[13] The composer's illness ("Wagner est une névrose") strikes chords in the ressentient souls of his listeners, those masses more comfortable with the elaborate and the weak than with the Dionysian forcefulness of true musical art.[14] Nietzsche extends this analysis to modern literature. He roundly criticizes modern novelists (predominantly French) in *Twilight of the Gods* for their use of "notebook psychology" instead of profound personal insight and scorns them for their elevation of style over substance, passivity over effectiveness, sickness over life.[15]

The Goncourts, Hugo, and especially Flaubert stand accused of creating an aesthetic in which "life no longer resides in the whole. The Word gets the upper hand and jumps out of the sentence, the sentence stretches too far and obscures the meaning of the page, the page acquires life at the expense of the whole—the whole is no longer a whole. But that is the simile for every style of *décadence.*"[16] Anticipating Sartre,[17] Nietzsche associates Flaubert's stylistic innovations with a deeper personal (and cultural) malaise:

In respect to artists of every kind, I now make use of this main distinction: has the hatred of life, or the superabundance of life, become creative here? In Goethe, for example, the superabundance became creative; in Flaubert the hatred. Flaubert, a new edition of Pascal, but as an artist with instinctive judgment at bottom: "Flaubert est toujours haïssable, l'homme n'est rien, l'oeuvre est tout." He tortured himself when he wrote. . . . They both felt "unegotistic." "Unselfishness"—the decadence principle, the will to end, in art as well as in morals.[18]

A significant strain in the modern "realist" novel—one thinks of Henry James—falls under indictment in these phrases. But even Dostoevski, whom Nietzsche usually admires, is associated in the Wagner essays with the resentful religious values which contribute to the artistic decadence of the nineteenth century:

There is the aesthetics of *decadence,* and there is *classical* aesthetics—the "beautiful in itself" is a chimera, like all idealism. —In the narrower sphere of so-called moral values there is no greater contrast than that of *master–Christian* valuation: the latter grown up on a thoroughly morbid soil (the Gospels present to us precisely the same physiological types which the romances of Dostoevski depict); master morality ("Roman," "heathen," "classical," "Renaissance") reversely, on the symbolic language of well-constitutedness, of *ascending* life, of the will to power as the principle of life. Master morality affirms, just as instinctively as Christian morality denies ("God," "the other world," "self-renunciation"—nothing but negations). The former communicates to things out of fullness—it glorifies, it embellishes, it *rationalizes* the world, the latter impoverishes, blanches, and mars the value of things, it denies the world. "The world," a Christian term of insult. These antithetical forms in the optics of values are both indispensable: they are modes of seeing which one does not reach with reasons and refutations. One does not refute Christianity, one does not refute a disease of the eye. . . . The Christian wishes to get loose from himself. Le moi est toujours haïssable.—Noble morality, master morality, has, reversely, its roots in a triumphing self-affirmation,—it is the self-affirming, the self-glorifying, of life; it equally needs sublime symbols and practices, but only "because its heart is too full." All *beautiful* art, all *great* art belongs here: the essence of both is gratitude.[19]

Nietzsche's forceful prose produces a vital judgment on art, identifying a spiritual emptiness which characterizes a major line in the post-Balzacian novel.[20] His critical methodology—a deliberate integration of ethics and aesthetics—is only now being understood and revived. But the Nietzschean sociology itself, the brilliant notion of ressentient injustice as the dominant factor in modern European culture—this was to generate immediate influence and elaboration.

2 Phenomenology and Prototype

MAX SCHELER AND THE MODERNITY OF RESSENTIMENT

As the century turned, it became increasingly hard to identify a valid system of values by which to lead one's life. We cannot overestimate the spiritual turmoil of a culture emerging from rigid hierarchies and expectations into apparent freedom and anomy. In a way, all thinking men and women could see themselves as Hamlets, as isolated beings maddened by responsibilities and unaided by meaningful moral absolutes. Nietzsche's vision of relativistic, reactive man, threatened by power but also bitterly seeking it, was coming to pass.

It is to this generalized relativism and its consequent resentments that Max Scheler, Nietzsche's student and a contemporary of Heidegger, turns his attention in his essay on ressentiment.[1] At the heart of his theory, which he elaborates in later essays equally useful to contemporary phenomenologists of sociology[2] and literature,[3] is the notion of intellectualized and recreative envy. Arising from the internalization of a negative sensation, "existential envy" (Existenzialneid) consumes the victim, who, deprived of absolute models for a positive resolution to his dilemma, cannot even take solace, like Hamlet, in self-chastising lucidity:

Envy does not strengthen the acquisitive urge, it weakens it. It leads to *ressentiment* when the coveted values are such as cannot be acquired and lie in the sphere in which we compare ourselves to others. The most powerless envy is also the most terrible. Therefore *existential envy*, which is directed against the other person's very nature, is the strongest source of *ressentiment*. It is as if it whispers continually: "I can forgive everything, but not that you *are*—that you are *what* you are—that I am not what you are—indeed that I am not *you*."(p. 42)

We may perceive traces of classical insights into envy in this essential paragraph: Paterculus' emulative man, Aristotle's disappointed man, Aquinas' sorrowful man, and, perhaps especially, Plutarch's obsessively cerebral man.[4] But Scheler's ressentient man surpasses even these. His entire world view becomes corrupted through his failure to resolve a profound negative sensation inspired by another. If such sensations are internalized, if they are resolved neither by action nor (where possible) by word,[5] they are likely to become generalized. That is, the specific envy or desire for revenge that the original "insult" inspired may be gradually dulled as the negative emotion spreads and begins to dominate the subject's psyche. The vital first stimulus—which is kept alive, but in an increasingly weakened form by the subject's continual resensing of the original incident—fades, and his negative response is transposed from its rightful object onto another person, a group, or even the whole world. As the original event is emotionally devalued, the possibility of resolving it through a positive act diminishes as well. Thus, for example, envy can no longer be overcome by acquiring the desired object, nor the impulse for revenge by taking vengeance.

In all cases, an alternative solution exists through what Scheler calls a "timely act of resignation," a notion directly traceable to Aquinas. The younger Scheler, unlike Nietzsche (who virtually equates ressentiment with what he considers the falsehood of Christian "love"), believed it possible within Christian structures to grant to the envied object a position of superiority in certain situations. In this regard, Scheler cites Goethe's phrase: "Against the great gifts of others there is no remedy but great love" (p. 53). But if, as usually happens in an age of relative values (and as happens consistently in novels), the victim cannot summon the requisite spiritual strength, then gradually his envy obsesses him and becomes generalized. When he reaches this advanced state of ressentiment, he not uncommonly strikes out at those who least deserve it—at friends or loved ones, for example—as a pathetic replacement for the original object of hatred. He may make scores of bystanders suffer in an effort to appease his unresolved rage.

Yet while the original event becomes dulled with time, the longer the original perpetrator is allowed to hold his implicit position of unchallenged mastery over the ressentient subject, the more he is idealized. Perplexing even to the bearer of ressentiment, such an "Umwertung der Werte" (overturning of values) may be temporarily offset by rationalization. Verbal deprecations of the mode of existence of the object (never declared to his face, however), or even an entire philosophical system justifying the failed original interaction, typically ensue. But although an articulated pattern of rationalization occasionally has the appearance of creativity, it can never relieve the subject's pervasive sense of negativity. The original object retains his position of superiority (either in fact or in memory), and the basic emotional response to the original incident, while weakened, can never fully be dissipated.

The longer the inverted emotion toward the original oppressor endures, the sicker the man of ressentiment becomes, until finally he falls prey to what Scheler calls "organic mendacity" (organische Verlogenheit). In this terminal stage of the disease, ressentient values absolutely replace positive ones. Instinctive and warm responses are virtually annihilated before they can appear; human contact becomes increasingly impossible, because sympathy has been overwhelmed by generalized vindictiveness. "Such people," observes Scheler, "never need to lie consciously," so ingrained is their perversity.

Scheler thus sees ressentiment as issuing from a specific sense of insult, followed first by an onslaught of unfulfilled reactive desires, then by a condition of existential envy of the unchallenged perpetrator, which the subject attempts to vent by lashing out at those closest to him. Finally, an almost organic impulse to misjudge or to lie and a constant sense of "being insulted" arise within the ressentient man.

Having concluded this description of the pathology of ressentiment, Scheler proceeds to categorize those people most prone to the phenomenon. The list includes priests (after Nietzsche's suggestion, itself, as we shall see, derived from Dostoevski), whose personal code of behavior and interpretation of Christian texts lead them to exploit the reactive emotions of their oppressed flock; subaltern bureaucrats (the nineteenth-century analogue to contemporary white-collar workers, lower-level corporate types, journalists, and even certain Chief Executives), who are at once envious of those they deem more powerful than themselves and incapable either of progressing beyond a certain point or of eliminating the envy by leaving the system; and the aged, who envy the young their vigor, resenting the bestowal of that gift upon their inferiors in knowledge and experience. "Ressentiment is always a sign of declining life," Scheler observes.

Like Hamlet when he (privately) lashes out at the king who sits on the throne intended for him, ressentient types generally sense a discrepancy between what they consider their theoretical worth and the actual position which others grant them. If they lack the personal or communal power to bridge this gap, their individual or collective behavior will become reactively defined by their envy of those who hold the positions they desire. Thus, in an age of bourgeois egalitarianism, an inclination to fits of vague rancor and generalized envy may be widespread.

The susceptibility of contemporary Western culture to ressentiment stems from the freedom from restrictions upon advancement that a democracy theoretically grants to any individual or group ("Anyone can grow up to be president of the United States"). Yet the very institutions of those democracies impose implicit handicaps upon many (a black person, for example, still has no great chance of becoming president of the United States). Even more poignant, advancement to the top of the hierarchy brings no particular satisfaction. Since power is disseminated throughout the democracy, one cannot assume that any given achievement will assuage the nagging sense that others are still "doing better." (Hence presidents aspire to be critics or sportscasters or waste their energies on "enemies lists.") The greater the sense of personal or social contradiction, the more fertile the soil for ressentiment.

Scheler, with some inspiration from Nietzsche, deduces that the criminal is not prone to ressentiment, because he successfully expresses his negative reaction to an individual or a society. The perception of the criminal act as a declaration of freedom from ressentiment is a fundamental contribution of modern literature, epitomized by writers such as Richard Wright, Jean Genet, and Anthony Burgess, as well as by those to be discussed here. In this vein, Nietzsche recognizes in an early aphorism the richness of Dostoevski's criminals.[6]

Almost diametrically opposed to the case of the criminal is that of the intellectual, defined in literary works as a character who has achieved a heightened form of narrative consciousness. Unable to locate any positive goals worthy of his talents, he turns to passive forms of behavior. He cedes power to less sophisticated mortals, yet audibly regrets the subsequent degradation of political institutions. To comfort himself, he assumes a seemingly disinterested, analytical stance,[7] but in fact his powerlessness galls him, and envy poisons his sense of superiority. "An intelligent man," declares Dostoevski's Underground Man, "cannot become anything in the nineteenth century." Convinced of the veracity of this questionable theorem, the intellectual adopts words as his private medium and ressentiment as his social contribution.

Continuing to elaborate upon Nietzsche's suggestions, Scheler also singles out the artist in modern democracies as a likely victim of negativity. The artist, unless he is totally unaware of his superior powers or—perhaps deliberately—denigrates their value, thinks highly of his enterprise. Yet society has come to regard the artist as a clown or, at best, as a "celebrity." The tension between the artist's self-conception and reality can often be overwhelming, and he may increasingly be driven to discuss as well as to display his alienation. The artist's stance toward society and his own enterprise in modern Western culture is more frequently ironic, often bitterly so, than in earlier Western epochs.[8]

Negativity in a large number of novels written contemporaneously with the theories of Nietzsche and Scheler is promulgated by intellectual and legalistic protagonists faced with challeging social environments which they soon come to regard as personally threatening. Where the protagonist most fully attains the "legalistic proclivity"—where the sensitized articulateness of the artist becomes embodied in his fictional hero—so, ironically, does ressentiment bare its destructive teeth.

THE FORMALISTIC MODEL: *NOTES FROM UNDERGROUND*

Against "Existentialism": Part 1 of the Tale

In Dostoevski's *Notes from Underground* (1864),[9] ressentiment achieves perhaps its most paradigmatic novelistic expression. This masterpiece of modern fiction is less representative of the independent "existential" philosophy for which it is known than of a personal history defined by frustrated vengefulness and distorted narrative formalism. The structure of the story, which still bears its original division into two distinct sections,[10] indicates that ressentiment is often motivated by external events working upon an overheated verbal imagination. The reverse chronology of the structure allows the reciprocity of this relationship to be clearly understood: the external events described in the second part have led to the romantic philosophizing of the first, just as the latter demonstrates the ressentient perspective from which the protagonist's youthful experiences are viewed some fifteen years afterward.

The two parts of Dostoevski's well-known story have allowed critics sympathetic to the Underground Man's philosophy to limit their analysis to the first and virtually to ignore the incidents in the second that inspired that philosophy. Apologists for the protagonist, from the existentialist critic Lev Shestov to many recent analysts,[11] often choose to forget that the outpourings of the first half of the novel flow from the fictional pen of the same character whose pathetic attempts at human interaction are described thereafter. For in his "relationships" with the tavern officer, Zverkov, Liza, and even the servant Apollon, the diarist in part 2 passes through every stage of the phenomenon of ressentiment; these few failed human interactions have sent him into the underground to resense forever the humiliation they have produced. But even if an analysis ignores part 2, the internal evidence of part 1 establishes the pathetic enslavement of this protagonist to a narrative mode which utterly inhibits a free response to people and even to ideas.

The recognition that we are treating a story, not a treatise, refines our understanding of the tale's ultimate meaning. For if the underground protagonist has become a spokesman for twentieth-century existentialists, and if, as I will argue, his diatribe in part 1 subtly disguises a goading negativity, the story may finally be perceived as a brilliant critique of those who flaunt their freedom, but whose philosophy actually derives from (and leads to) passive resentment and repressed violence.

Part 1 establishes three fundamental aspects of the protagonist's character: his bellicosity, his obsessive self-awareness, and his verbosity. The very first paragraph centers on the adjective *zloi*, the closest Russian equivalent to the word *ressentient*, and one associated in all of Dostoevski with intellectual types. "I am a sick man, a spiteful [zloi] man," begins the underground "confession" (p. 179). We are immediately launched into a spiritual mode utterly at odds with that of the noble heroes of premodern literature. The Underground Man recognizes that he is no Achilles; the wordy Thersites has come home to roost as epic hero, and spitefulness has advanced from the fringes of Western literature to its very center.

The Underground Man quickly seeks an object for his characteristic rancor and chooses the reader of his diary. He gratuitously grafts onto us his own mocking insensitivity: "No. I refuse to consult a doctor from spite [zlost'i]. That you probably will not understand. Well, *I* understand it." And again, "Now, are not you fancying, gentlemen, that I am expressing remorse for something now, that I am asking your forgiveness for something? I am sure you are fancying that. . . . However, I assure you I do not care if you are" (p. 181). In a deliberate parody of the style of Rousseau's diarists, and presaging that of Camus' Clamence, Dostoevski's protagonist reveals his lack of genuine self-analysis. The mutual spite imposed on the relationship between speaker and listener by the Underground Man contrives to eliminate within all of part 1 any forthright communication.

Using his exquisitely crafted tool of rationalization, the Underground Man generalizes from his own apparent negativity: *all* intelligent men suffer from the "illness of overconsciousness," he explains. Intelligence is thus depicted as a weakness imposed by hated "laws of nature" upon certain unfortunates. These people consequently lose the capacity for self-actualization, because "an intelligent man [*umni čelovek*] cannot become anything in the nineteenth century." Only in the act of writing can he become ("I have taken up my pen to explain this phenomenon," the protagonist says), for only writing can express his sole remaining emotion, "the enjoyment of one's own degradation." No meaningful approach to life is possible other than through narrative forms, and from these the protagonist significantly singles out the paradigm of insult and revenge:

Finally, even if I had wanted to be anything but magnanimous, had desired on the contrary to revenge myself on the assailant, I could not have revenged myself on any one for anything because I should certainly never have made up my mind to do anything, even if I had been able to. Why should I not have made up my mind? About that in particular I want to say a few words. (pp. 185–86)

Many readers have taken chapter 2 to heart, seeing in it the noble alienation and sensitivity of an existential hero. An alternate view identifies this chapter and the "few words" that follow as the expression of a hopelessly static or nonexistential consciousness. Causes are casually intertwined with effects in this masterpiece of rhetoric. Intelligence is gratuitously linked with nonactualization, and an idiosyncratic illness with a widespread social condition. Instead of proceeding from an awareness of some personal malady to a search for its cause (the usual path to cure), the narrator manages to work backward. He posits the cause first, the intangible "nineteenth century," and perversely concludes that a negative symptom (vindictiveness) must reflect a positive condition (intelligence). There is no way out of this logical fantasy, the first significant literary example of "mauvaise foi" since Hamlet observed, "The time is out of joint, O cursed spite, / That ever I was born to set it right!" Both characters grandiloquently blame their own most glaring inadequacies on an outside force, temporality.[12]

With immense sensitivity to the obsessive interests of such protagonists, Dostoevski now has the Underground Man advance his treatise with a dialectic on the subject that seems most to interest him: insult and revenge. When a nonintellectual senses himself to have been insulted, we learn, he rushes "straight toward his object like an infuriated bull with his horns down, and nothing but a wall will stop him." On the other hand, the overconscious man, the self-defined "mouse," so complicates the issue of revenge that he does not even begin to charge. For decades, critics have quarreled over the meaning of the "wall," the force to which even the man of action "defers," and about which the "mouse" endlessly theorizes from the beginning of chapter 3.[13] The wall evidently stands between all men and a necessary act. When the "normal" man, in quest of such acts, confronts the wall, he concedes its unmistakable dominance over him and resumes other activities. He perceives the wall for what it is, a given:

as though such a stone wall really were a consolation, and really did contain some word of conciliation, simply because it is as true as twice two makes four. (p. 189)

Existentialists such as Shestov embrace the protagonist's articulate refusal to accept unthinkingly even this basic external reality:

> But what do I care for the laws of nature and arithmetic, when, for some reason, I dislike those laws and the fact that twice two makes four? Of course I cannot break through the wall by battering my head against it if I really have not the strength to knock it down, but I am not going to be reconciled to it simply because it is a stone wall and I have not the strength. (p. 189)

Indeed, these passages superficially embody a fierce rejection of rationalism in the name of freedom. No wonder that Shestov, for example, compares the Underground Man to Nietzsche, Kierkegaard, and even Socrates.[14]

A careful look at the quality of the assumptions in the argument, even without an analysis of its source, reveals the protagonist's underlying deterministic stance. From the depths of his negative spirit, the narrator first assumes that even the man of action will always defer to the stone wall. Such a man at least begins to act, however, whereas the protagonist has already identified himself as one who "could not have revenged myself on anyone for anything." The mouse would never dream of rushing toward the wall, much less of battering his head against it; instead, he creates so many doubts for himself about the wall that he does not even make a move toward resolving a deeply felt insult. Primary causes (the justice of the charge against the oppressor, no matter what the odds of success) are replaced by endless second-guessing (Should I act? Will there be a better time to act? Was my enemy really wrong? Don't I admire him deep down? Will I look ridiculous? etc.).

But the wall that occasionally hinders even the active man by definition does not allow for a great deal of inquiry. It is an axiom of human experience. Two plus two *does* equal four. There are things in the universe which are materially true, and which are insusceptible to human change. In Nietzsche's words (and the Underground Man is no Nietzschean!), "such truths do exist." The willingness at least to test his natural capacities to the fullest ennobles the not unintelligent "homme de la nature"; he will not allow imponderables to prevent him from confronting his destiny head-on. Thus, even if he is as mediocre as the Underground Man resentfully claims, the average nineteenth-century man is a step ahead of the narrator. The two are equally fascinated with the stone wall; neither has the heroic capacity to defy it. But whereas the normal man accepts its incontrovertible presence, the ressentient man makes it his personal enemy and determines his life in reaction to it. Thus the Underground Man, and not, as it may first appear, the natural man, converts a fundamental truth into a "satisfying determinism."[15]

Victor Shklovski, the gifted Russian formalist critic, recognizes the intrinsic fallacies of, and the autobiographical impetus for, the Underground Man's declaration of "freedom." As he puts it, "The narrator cannot even go to the wall to try his luck at bringing it down. Weakness thus becomes his amusement [B'essilie stanovitse evo razvlečeniem]." Unlike Shestov, Shklovski makes effective use of part 2, observing that "the stone wall is realized in the form of the officer who shoves everything aside as he walks. . . . The narrator cannot live because he is surrounded by *walls of this sort*. . . . The man, well-dressed, socially successful, is already a wall for the underground inhabitant."[16] Shklovski's approach is close to my own in that it affirms the unity of the story and the interaction of its parts. Indeed, the "stone wall" passage early in the tale merely restates and rationalizes the ressentient frustrations, weaknesses, and inaction of all of part 2. For there he recounts the galling truth that just such "normal" types as Zverkov and the tavern officer have "insulted" him by their self-confidence and popularity.

In the midst of the deceptive narrative in part 1, chapter 5 stands as a small oasis of veracity. It could be called the "soliloquy chapter," for in its single paragraph, the Underground Man expresses himself in a manner that echoes Hamlet at his most lucid. He tells us that he has "made up a life, so as at least to live in some way." Rejecting reality out of hand, he finds constant excuses for isolation and inaction; "the legitimate fruit of consciousness is inertia, that is, conscious sitting with the hands folded." And, although he continues to pretend to himself that only stupid men can act, he ends, like Hamlet, in an astounding confession:

Oh, gentlemen, do you know, perhaps I consider myself an intelligent man only because all my life I have been able neither to begin nor to finish anything. Granted I am a babbler, a harmless vexatious babbler, like all of us. But what is to be done if the direct and sole vocation of every intelligent man is babble, that is, the intentional pouring of water through a sieve? (p. 194)

This comment, a strikingly and singularly honest one for the Underground Man, confirms that the internal logic of his diatribe against the "laws of nature" and the nineteenth century is organically false. The protagonist manages a brief confession; he admits that his sole virtue, intelligence, may itself be a figment of his mendacity. Having undermined this defining trait, the Underground Man is truly relegated to what Shklovski calls *ničtožnost'* (nothingness).

But while nothingness defines the protagonist, he paradoxically insists upon giving a narrative form to it. Could it be, he queries, that I only call myself intelligent to rationalize my inaction? For the Underground Man's diatribe in part 1 against observable reality is only partially justifiable as a critique of mediocre technological positivism. After all, the "homme de la nature" is far less a positivist than is the protagonist. The natural man spontaneously partakes of all the fullness of reality; the protagonist's only act, on the other hand, is to delimit that reality to the comforting material boundaries of his four underground walls and the pages of his diary.

From Insult to Mendacity: Part 2

Far from wanting to live, the protagonist has chosen a hermetic, moribund mode of mere existence. Yet he has adopted this stance not through rejection of alienating society, but by a cowardly acceptance of his own proclivity toward ressentiment.

The protagonist had been a middle-level bureaucrat before his "retirement." He despised his work but "did not openly abuse it" because he "got a salary for it." He considered himself intellectually superior to his fellow clerks ("they were all stupid"), but he envied their unselfconsciousness and feared their ridicule. "It somehow happened quite suddenly," he informs us, "that I alternated between despising them and thinking them superior to myself." He led a solitary existence; his only pastime was reading. By virtue of this reading he became what he calls a "romantic": an intelligent man who forms an ideal but "never stirs a finger for that ideal," and who "would rather go out of his mind—a thing though that very rarely happens—than take to open abuse." He was often "seething within because of external impressions," but smothered the flames in the "pleasure and pain" of reading and solitary acts of "filthy vice." "Even then I had my underground world in my soul."

With this background, only one or two specific events were needed to develop the seeds of envy and vindictiveness into a mature case of underground ressentiment. The narrator describes these few experiences in great detail, for petty as they are by normal standards, they are the only instances of human contact in his life. Dostoevski means us to test the compelling language of the Underground Man's philosophical freedom against the details of his biography.

The first of these "happenings" commences when the young clerk observes someone being thrown out of a tavern by an officer. Since, as he tells us, he "actually envied the gentleman thrown out the window," he naturally wishes to meet the perpetrator of the deed. By entering the tavern, he expresses the same mixture of fascination and fear which he has often felt toward his fellow clerks.[17] In addition, he hopes to place himself in a "literary" situation, but the defeat in violent battle which he romantically craves does not come to pass. Instead, he is bodily lifted and set down by the officer who "passed me by as though he had not noticed me." This ignominious confrontation, which has none of the anticipated frills, deeply offends the Underground Man's sensitivities. But even though he senses that he should protest, he "changed his mind and preferred to retreat resentfully [ozloblenno]."[18]

In the face of a direct insult, the young man can neither strike back nor even verbalize his outrage. Instead, he adopts Hamlet's "wait until next time" philosophy,[19] that fatal hesitancy derived from the verbal individual's legalistic approach to confrontation. As Hamlet sheathes his sword during Claudius' "prayer," so the Underground Man suppresses all outward reaction to the sense of insult. And, like the prince, he consoles himself with the promise that vengeance will occur in the context of a more perfect "justice." He returns to the tavern the next evening, but as the consciousness of his original weakness has been heightened, so too his consequent resentment has become generalized; thus, the entire group assembled in the tavern, "every one present, from the insolent marker down to the lowest, stinking, pimply clerk in a greasy collar," now becomes the object of his vindictiveness.

The effects of his pervasive negativity persist and expand as the Underground Man takes his problem to the fashionable milieu of the Nevski Prospect. Even here, however, he cannot translate his hatred of the officer into meaningful physical or verbal form. Instead, he adopts the visual mode of Plutarch's envious man: "But I—I stared at him with spite and hatred and so it went on . . . for several years! My resentment [zloba] grew even deeper with years. . . . Sometimes I was positively choked with resentment" (p. 223).

Chapter 3 introduces Zverkov, the character who inspires the Underground Man with Existenzialneid, the penultimate stage in the process of negativity. The protagonist notes that his former schoolmate had been "a pretty, playful boy whom everybody liked. . . . He was vulgar in the extreme, but at the same time he was a good-natured fellow even in his swaggering" (p. 233). Furthermore, Zverkov was the object of reverence to many "simply because he had been favored by the gifts of nature." How wonderfully the polemic against "the laws of nature" may now be understood in its personalized context, and how brilliantly Dostoevski demolishes complex statements of social criticism!

I had hated him . . . just because he was a pretty and playful boy. . . . I hated his handsome but stupid face (for which I would, however, have gladly exchanged my intelligent one), and . . . the way in which he used to talk of his future conquests of women. (p. 233)

Our understanding of this protagonist largely determines our sensitivity to modern fiction, and he deserves our pity, not our admiration. The Underground Man represents a culture whose lack of coherent values makes it necessary to compare ourselves to others, to adopt rather than to create a personal world view. The *imitatio Christi*,[20] in other words, has degenerated into a relativistic pattern of *imitatio alterorum*. The merest Zverkov may potentially inspire ressentiment. In such a culture, admiration rather than envy is made possible only through what Nietzsche (here somewhat anticipating John Rawls) calls an act of "good will operating among men of roughly equal power."[21] Neither reactive Christian "love" nor, for that matter, any legal system provides the modern protagonist with this sense of equanimity. Still less is it to be found in wordy philosophical or critical analyses uninformed by sympathetic values.

Few readers soon forget the picture of the protagonist during the party scene, desperately craving the attention of the envied be-ing. "No one paid any attention to me, and I sat crushed and humil-iated. . . . Zverkov, without a word, examined me as though I were an insect. I dropped my eyes" (pp. 246–47). Once again, the narra-tor's shining dreams are brought down to the level of cold reality, just as they had been in the tavern and on the Nevski Prospect. Again, too, the Underground Man casts himself in the absurd role of avenging hero, challenging an irrelevant outsider, Ferfitchkin, to a duel. When others at the party greet this unexpected and incon-gruous challenge with mockery, the scene is set for the novel's quin-tessential act of repression:

"Now is the time to throw a bottle at their heads," I thought to myself. I picked up the bottle—and filled my glass. (p. 248)

The brevity of the phrase belies its significance, for it describes a nonact which is the consistent trademark of intellectual and legal-istic heroes. The lowered bottle symbolizes, as does Hamlet's sheathed sword ("Now might I do it, pat"), the failed attempt of a frustrated character to resolve a profound sense of personal injury. It also literally depicts the process of internalization. Rather than con-summate the externally directed action—hurling the bottle at the others—the Underground Man merely consumes its contents. Hamlet's returning his sword to its sheath may symbolize a denial of manliness in a Freudian sense—again, an act of internalization. However petty the more modern situation as compared to Hamlet's, its implications for the pervasive negativity of novelistic heroes are profound. Neither protagonist effectively "lowers his horns."

As the ensuing brothel scene begins, Liza, the protagonist's last chance for human intimacy before he creeps underground for-ever, becomes the passive object on which he projects all his frus-trated inclinations for revenge. As when he challenged Ferfitchkin, instead of Zverkov, he plans to avenge himself on Liza instead of on his truer "enemies." We also know that the Underground Man has always rejected those seeking to understand him; for example, the total devotion of the "one friend" he made in school, "a simple and devoted soul," caused the protagonist to "hate him immediately" and to "reduce him to tears and hysterics." Predictably, the Under-ground Man begins to work the gentle and quiet Liza into his gran-diose fantasies. She will be the slavishly oppressed heroine of his "book." He will save her. But as he acts out in his mind the literary role of hero, he destroys her real existence just as the tavern officer and Zverkov had crushed his own. Liza's rejection of her role in this scenario is the insult that permanently debilitates the protagonist. Like several among Dostoevski's women, Liza possesses an indigenous and nonintellectualized sympathy for others which allows her remarkable insight into complex personalities. For just this reason, she cannot append herself to the hero's romantic forms. Her simple statement, "Why, you speak somehow like a book," shatters his glorious plans and warns him that she is a force to contend with.

Liza's insight, however threatening, almost succeeds in curing the narrator's soul of its bitterness. With her, he experiences the only moments of direct emotional response he reports. His admission that his bookish harangue was meaningless, his grasping of her hand, his sincere invitation to his house, his warm acceptance of her "self-defense" (the student's love letter)—all this implies that Liza has unexpectedly moved the young man. But because he is unused to such emotions, because he cannot defend against them with verbal structures (he says virtually nothing in the concluding paragraphs of chapter 7), he must run out of the brothel and return home.

Unfortunately, the moment of elation which might have saved him lasts only long enough for him to sink into an exhausted sleep. Soon enough, the "inversion of the table of values" recommences. Vindictiveness so determines him that he makes good into evil and perverseness into an ideal. He retreats once again into formalism, almost forgetting Liza and writing a conciliatory note to one of the party-goers who had insulted him. His resentful proclivities vie with Liza's positive but too brief influence upon him. A passage in Scheler captures this tension in such types:

Such phenomena as joy, splendor, power, happiness, fortune, and strength magically attract the man of *ressentiment*. He cannot pass by, he has to look at them, whether he "wants" to or not. But at the same time he wants to avert his eyes, for he is tormented by the craving to possess them and knows that his desire is vain. The first result of this inner process is a characteristic *falsification* of the *world view*. Regardless of what he observes, his world has a peculiar structure of emotional stress. The more the impulse to turn away from those positive values prevails, the more he turns without transition to their negative opposites, on which he concentrates increasingly. He has an urge to scold, to depreciate, to belittle whatever he can. Thus he involuntarily "slanders" life and the world in order to justify his inner pattern of value experience. (*Ressentiment,* pp. 74–75)

But this instinctive falsification of the world view is of only limited effectiveness. Again and again the ressentient man encounters happiness (the Nevski passers-by), power (Anton Antonitch Syetotchkin), beauty (Zverkov), goodness (Liza), and other positive forms of life. They exist and impose themselves, however much he shakes his fist against them and tries to explain them away. He cannot escape the tormenting conflict between desire and impotence. Averting his eyes is sometimes impossible and in the long run ineffective. When a positive quality irresistibly forces itself upon his attention, the very recognition produces hatred against its bearer, even if he or she has never hated or insulted him.

It is of the utmost importance to recognize that a single unresolved incident, when perceived by a complex sensitivity as a reproach to its existence, may well lead to a generalized vindictiveness which sees everything and everyone as potential sources of insult. Hence, prior even to any real attachment, another person may be perceived as threatening. Moreover, as the Underground Man's reaction to Liza illustrates, ressentient personalities perversely confuse goodness with enmity. Since everyone attacks me, says the ressentient man, surely those who most embody what others call "positive" traits pose the greatest threat to me. Against them especially I must be on guard.

This perversion of perception through ressentiment is exemplified in the Underground Man's confrontation with his servant Apollon, a scene whose significance is frequently overlooked. Apollon's role is similar to that of Smerdyakov vis-a-vis Ivan Karamazov; he is the constant reminder to the Underground Man of his degradation. Each of these two obsequious figures contrives to reverse the master-servant relationship which ostensibly obtains. As in the brilliant Harold Pinter film *The Servant,* a seeming dependent assumes the status of moral better to his supposed superior, to the ultimate detriment of the latter. The table of values, implicitly reversed in the tortured minds of the Underground Man and Ivan, is explicitly reversed in these two demonic Dostoevskian relationships. Flustered, the Underground Man only with great difficulty brings himself to dismiss Apollon. "I will kill him!" he shouts, and bursts into tears. But then, strangely enough, "a horrible spite [strašnaya zloba] against *her* surged up in my heart; I believe I could have killed *her*" (emphasis mine).

In the space of seconds, the Underground Man's overheated imagination has substituted Liza for Apollon. Whatever "revenge" the narrator could not wreak upon his manservant (or upon the officer or Zverkov), he will wreak upon her. But still his vengeance takes the form of a Hamlet-like torrent of words directed against an irrelevant object. Few innocent victims of ressentient frustrations in all of literature since Ophelia endure so gracefully the verbal "daggers" hurled by the anguished protagonist. Finally, incredibly, he attempts to pay the girl for her time with him. The cruelty of the gesture amazes even Liza, and she flees her tormentor forever. Unable to accept love, and shorn of the heroic stature of his elaborate fantasies, the protagonist now has no recourse but to the underground.

As noted earlier, the vocabulary and style of part 1 match the mendacity of the narrator; the consistent use of irony, paradox, and diatribe forces the reader to adopt an unflinching hermeneutical approach to the "diary." Nothing is to be taken at face value. But the compulsive aspect of the rhetoric of part 1 may be best understood in the protagonist's own terms during his outpourings to Liza:

I knew I was speaking stiffly, artificially, even bookishly [knižke], in fact I could not speak except "like a book." (p. 272)

In a sense, all of part 1 can be analyzed as though it were a recapitulation of the pompous verbiage of the Liza-incident, as though "from a book" and not from the spontaneous workings of an existential consciousness. Organic mendacity becomes perpetual in the underground. We, and no longer Liza, are its victims.

Dostoevski's brilliant depiction of ressentient negativity thus succeeds in associating a seemingly "free" philosophy with the most falsifying and obsessive tendencies of a certain type of formalistic existence. As we shall see, the writer implicates his own enterprise when he makes such an association: the urge to structure reality within the artificial confines of a "book" is, of course, the writer's own. More explicitly, the two parts of the tale reveal the need to examine the premises upon which lofty articulations are based. This insight will enrich our understanding of such characters as Ivan

Karamazov, Captain Vere, and Jean-Baptiste Clamence; but it is Dostoevski's next work, *Crime and Punishment,* that expands the verbalizing tendency beyond the confines of the underground mentality and into the courts of law. In his careful progression toward *The Brothers Karamazov,* Dostoevski came to recognize the social, as opposed to the merely personal, consequences of narrative ressentiment.

The Jews would have been deeply puzzled by the idea that the aesthetic and the moral are distinct realms. One spoke not of a beautiful thing but of a beautiful deed.
                    —Irving Howe, World of Our Fathers

For the last twenty years, . . . I have felt agonizingly—and I see it more clearly than anyone, that my chief literary defect is—verbosity, and I simply cannot get rid of it.
                    —Dostoevski, letter to Mikhail Katkov,
                    19 July 1866, cited in David Magarshack,
                                        Dostoevski

PART 2   The Failure of the Christian
          Narrative Vision:
          Dostoevski's Legal Novels

The notes will serve as a reminder, perhaps, that the Dostoevsky of the magnificent conceptions, Miltonic imaginings, and Dantesque visions was also a writer who had to find the mesh of expressive details, without which the imaginings and the visions would never have found their sensuous embodiment and would never have achieved their magnificent effects. We have in many respects a "denuded" novel in the notes, and the interest in the notes may consist in reminding us how much the details and complexities that Dostoevsky found between notes and novel added to the conceptions and imaginings.
—*Edward Wasiolek, introduction to*
The Notebooks for "The Brothers Karamazov"

3 "Artistic Legality" and the Figure of the Examining Magistrate

AN AUTHOR FIGURE DERIVED FROM THE CRIMINAL CODE

Fyodor Dostoevski knew his czarist law, and his novels demonstrate a detailed expertise intimately integrated into the works' larger significance. From *Crime and Punishment* (1866) through *The Brothers Karamazov* (1881)—a period of intense legal reform in Russia —Dostoevski approached criminal procedure with the zealotry of an ambitious law student. All of the formal, structural, and spiritual elements discussed in earlier chapters unite in Dostoevski's great legal novels. Continuing his treatment of the resentful intellectual, Dostoevski extends the theme in his last novels to portray a lawyer unique to Continental systems of criminal procedure, the "examining magistrate."[1] While this figure may remind American and English readers of a police detective, the "examining magistrate" is a *lawyer*. His advanced education, psychological acumen, and verbal

45

skills commend him to the imagination not only of Dostoevski but of other seminal Continental novelists, including Camus. He merits our detailed attention here.

With precursors in the Roman and ecclesiastical systems,[2] the "examining magistrate" (originating in the "juge d'instruction" of the French criminal procedure code of 1808)[3] is basically the same figure seized upon by Camus as part of *The Stranger*'s Algeria in 1942.[4] In Dostoevski's Russia, the new codes of 1864 emphasized the growing powers of the analogous "sudebni sledovatel'," powers which the knowledgeable writer explicitly notes in *Crime and Punishment*, which was written in the midst of the reforms of the 1860s.[5]

This functionary must have appealed to the imaginative writer in many ways. Standing at the center of the process of criminal investigation, the examining magistrate possessed, and exercised, enormous control over the life of any given suspect. Indeed, his techniques were directed at the realistic goal of eliciting a confession from the person finally believed to be culpable. To enable him to uncover the "truth" (who did it and why), Continental law granted this figure powers of interrogation, search and seizure, fine, and arrest which would largely be unconstitutional under American law. Perhaps better called the *inquisitor* for our purposes, the figure's responsibility was thus less adversarial, as in our system, than educational and ultimately accusatory. For Dostoevski, the psychological brilliance of the real-life interplay between inquisitor and suspect became the glittering source of many a fictional chapter.[6]

As the sole investigative arm of the state in any serious criminal case (albeit with full authority and funds to invoke police assistance), the inquisitor is quickly called into the case by the prosecutor (called here the "procurator," a term that reflects the differences between the French "procureur" or the Russian "prokurator" and their American counterparts).[7] From this point on, the inquisitor proceeds to establish the existence of a crime or crimes, to interview in great secrecy suspects, witnesses, and interested parties, and to prepare a dossier on the full matter. In the roughest sense, as many Continental observers have noted, the inquisitor seems to combine in one man the functions of the Anglo-American police detective and grand jury.[8] The parallel is weak, however, in that the inquisitor is charged with exploring any and all aspects of a given criminal matter and theoretically plays neither an adversarial nor a judgmental role.[9] His function frequently commences before a single suspect has been established; and rather than amass only the data necessary to arrest or indict—the necessary prerequisite to the Anglo-American adversarial process—the inquisitor seeks out the full background of the case.

As his French title implies, the inquisitor strives to "instruct" himself about a given crime. Yet, like his ecclesiastical predecessors who passed on their techniques to him,[10] the secular inquisitor has broad control over those who do become suspects in the case. Endowed with an arsenal of powers to aid his "instruction," the inquisitor may covertly interview a host of character witnesses, as well as the suspect himself, before formally declaring the latter to be under criminal investigation and hence protected by the rights of an "inculpé." Far more than in the American system, Continental pretrial procedures aim to elicit a confession; hence the inquisitor's curiosity legally extends to every aspect of a suspect's personal life. All secret findings become a part of his dossier, for even if the suspect does confess, a full trial must still ensue to decide the measure of culpability and extent of punishment.[11]

As depicted by European novelists, the inquisitor possesses a degree of insight into others shared only by the literary artist himself. Endowed with clearly superior powers of observation and articulateness, as he may often be in reality, the inquisitor duplicates the methods and the creative deeds of the novelist. His professional duties frequently require that he direct at the subjects of his investigation the faculty of perception which is the novelist's primary power. Ultimately, his observations become part of a written dossier which forms the backbone of the procurator's presentation at the trial. Thus, in both the inquisitor and the novelist, acuity of perception serves to uncover and to record reality in its fullness. The inquisitor (like the narrative-prone intellectual) embodies the author's verbal proclivity.

Here is a case, then, in which a legal institution provides the basis for an artistically compelling description. Not content, however, with minor caricatures of the inquisitor, Dostoevski depicts him in a manner both precisely congruent with the smallest details of the codes and eminently evocative of his strong aesthetic possibilities. In the words of Porfiry Petrovich, the inquisitor in *Crime and Punishment,* "An inquisitor's . . . business is, so to speak, some sort of art."

THE BRILLIANT REACTOR: THE INQUISITOR
IN *CRIME AND PUNISHMENT*

The tortured law student, Raskolnikov, has committed two murders to test his theory that an individual can "step across" the ordinary legal limits and say "a new word." Burning with fever and guilt, caught up in the seamy yet inspiring world of the second most artificial city in Europe (St. Petersburg being to Dostoevski what Venice was to Schiller and Mann), the troubled intellectual maintains a tenuous grip on reality and on his own theoretical superiority. But this begins to disintegrate rapidly the moment he meets the inquisitor assigned to investigate the murders. To an informed reader, the dynamic between inquisitor and suspect in *Crime and Punishment* surpasses even the perennially fascinating relationship between the police officer and Jean Valjean in Hugo's *Les Misérables.*

As Dostoevski's attention to detail might lead us to expect, the investigation in *Crime and Punishment* parallels the criminal procedure in the Alexandrine Russia of the 1860s. After the typically brief role of the police in serious crimes,[12] the inquisitor Porfiry Petrovich is called in to commence formally the "preliminary inquiry" (*predvaritel'noe proizvodstvo*); a few days later, his first meeting with Raskolnikov occurs, almost halfway into the novel. Prior to this meeting, Raskolnikov has had only tangential brushes with two police officials, Zametov and Nikodim Fomich. While the student's behavior and remarks have inspired some suspicion on those occasions, Porfiry alone sufficiently grasps Raskolnikov's subtle mind to consider him a possible murderer of the old pawnbroker and her sister, Lizaveta.

Porfiry is inaccurately called the *zdešni pristav sledstvennikh del'* (the local police investigator of the case), first by Razumikhin, Raskolnikov's friend and Porfiry's distant cousin (part 2, chapter 4) and again later by Raskolnikov (p. 343); Porfiry, however, calls himself either the *sledovatel' kotoromu poručeno delo* (the investigator charged with the case; p. 240) or, more simply, the *sledovatel'.* The lay misapprehension that Porfiry is a police official, instead of a lawyer and officer of the court, is representative of the public confusion

about criminal procedure in general, which contributed to the reforms that Porfiry specifically mentions to Raskolnikov later—
"inquisitors are all at any rate to be called something different soon"
(p. 241). Here as elsewhere in his works, Dostoevski demonstrates
through these variations on the inquisitor's title both interest and
competence in procedural law. Indeed, the Code of 1864 denomi-
nates the position *sudebni sledovatel'* (literally, "judicial investigator"), a clearer title which Dostoevski uses only for the inquisitor in
The Brothers Karamazov, published fifteen years later.[13]

As soon as he enters the case, Porfiry enjoys predominance
over both Police Chief Fomich[14] and the procurator, who is his hi-
erarchical superior but must cede power to the inquisitor until the
dossier is given over to him.[15] In such a case, an actual inquisitor
would have had no trouble assuming Porfiry's broad powers. He
would have had only to show that a crime of sufficient seriousness to
engage his office had been committed, a fact already established
during the police inquiry. The absence of an immediate suspect
would not have prevented the inquisitor from interviewing anyone
even vaguely connected with the incident. Hence, Porfiry can and
does examine character witnesses in regard to Raskolnikov, legiti-
mately probing into incidents which are totally unrelated to the
crime;[16] he searches Raskolnikov's rooms in the latter's absence
and without even the permission of the landlady. Continental inquisitors to this day may legally emulate Porfiry's techniques (many
of them unconstitutional under American law) wherever such procedures will serve "the truth," and without prior judicial interven-
tion.

Summarizing the virtually unparalleled powers of the Continental inquisitor, a Russian jurist of Dostoevski's time observes:

All such functions demonstrate that our legislation entrusts to the inquisitor not only the responsibility to adjudicate fairly, but also the responsibility inherent in the function of criminal investigator and uncoveror of proof
of guilt and innocence.[17]

But it may be precisely the need to be impartial (Article 265 of the
Code of 1864 orders that the inquisitor must "*without prejudice* investigate all the favorable circumstances regarding the accused, as
well as the unfavorable ones"), and the absence of the American
prosecutor's political zeal to "get a conviction," that leads Porfiry to

establish the ambivalent tone toward Raskolnikov which provides the operative tension behind their relationship.

Indeed, *Crime and Punishment* dissects the subtle nature of what might be called the inquisitor's pragmatic befriending of the protagonist. In contrast to the general absence of specific motive in other friendships, the attraction of inquisitor to suspect combines genuine human interest with the desire to elicit a confession. The inquisitor rarely hesitates to bring his great investigative powers to bear, occasionally assuming a virtually omniscient dominance over his increasingly befuddled "friend." Yet Porfiry's genuine interest in the criminal personality, which from time to time appears as envy of a man who can "step across" externally imposed social boundaries, lends an equality to the relationship and renders it both artistically compelling and immensely significant to our discussion. Throughout the second half of the novel, Porfiry engages in a battle of wits with Raskolnikov. Their verbal joust consists of three distinct "passes," culminating in the inquisitor's two-pronged victory: a confession of guilt and a thorough comprehension of the accused. As we shall see, Porfiry's subsequent willingness to conceal from his legal superiors parts of what he has learned both saves Raskolnikov's life and (somewhat precariously and artificially) preserves Dostoevski's Christian world view.

In part 3, chapter 5, Raskolnikov deliberately sets a tone of gamesmanship in the relationship, by staging an entrance into Porfiry's apartment in which he light-heartedly banters with Razumikhin. Raskolnikov, whose every meeting with and ultimate confession to Porfiry are legally (though not psychologically) voluntary, wishes immediately to give an impression of total insouciance regarding the criminal investigation. While the inquisitor joins in the cordiality, nonetheless he "did not once take his eyes from the guest." Porfiry may have the caricatured physical appearance of a Dickensian lawyer, with his "fat, round, rather snub-nosed, dark-skinned face which had an unhealthy yellowish pallor, and a cheerful, mocking expression" (p. 329), but he possesses the subtle and careful mind essential to his profession.

In addition, he works hard. By the time Raskolnikov visits, the lawyer has already interviewed Zametov and other witnesses to Raskolnikov's strange behavior at the police station a few days earlier (pp. 89–101). He has also taken the time to read the suspect's recent article, "Concerning Crime." By reiterating at the interview Raskolnikov's argument in the article, Porfiry cleverly insinuates his suspicion that his guest may well have effectuated his "extraordinary man" theory by murdering the two women.

It is this . . . really, I hardly know how best to express it . . . it is a very tri- fling little idea . . . Psychological . . . Well, this is it: when you were com- posing your article—surely it could not be, he, he, that you did not con- sider yourself. . . just a tiny bit . . . to be also an "extraordinary" man, one who was saying a *new word*—in your sense, that is . . . Surely, that is so? (pp. 254–55)

Such maneuvers torture Raskolnikov, and by the end of the scene his feigned cheerfulness has changed to evident disequilibration. Tactically naive, he even blurts out, "Do you wish to interrogate me officially, with all the formalities?" failing to recognize that the unique procedural role of the inquisitor renders an overt accusation "quite unnecessary for the present," in Porfiry's own words. An ar- rested suspect is far less likely to confess than a confused man left free to implicate himself further.

Becoming gradually addicted to the game he is already losing (like Kafka's Joseph K. before the mysterious "court" of his undo- ing), Raskolnikov demonstrates the efficacy of Porfiry's strategy. He voluntarily returns for a second meeting the very next morning, this time at the inquisitor's office. Unlike his earlier entrance, Raskolni- kov's second appearance displays fear, outrage, and even hatred to- ward his "friend." Porfiry continues his verbal undermining of Ra- skolnikov by establishing a tone of familiarity, even referring to him as *batjuška* (old boy). The unclear nature of his situation forces Raskolnikov to stifle all outward expression of his growing resent- ment (*zlost'*):

"I think you said yesterday that you wished to question me . . . officially . . . about my acquaintance with the . . . murdered woman," began Raskolni- kov again. "Why did I put in that *I think?*" flashed through his mind. "And why am I so worried at having put it in?" came in another flash. Suddenly he felt that, simply because he was in Porfiry's presence, and had ex- changed a couple of glances and a couple of words with him, his uneasiness had instantly increased to gigantic proportions . . . and that this was terri- bly dangerous: his nerves were tense, his emotion was increasing. "This is disastrous! . . . I shall say too much again." (p. 320)[18]

As for Porfiry, a growing certainty of Raskolnikov's guilt, to-gether with a continuing sense that arresting such a suspect will only forestall confession, move him to prolong the contest. But it is something beyond these factors, something beyond even Porfiry's obvious delight in the game itself, which inspires him to broaden the inquiry. For the lawyer, too, begins to experience a personal, re-active fascination with his adversary. Indeed, suspect and lawyer create, in this novel, the poignant duality which has marked much of recent literature's perplexing stance on criminality. As Porfiry's investigation closes in on Raskolnikov's guilt, the lawyer grows spir-itually closer to the transgressor. The two unite in what Raskolni-kov recognizes as their uncommon mutual brilliance:

"Do you know," he said suddenly, looking almost insolently at Porfiry Pe-trovich, and delighting in his own insolence, "there must exist, I believe, a lawyer's procedure, a legal method, applying to all sorts of investigations, by which they begin with trivial matters, far removed from the real subject, or even with something serious, so long as it is quite irrelevant, so as to en-courage the person being interrogated, or rather to distract his attention and lull his mistrust, and then suddenly and unexpectedly stun him by hitting him on the crown of his head with the most dangerous and fatal question. Am I right? Isn't the principle enshrined in all the rules and pre-cepts to this day?" (p. 321)

Porfiry's own explanation of the inquisitor's ultimate success is "double-edged." "The criminal's nature comes to the rescue of the poor investigator" (p. 328); but only the inquisitor's wit discerns that nature and recreates it verbally in a legal context. Like the per-ceptive novelist, Porfiry ferrets out the individual subject's deepest meanings, then uses his verbal skills to formulate a portrait which will further his own subjective goals. If the end of justice is to apply codified legal wisdom fairly in each particular case, the inquisitor's aim is to make of every case a generalized portrait.

As their fascinating relationship progresses toward Porfiry's in-evitable victory, Raskolnikov's internalized resentment grows to a level matched in Dostoevski only by the Underground Man and by Ivan Karamazov when he is faced with the insidious Smerdyakov during the comparable three interviews of that final novel. In the last of their dialogues (part 6, chapter 2), Porfiry displays an almost genuine fondness for the debilitated suspect, occasionally patting his knee or shoulder, and alternating his self-styled giggling "clown-ishness" with a seeming melancholy at the imminent termination of the game. It was "as if he now scorned to use his earlier tricks and stratagems" (p. 430); but his sincerity, while not entirely feigned, also serves his strategic purposes.

After "confessing" his own technique as a lawyer, during a lengthy statement about the immense power of the inquisitor, Porfiry can quite naturally proceed to articulate Raskolnikov's actions as a murderer. Porfiry admits to secret violations of Raskolnikov's existence: covert searches and seizures, interviews with his closest friends, spreading rumors to confuse the suspect, staging spurious confessions, and subtle verbal manipulation of people and events. From a theoretical point of view, Porfiry's decision to lay bare his own amoral or excessive, though legal, procedures in investigating the guilt of Raskolnikov is fascinating. Drawing close to the desired confession, Porfiry decides that he owes the tortured intellectual suspect a "statement of his own transgressions." In acknowledging these excesses, Porfiry accomplishes at least two things. First, he boasts of a "stepping across" which Raskolnikov thought could be accomplished only through crime. Lawyers, too, he seems to say, act on a moral level quite different from that of the ordinary bour-geois. But second, Porfiry associates himself with the novelist who has created him; for his "laying bare" of professional techniques du-plicates the self-conscious use of narrative techniques within the novel. This may be why the interviews culminate in Porfiry's lengthy third-person narration of Raskolnikov's homicidal actions (beginning on p. 435). The inquisitor's recapitulation of the crime embellishes upon the original account in part 1, but remains essen-tially truthful to it.

As the more perfect evocation of the legal theme in *The Broth-ers Karamazov* exemplifies, the association in *Crime and Punishment* of lawyer with criminal on the one hand and with author on the other raises questions which the earlier novel does not fully answer. Since Porfiry's account of the crime and the criminal during this fi-nal interview achieves essential accuracy, it would appear that Dos-toevski was not yet fully ready to face the self-critical implications of legalistic ratiocination. This task was left to his last masterpiece. However, he plants the seeds of that recognition during the ex-tremely brief trial scene at the end of *Crime and Punishment*.

Fittingly placed in the epilogue, which contains several aesthetically weak reversals, the description of Raskolnikov's trial emphasizes the creative falsehood of the inquisitor. The defendant (with Porfiry's tacit consent) pleads poverty and even emotional instability as the reasons for the double homicide. While these lies definitively bar Raskolnikov from the superhuman status he vainly sought, they also indicate the way in which legal recreation of events sometimes serves more to fulfill the psychological and artistic goals of the lawyer than to achieve justice in the individual case. Porfiry, having totally dominated Raskolnikov in the pretrial interviews, has no enduring personal need to see the defendant pay the supreme penalty for what was, after all, at least one premeditated murder. The inquisitor therefore deletes from his dossier (and hence keeps from the procurator) his firm insight into the utterly intellectualized nature of the crime. At the trial, Raskolnikov is presented as just another starving student, and thus deserving of a sharply mitigated sentence in exile (p. 513).

Foreshadowing the theme fully expressed in his final work, and in Camus' novels about the law, Dostoevski indicates that the process of legal investigation contains the potential for imaginative artistry. Porfiry, fascinated by the criminal mind, perhaps even envious of it, plays a game of life and death within the context of a perfectly respectable professional position. The lines between lawyer and criminal start to blur; the lines between lawyer and novelist begin to appear. But since Porfiry's artifice at the end of *Crime and Punishment* allows the reader to take from his experience the satisfaction that a protagonist for whom he has oddly sensed tremendous sympathy despite two brutal murders emerges from the novel a free and changed man, Dostoevski perhaps saw no reason, for the moment, to explore those lines of identity. Fifteen years later, having added greatly to his store of legal knowledge and artistic experience, Dostoevski was again ready to grapple with the crucial significance of imaginative legal investigation.

"REASONABLENESS" AND MISCALCULATION OF GUILT: TEMPORAL LAW IN *THE BROTHERS KARAMAZOV*

Any complex literary text generates a series of critical responses which directs each generation's attention to certain specific passages, at the expense of the whole. Thus, even in the face of numer-ous sources who testify to Dostoevski's virtual obsession with the criminal law of Russia throughout his postexile life,[19] the lengthy and detailed legal description in The Brothers Karamazov receives scant attention compared to certain less concretely drawn sections of that novel.

In fact, during the years separating its publication from that of Crime and Punishment, the czarist reforms were of topical interest in lay and legal circles. But for Dostoevski, who had recently partici-pated in the famous Kroneberg case of 1876,[20] the courtroom, and the procedures which culminated in the criminal trial, appeared to generate a particular fervor. Almost one-fourth of the text of The Brothers Karamazov explicitly concerns the two major components of Continental criminal procedure: the "preliminary investigation" (book 9) and the trial itself (book 12).[21] Not surprisingly, the figure of the inquisitor plays a significant role in the first part of the proce-dure; but since the defendant, Dmitri Karamazov (Mitya), persists in maintaining his innocence of the murder of his father, the procu-rator and defense attorney ultimately become the center of narrative interest during a trial scene considerably longer than the "plea-bar-gained" trial of Raskolnikov.

Arrested as a consequence of the first series of interrogations at the Mokroe Inn, Mitya differs from Raskolnikov not only in his unwillingness to confess to the crime, but also in his rapid incarcer-ation by order of the inquisitor. While the inquisitor continues to gather further data on the case, in the absence of an ensuing rela-tionship with a defendant at large, he is not really compelled to play the kind of psychological game engaged in by Porfiry Petrovich in the earlier novel. The legal figures in The Brothers Karamazov (in-cluding Fetyukovich, the defense attorney), immediately convinced of Mitya's guilt, seek only to emphasize those aspects of the suspect's personality which appear to indicate his culpability, and then to narrate a version of the Karamazov reality in accordance with their preconceptions. Thus, where Porfiry had to be an exceptional figure in his own right to fathom the mind and motives of Raskolnikov, the lawyers in The Brothers Karamazov must be conventional enough not to comprehend the unusual behavior of Mitya, and thus to find him guilty of a crime he really has not committed.

This ironical development of the use of the inquisitor in Dostoevski finds expression in the differences between Porfiry and his later counterpart, Nikolai Parfenovich Nelyudov. A diminutive, pleasant looking young man, Nikolai shares Porfiry's extensive legal education, the high-level jurisprudential training required of inquisitors (p. 406). But in practice Nikolai demonstrates more of the qualities of a social gadfly—he is gossipy, distracted even by people like Grushenka who are involved in his own inquisitions, and ambitious in a mediocre way. His lack of exceptional talent is further indicated by his ceding his legal dominance over the preliminary inquiry to the procurator, Ippolit Kirillovich.[22] Whereas Porfiry never looks to anyone for advice on conducting his inquiry, Nikolai is almost wholly dependent on the legal skills of his superior during the questioning of suspect and witnesses: "The sharp-witted junior caught and interpreted every indication of his senior colleague's face, at half a word, at a glance, or at a wink" (p. 426).

Despite Nikolai's procedurally questionable deference to the procurator (who theoretically must ask permission of the inquisitor before speaking if he happens to attend a preliminary inquiry),[23] he does retain the symbolic appurtenances of his office. As the "sub-debni sledovatel'," he assumes authority over the policemen, Makarov and Schmertsov, commissions a police inspector to conduct a formal search and seizure (p. 417),[24] confronts Mitya at the Mokroe Inn, interrogates Mitya and the witnesses,[25] and, finally, detains Mitya for the suspected parricide. Indeed, Nikolai imposes on Mitya the three Dostoevskian "ordeals" described in book 9, entitled "Predvaritel'noe Sledstvie" ("The Preliminary Inquiry").[26] However, where Raskolnikov is tortured by Porfiry's increasing insight into his personality, Mitya is terrorized by Nikolai's consistent inability to understand him.

Mitya also senses the full humiliation of the procedural situation he finds himself in prior to arrest, a situation theoretically impossible under American law, but to this day quite proper in Europe. He is seated at a table, under the scrutiny of several interrogators; his every gesture is noted by the inquisitor, who makes them a part of his dossier and later of a lengthy narrative admissible in court. Although the inquisitor informs him on several occasions of his right to refuse to answer any question (see pp. 428, 438), Mitya nonetheless has no right during this first interrogation to the advice of an attorney as to which silences might be prejudi-

cial. Nor is Nikolai Nelyudov, despite his overall inferiority to Porfiry Petrovich and his unwarranted deference to the procurator, an
easy interrogator. During the intense questioning around the table,
Mitya learns that the inquisitor is "a skillful lawyer" (*iskusnejši sledovatel'*),[27] competent in the psychological artistry of his position.
Among the tactics common to Nikolai and Porfiry is the clever al-
ternation of an amiable tone with insinuating verbal mannerisms
(Porfiry's giggle, Nikolai's prattling lisp) and disconcerting suggestions. An example of the latter ploy is Nikolai's insistence—a slight
and probably justified exaggeration of his powers of search and
seizure—that Mitya undress himself in the presence of several peasants (p. 442). Since Nikolai has observed that the suspect's clothes
are covered with blood, his order is quite reasonable in terms of uncovering evidence, but the necessity of disrobing in front of others
humiliates Mitya, making him feel "almost guilty." Embarrassed especially by his feet ("All his life he had thought both his big toes
hideous"),[28] Mitya compares his predicament to "flogging" and
later calls the lawyers his "torturers" (p. 455).

The incident fully reveals the powers and the medieval origins
of the inquisitor's office. Even an innocent man like Mitya, who is
able to articulate his rage, can be made to feel culpable through the
subtle machinations of the inquisitor. Nikolai's order fulfills his historical role: coerce the suspect into a guilty state of mind in which
he actually comes to relish the possibility of confession. Like
Camus' Meursault when faced with the inquisitor brandishing a crucifix, Mitya almost capitulates to the tactics of European criminal
procedure. Dostoevski's awareness of czarist criminal procedure at-
tends to the smallest details of Nikolai's technique. His careful
maintenance of the "procès-verbal" by asking Mitya to affirm its accuracy and to sign it before making it a part of the larger dossier (p.
454), his interrogation of the witnesses in chapter 8 (oddly enough
in Mitya's presence, and plainly more a tactic than a legal commonplace), and his ultimate arrest of the suspect ("under the provisions
of the Criminal Code," p. 465) all provide the formalistic backbone
of his office.

The ultimate significance of the legal process in this masterpiece, however, finds expression more in the procurator (and, as we
shall see, in the "Grand Inquisitor") than in the preliminary inquisitor himself. This development beyond *Crime and Punishment* em-

phasizes Dostoevski's belief that the legal investigator, like the novelist himself, is motivated by an essentially personalized vision of reality. The myth of legal "objectivity" is explored in these pages, not for the sake of social satire alone, but for its association with narrative self-expression in general.

In Mitya's case, neither Nikolai nor Ippolit grants credence to what they call his "romaničeski" (literary or romantic) alibi (pp. 438, 440, 459, and 462). Nor do they really listen to Mitya's desperate attempt to communicate to them his own system of values, predicated on honor rather than "reason." On the other hand, they delight in stressing details Mitya deems irrelevant (pp. 427, 436). When confronted with the suspect's perfectly accurate, if highly improbable, account of why he carefully preserved the money given to him long before by Katerina Ivanovna and thus had 1500 roubles to squander at the Mokroe Inn (p. 449), Nikolai calls the story "čudesno" (fantastic), and the procurator responds with overt resentment (zlobi).

Conversely, when Ippolit Kirillovich propounds his own "reasonable" theory of the case (Mitya killed his father out of jealousy over Grushenka, stole the 3000 roubles from the victim's bedside, and spent the money at Mokroe), Mitya says he is "joking" and calls him "base" (podlo, p. 452). The procurator cannot understand how anyone could so flout "reasonableness" as first to sew 1500 roubles into a handkerchief in order not to spend it, and then suddenly to dispose of it all during one night of passion. Katerina's roubles "must" have been squandered long before, and the money spent at Mokroe "must" have been taken from the murder victim.

The dichotomy in Dostoevski is not between passion and reason, however. Rather it opposes two value systems, one spontaneous and the other formulaic, each striving aggressively to prove its own supremacy. The process of legal investigation, for Dostoevski, displays subtly but insistently its own narrative standards, and it will have its way even if it must create a falsehood to fit the individual suspect into its required patterns of behavior. Hence the inquisitor and the procurator (and, at the trial, the defense attorney)[29] have a vested interest in establishing for Mitya a motive that will explain his crime in a manner conducive to narrative rearticulation. This interest spirals into a "passion" in the figure of Ippolit Kirillovich (see pp. 414, 421, and 433), whose eminently reasonable methods and arguments, like those of the criminal process itself, mask a deep-seated allegiance to a purely personal world view which Dmitri Karamazov simply does not share.

As Professor W. Wolfgang Holdheim has noted, Ippolit Kirillovich, "als typische Ressentiment-figur," strikes out resentfully during the criminal procedure not only at Mitya, whose charms had evidently attracted the lawyer's wife, but also at his intellectual betters Fetyukovich and Ivan.[30] More generally, the procurator may be responding, in the tradition of Porfiry Petrovich, to the *active* man. For, even though in reality Mitya has not committed the homicide, the lawyer's persuasion that he has (together with the defendant's forceful, outgoing nature) marks him as an object of fascination and bitterness.

The entire thrust of the legal procedure, and the task for which "artistic legality" is eminently suited, is to recreate verbally, and thus to devalue, the existence of the spontaneous, vital individual who stands accused. Like the modern novelist, the lawyer employs his verbal gift to produce ironic or negative portraits of positive heroes. The personal problems of the examining and prosecuting lawyers (which in many cases fall under the category of ressentiment) become institutionalized in the *seemingly* rational procedures of criminal law.

Thus Ippolit's training as a "reasonable man," although it does not outweigh the subjective elements which truly motivate even those who seem most disinterested, makes it difficult for him to understand the code of honor which allows Mitya to say he would be "a scoundrel, but never a thief" (p. 45). As I shall show, the lawyers' incredulity at the honorable man's personal code, and their vigorous insistence upon ignoring "details" which are vital to an understanding of Mitya's actions, lead them to construct a theory of guilt based on robbery and personal greed, motives foreign to Mitya's nature.

Developing many of the legal aspects of *Crime and Punishment*, Dostoevski again has a procurator erroneously impute a robbery motive to the murder suspect. In Raskolnikov's case, the robbery theory ultimately gains official acceptance. Since the preliminary investigation has allowed Porfiry first to identify with and then to triumph over Raskolnikov, he has no further personal stake in the matter and allows a falsehood to prevail at the trial. In Mitya's case, the lawyers fail to reconcile the nature of the suspect with their false perceptions, and hence become more and more vigorously committed to them. Both trials therefore generate false conclusions, even though only Mitya's ends in an error as to actual guilt.

Throughout, Dostoevski brilliantly depicts artistic legality, with an attention to detail that clearly reflects self-identification. By the time the creative lawyer comes to formulate the official portrait of the defendant Mitya Karamazov at the trial, his analysis has undergone a series of fateful (if tiny) errors produced by the overall narrowness of his idiosyncratic vision.[31] Thus, when Mitya insists at the preliminary inquiry that the money he has just spent at Mokroe represented half of the 3000 roubles that earlier came from Katya (and not from his dead father's room), the following dialogue occurs, in which three testimonial mistakes can be discerned by a very perceptive reader:

"I brought [Grushenka] here to Mokroe then, and in two days squandered half of that damned three thousand. But the other half I kept on me. Well, I kept that other half, that fifteen hundred, like a locket around my neck. But yesterday I undid it and spent it . . . "

"Excuse me. How's that? Why, when you were here a month ago you spent three thousand, not fifteen hundred. Everybody knows that" [first error].

"Why you told everyone yourself that you'd spent exactly three thousand" [second error].

"It's true, I did. I told the whole town that . . . But I didn't spend three thousand, only fifteen hundred. And the other fifteen hundred I sewed into a little bag. That's how it was, gentlemen. That's where I got that money yesterday."

"This is almost unbelievable" [čudesno: miraculous], murmured Nikolai Nelyudov. "Let me ask," observed the procurator at last. Have you informed anyone of this circumstance before?"

"Absolutely no one. No one and nobody" [third error].

"What was your reason for this? What was your motive for making such a secret of it? . . . "

The procurator stopped speaking. He was provoked. He did not conceal his irritation, his ressentient reaction [zlobi], and he gave vent to all his accumulated spleen, without choosing words, disconnectedly and incoherently.

"It's not the fifteen hundred that's a disgrace, but that I put it apart from the rest of the three thousand," said Dmitri firmly. . . . "I squandered it, but I didn't steal it. . . . So in that case, I would be a scoundrel, but not a thief. Not a thief!"

"I admit that there is a certain distinction," said the procurator, with a cold smile. "But it's strange that you see such a vital difference."

The first error, revealed by reference to pages 116 and 149–50, indicates that at least one person could have surmised that Mitya had only spent 1500 of Katya's roubles and then preserved the other 1500 in a little bag around his neck (which he finally spent on Grushenka just prior to being arrested). This person, Alyosha, eventually does recall the relevant conversations when he testifies during the trial (p. 614), but the tardiness of his recollection renders the testimony too weak to impede the convincing flow of the procurator's narrative version of the case.

The second error is more explicit still. Even Mitya forgets that he told the innkeeper Plastunov that he "spent more than 1000 [not 3000!] roubles the last time I was here," and that he has "come to do the same again" (p. 381). These remarks, if they had been brought out by the inquisitor or procurator, would have exonerated Mitya, since they indicate that he could not have spent 2000 newly found roubles on the second spree at Mokroe. But Plastunov, one inaccurate witness among many, has lied about this issue at the preliminary inquiry (p. 458), stating with great certainty that Mitya "told him" he had brought 3000 roubles with him both times.

Such small falsehoods as these, ironically reinforced by Mitya himself in this third error, allow the lawyers to write a comprehensive and distorted narrative exposition of Mitya's motives and actions. Thus, at the end of the trial, Ippolit Kirillovich, in the lengthiest verbal formulation in the novel since Ivan's narration of "The Grand Inquisitor," can convincingly say:

But no, he did not touch the money in the little bag. And what is the reason he gives? The chief reason, as I have just said, was that when she would say "I am yours, take me where you will," he might have the wherewithal to take her. But that first reason, in the prisoner's own words, was of little weight beside the second. While I have that money on me, he said, I am a scoundrel, not a thief. I can always go to my insulted fiancée and laying down half the sum I have fraudulently appropriated, I can always say to her: "You see I've squandered half your money, and shown I am a weak and immoral man, and if you like, a scoundrel" (I use the prisoner's own expressions), "but though I am a scoundrel, I am not a thief, for if I were a thief, I wouldn't have brought back this half of the money, but would have taken it as I did the other half!" A marvelous explanation! This frantic but weak man, who could not resist the temptation of accepting the three thousand roubles at the price of such disgrace, this very man suddenly develops the most stoical firmness, and carries about fifteen hundred roubles without daring to touch them. *Does that fit in at all with the character we have analyzed?* No, and I will venture to tell you how the real Dmitri Karamazov would have behaved in such circumstances, if he really had put away the money. At the first temptation—for instance, to entertain the woman with whom he had already squandered half the money—he would have unpicked his little bag and have taken out some hundred roubles. For why should he have taken back precisely half the money, that is, fifteen hundred roubles; why not fourteen hundred? He could just as well have said then that he was not a thief, because he brought back fourteen hundred roubles. Then another time he would have unpicked it again and taken out another hundred, and then a third, and then a fourth. And before the end of the month he would have taken the last note but one, feeling that if he took back only a hundred it would answer the purpose, for a thief would have stolen it all. And then he would have looked at this last note, and have said to himself: "It's really not worth while to give back one hundred; let's spend that too!" *That's how the real Dmitri Karamazov, as we know him, would have behaved.* One cannot imagine anything more incongruous than this story of the little bag. Nothing could be more inconceivable. (pp. 634–35; emphasis mine)

Like Porfiry Petrovich's narration of Raskolnikov's crime and motivation at the end of their third dialogue, this last narration deserves close scrutiny. The culmination of the preliminary investigation, this speech to the jury displays the creative world view, and the spiritual essence, of the lawyer who utters it. Observing Mitya from a subjectivity marred by resentment, the procurator institutionalizes as a narrative work of art his peculiar perspective on reality. We know that his version of Mitya, unlike Porfiry's of Raskolnikov, totally misses the mark. But his position of legal power, and his acute ability to structure into flowing language his own ressentient errors, convinces the less knowledgeable jury and assemblage both of Mitya's guilt and of his motives.

As we shall see repeated in much of the mainstream of legal fiction, after Dostoevski, a prosecutor confronted with a defendant who displays some form of justice itself (Captain Vere and Billy Budd, for example), raises his own confused reaction to a level of seeming objective legality. The embodiment of honor, of morality, of justice, must be destroyed through legal means.

But as Ippolit Kirillovich's creative act exceeds in its distortion and its effect even Porfiry Petrovich's, so are its implications for Dostoevski's enterprise also immeasurably heightened. A first clue to our understanding of this is that the procurator's initials are the same as those of the most tortured intellectual verbalizer in the novel, Ivan Karamazov. Almost entirely defined by ressentient rage against his grotesque father, Ivan's increasing dependence in the book on his idiot half-brother Smerdyakov (with whom he, too, must tolerate three debilitating "interviews"; book 11, chapters 6–8) renders him ineffective and even cruel to all those he should love. Lise Hohlakova, Katerina Ivanovna (who shares part of his name and his ressentiment), the servant Grigori, even Alyosha, and of course Mitya become the objects of his futile rage, while, pathetically, the true source of his sense of insult remains unavenged. Smerdyakov alone can finally vanquish that constant, irksome paternal presence. But Ivan, for all his talk of a more just world, permits his older brother to be convicted of the parricide.

Like Ippolit Kirillovich, Ivan achieves creative brilliance only through narrative formulation. His conversations are really structured discourses. Like the Underground Man who is his spiritual precursor, Ivan organically rejects the highest Dostoevskian state: spontaneous, unstructured love. His ressentiment leaves him insusceptible to all human experience except narrative formulation. And his theories, like those of the Underground Man, mask behind mere words about freedom and effective action their author's subjective enslavement to spiritual disease.

Ippolit Kirillovich, too, achieves fullest self-expression by generating, from the depth of an essentially resentful spirit, a series of lengthy narratives; when he, like later legalistic characters such as Captain Vere and Clamence, manages to disguise a ferociously negative subjective tendency with a cooly rational outer form, the ramifications for the novel's meaning exceed mere social criticism. Dostoevski submits, through the legal theme, that whoever brings ressentiment to the act of formulating life through words only succeeds in producing an artistically convincing but essentially *unjust* portrait of reality. No juror apprehends the motives and ultimate errors of the artistic lawyers who reorganize the original circumstances of the parracide; the deliberately falsified or unconsciously distorted testimony of witnesses such as Grigori and Katerina Ivanovna, who both harbor some of Ippolit-Ivan's bitterness against the defendant,[32] buttresses the unbreachable wall of prosecutorial language.

The innocent Mitya stands convicted.

4 Dostoevski's Broken Structure

THE GRAND INQUISITOR

The legal sections of *The Brothers Karamazov* point to the negative
social consequences of narrative structures uninformed by a just substantive vision. Lives are destroyed and falsehood triumphs as legalisms bend reality. But like a jury, the reader may all too often fall
prey to the verbalizer's grandiose performance. For the essence of reality, disclosed only by the formulator's underlying urge to "lay bare"
his procedures and never in the overt meaning of his major pronouncements, must be discerned through an awareness of the details and the structure of the whole narration.

Inquisition provides a subtle, diadic structure to *The Brothers
Karamazov*. Until the two parts are linked, the artist's intention remains hidden. Although the temporal inquisition fills nearly ten
times as much narrative space, and although its two full sections
pertain more centrally to the "plot" of the novel, the other, meta-

physical one suffuses most critical reactions to the text. And yet the craftsman's placing of the two levels into a single structure would seem to invite observations stressing their complementary nature.

The finest creative emanation of Ivan Karamazov's narrative abilities, the shorter investigation bears the name of one of its principals, "The Grand Inquisitor."[1] This figure, who embodies organized modern Christianity, confronts in sixteenth-century Spain the returning founder of the now-prevalent religion. Amazed and disturbed by the sight of the Nazarene, the Inquisitor hastens to banish him from the midst of his impressionable flock. He deems Jesus an unwelcome intruder, an example of the kind of freedom which is anathema to his own ordered system; he acknowledges that the religion now has absolutely no place for spontaneity. No judicial process takes place, however, only a lengthy verbalization by the Inquisitor, an apology for valuing externally imposed order over individually willed action. But this unilateral presentation, unanswered, prevails. Without uttering a word, Ivan's Nazarene substitutes a single gesture for volumes of narrative: he bestows a kiss upon his adversary. Ironically, Ivan's story inverts the model of insult and repression which frequently informs the private confrontations of two characters in Dostoevski's works. The wordy formulator inflicts the insult here, and the loving free agent retreats from the scene. The Nazarene's gesture, though touching on a purely abstract level, thoroughly fails to answer the particular injustice of the Inquisitor's aggression toward him, just as the passivity of his religion's followers has often allowed, and sometimes encouraged, the dominance of injustice on earth during the two millenia of Christian culture.[2]

Listening to Ivan's story, Alyosha remains relatively silent, limiting himself to a few loving remarks. But no effective answer to Ivan's powerful indictment of Christianity, both in the story and in other conversations with Alyosha, is forthcoming. Like the Nazarene's, Alyosha's solution to the state of temporal injustice remains, until the end of the novel, in silence coupled with love.

Jesus and Alyosha, representing (with the saintly Father Zossima) the strongest Dostoevskian answer to the falsehood of narrative enslavement, appear to have failed. Their day in the court of human history has only compiled sufficient evidence against their passive mode to place it in strong doubt. Christian man, lulled by the lovely theoretical voice of love, faith, hope, and charity, has ceded power to those who terrorize the earth. Assured of his own eventual salvation, he frequently has permitted actual, nonmetaphysical atrocities to occur and sometimes has willingly participated in them. "Outsiders," those who refuse to organize their lives according to the imposed structures of the "true faith," have been punished with particular gusto.

Ivan Karamazov employs the Inquisitor to demonstrate the inevitable fate of such a religion, grounded not in law and ethics but rather in the most metaphysical and personal realm of human emotions: love. But if Ivan's story graphically indicates how quickly the notion of love, elevated to a communal precept, turns into chilly formalism and mass hatred, he himself, when he is not creating, adopts that negative mode fully. In a sense, Ivan reincarnates the Inquisitor, rejecting his medieval vocabulary but preserving his reactive, formal approach to those who fall in his sphere of influence. "Freedom" may have replaced "love" in Ivan's personal creed, but only as its theoretical foundation. The actual result, resentful formalism and cruelty, is no different.

Ivan is too intelligent to ignore this supreme irony in his world view. Like Dostoevski (and the lawyer Ippolit), he expresses it in his major artistic portraits. In the Grand Inquisitor, his finest creative characterization, Ivan depicts his own urge to bring order to what is otherwise free. Like many modern intellectuals, he brings to the service of a seemingly nihilistic world view a paradoxical tendency to construct forms. But in the realm of human interaction, Ivan's mode, like the Inquisitor's, only stifles others or leads them to violent thoughts or deeds. He cannot inspire them with a sense of their own free potential.

The Inquisitor's schemes for the happiness of man reflect his exaggerated notion of himself as one of the unhappy few upon whose shoulders the fate of all mankind descends. We are reminded of Nietzsche's brilliant aphorisms about priests, in the *Genealogy of Morals*, and of his debt to Dostoevski:

We must look upon the ascetic priest as the predestined advocate and savior [Heiland, Hirt und Anwalt] of a sick flock if we are to comprehend his tremendous historical mission. His dominion is over sufferers. . . . He must be sick of himself . . . yet he must also be strong, master over himself even more than over others, with a will to power that is intact, if he is to be their support, overlord, disciplinarian, tyrant, god. They are his flock and he must defend them—against whom? Against the healthy, obviously, but also against their envy [Neid] of the healthy; he must be the natural antagonist and *contemner* [Verachter] of all rude, violent, savage health and power. . . . He fights a clever, hard, secret battle against anarchy and disintegration, always aware of the piling up of rancor [ressentiment], that most dangerous of dynamites. In other words, it is up to the priest to redirect resentment toward a new object. The release of aggression is the best palliative for any kind of affliction. The wish to alleviate pain through strong emotional excitation is, to my mind, the true physiological motive behind all manifestations of resentment. I strongly disagree with those who would see here a mere defensive or prophylactic reaction to sudden injury or jeopardy, a mere reflex, such as a headless frog makes to throw off an acid. There is a fundamental difference between the two processes: in the one case the effort is simply to prevent further injury, in the other to *dull* by means of some violent emotion a secret, tormenting pain that is gradually becoming intolerable—to banish it momentarily from consciousness. For that purpose an emotion of maximum violence is required, and any pretext that comes to hand will serve. "*Somebody* must be responsible for my discomfort." . . . All sufferers alike excel in finding imaginary pretexts for their suffering. (*Genealogy* 3.15:262–64)

Ivan takes upon his own sick and tortured soul the need to redirect and to reformulate the emotions of those around him. But negativity breeds only negativity; like that of the Inquisitor, Ivan's flock is led astray. Alyosha, Katerina, Lise, and Smerdyakov suffer tangibly from the guilt Ivan imposes in his role of latter-day inquisitor-priest. Their emotions are aroused to fever pitch, but they are offered no direction except reactive violence.

Camus, stressing Ivan's philosophical arguments, saw him as a rebel.[3] But observing him in the fullness of his character, Nietzsche might have joined us in calling him a *priest*. Rebellion requires more than words—it requires an act; but priestliness, like exaggerated legality, thrives on the cleverness of a merely reactive formalism. Rebellion involves, after an initial *no*, a concrete deed; but priestliness strives to preserve the original negation, propagates it, and then instills it in others. For Ivan, life has been reduced to reaction. Just as the Grand Inquisitor's schemes are negative responses to Christ's example of freedom and spontaneity, so Ivan infuses everyone he meets with his bitter resentment, inspired first and foremost by his father. For Ivan creates more than the story of the Inquisitor. While he cannot act himself, he succeeds in communicating a violently reactive idea to the overly receptive mind of at least one member of his audience. The servant and bastard half-brother, like the Christian flock, absorbs the resentments of his "priest" and translates narrative structures into violent deeds. And for this violence an innocent outsider is condemned.

The "doubling" of Ivan and Smerdyakov in their virtual conspiracy to kill their father, parallels Dostoevski's deepest fears about Christian appearance versus reality. Ivan's noble pronouncements, like those of the Christianity he purports to reject, produce no tangible earthly good. Only a fragment of the central idea reaches the flock. Smerdyakov, linked to Ivan since childhood by their mutual resentment of Fyodor and by their perverse precociousness (his hanging of cats is the active equivalent of Ivan's "sullen and introverted" intelligence), can absorb only the venomous aspects of his brother's pronouncements. Ivan's priestly bearing and words motivate Smerdyakov to the violent act, while Smerdyakov's capacity to act fills Ivan with increasing rage. The homicide accomplished, Ivan retreats into self-flagellation and madness, passively permitting his innocent older brother to take the blame. For all his protestations of philosophical freedom, he has bound his fate to that of the repressed and violent servant. Ivan's ressentiment takes the nightmarish Dostoevskian underground to its limits. All positive values have been subverted.

So we may come to understand "The Grand Inquisitor" in context. The Nazarene represents an affront to the Inquisitor's authoritative formalism. So Mitya, equally innocent of the accusation levelled against him, but also equally offensive to the procurator's resentful sense of order, stands unjustly condemned. Dostoevski's Christian epistemology, translated into the narrative structure of the novel, thus generates a deeply anti-Christian statement. Christ unwittingly founds an institution whose negative precept of order evolves to exclude even him. That negation, carefully engendered in the flock, is then translated into violence inflicted upon, and ultimately ascribed to, outsiders.

The spontaneous beauty of the new religion, nineteen centuries into its history, has ceded to narrative authoritarianism and tangible temporal injustice. More damning yet, it has led to a culture so saturated with reactive guilt that even its intellectual "rebels" fail to effectuate their theories of freedom and justice. Little more than half a century after Dostoevski's statement, the participation

of all Christian institutions in an unthinkable victimization of innocents, a participation now increasingly recognized by courageous
Christian theologians,[4] was to demonstrate the novelist's prophetic
brilliance.

Despite Alyosha's professed faith in his innocence, Mitya, an
outsider by virtue of his nonformulaic approach to reality, is condemned for the crime committed by his half-brother Smerdyakov
and actually "created" by Ivan. The structured word vanquishes the
representation of life itself, both in the double-leveled inquisitorial
scenario and in the intermediary between the two levels, the intellectual Ivan. For if unaided tacit love is shown to fail on this earth,
so does the "narrative tendency," whether in the lawyer, the intellectual, or the literary artist. A just vision of the world requires a
vigorous ethic of moral autonomy and communal responsibility.
Love, which arises only within individuals, never within communi-
ties, will thrive when it is least discussed. Once it loses its essentially nonnarrative quality and is made the basis of a social system,
it will produce only its opposite, ressentiment.

DOSTOEVSKI AS IVAN: NOVELISTIC RESSENTIMENT

Ivan's Devil

Existenzialneid, the impotent rage of one who envies the being-in-
itself of another, engulfs Ivan's spirit as his horrifying relationship
with Smerdyakov draws to a close. His older brother is on trial for
the crime committed by Ivan's protégé and lackey, but that crime
has placed Ivan forever in his servant's debt. Only by his co-conspir-
ator's suicide can the hideous situation be relieved. But even in this
act Smerdyakov usurps Ivan's fate; his death forces Ivan to succumb
to a figurative death of his own. The bastard brother who successfully plundered Ivan's homicidal idée fixe in life takes his booty with
him in death.

Ivan Karamazov actually "loses his mind." Yet as he takes leave
of Smerdyakov for the last time, he intuits an imminent improve-
ment in his condition. Perhaps he realizes he will never see Smerdyakov again; perhaps he senses the curative power of his impending madness. In any case, a "sort of happiness was entering his

soul." As he leaves, he experiences his first brief sense of joy since the few spontaneous conversations with Alyosha much earlier in the novel. This spiritual upturn finds overt expression. Uncharacteristically repenting for a moment of resentful violence, Ivan lifts from the frozen earth a drunken peasant whom he had knocked down just before the final scene with Smerdyakov and sees to his medical care as well. Without thinking, he achieves his one and only charitable deed.

The significance of this act lies in its unprecedented generosity. In losing his mind, Ivan loses the constricted narrative character, so to speak, which had negatively determined his earlier existence. Unfortunately for the intellectual, the process of ressentiment, once it has reached its ultimate stages, possesses a ferocious negative momentum. Even as Ivan rescues the peasant, his intellect continues to deceive him; he finds himself thinking that the charitable act was "a waste of an hour." Furthermore, he is certain that he will not go mad, and that the opportunity to testify in Mitya's case will somehow prove his own innocence.

Like the Underground Man fleeing from Liza, Ivan returns home to isolation, to his personalized falsehood. But in Ivan's case, the spectre of falsehood actually achieves diabolical embodiment. A devil, a grotesque figment of Ivan's overworked imagination, greets him amicably at his door. Like Faust's Mephistopheles, Ivan's devil is shaped by a modern intellectual's narrative consciousness; he is not at all the traditional horned creature spewing fire.[5] In our terms, the bourgeois *chort* is organic mendacity personified, a lie evoked by the artist figure Ivan. It is the equivalent in artifice of the diary in part 1 of *Notes from Underground*. All human contact has gradually been removed from Ivan's life. Finally even his double has been eliminated. Alone with his lie, he finds his inner falsity rendered palpable. He soon grasps the essential meaning of the witty demon who addresses his sick creator with sarcasm and in the familiar (a liberty otherwise foreign to Ivan's relationships):[6]

"Never for one minute have I taken you for reality," Ivan cried with a sort of fury. "You are a lie, you are my illness, you are a phantom." (pp. 577–78)

"No, you are not someone apart, you are myself, you are I and nothing more! You are rubbish, you are my fancy!" (p. 582)

The devil is merely a projection of the "trash" which is Ivan's internal state. Every idea that he elucidates in his self-described "literary way" has already been expressed by Ivan in a story, essay, or article. Piece by piece, the devil holds up to ridicule Ivan's philosophical system—the notion of the "man-god," the formula "everything is lawful," the theory that each individual must insist on retaining his freedom at the expense of his grace (the equivalent of the Underground Man's "two plus two equals five").

Ivan's reaction to himself duplicates Raskolnikov's resentful gnashing of teeth and absurd threats of violence in the face of Porfiry Petrovich. Like an artist suddenly overly conscious of his own processes and creations, Ivan perceives his whole life as irony, hypocrisy, and unparalleled enslavement to falsifying forms. His devil, like the novel, is a structured lie which captures the intellectual and spiritual essence of its creator. By parroting Ivan's verbalizations, the demon satirizes the detached narrative existence he has led. In a sense, then, when the devil makes his traditional complaint, he speaks through Ivan for all modern "literary men":[7]

"Why am I, of all creatures in the world, doomed to be cursed and even kicked by all decent people. For if I put on mortal form I am bound to be cursed and kicked." (p. 587)

The writer's "mortal form," which paradoxically divorces him from the world of human emotion, is his literary statement. Ivan, whose earlier forms included scholarly articles and "The Grand Inquisitor," finally creates the devil, the rejection of love and the epitome of falsehood.

My interpretation of Notes from Underground sees part 1 as the protagonist's expression of the last stage of ressentient negativity, organic mendacity. Like Ivan's devil, its ironic structure gives voice to a life of mere reaction and repression, through the absolute negation of human sympathy and the elevation of words above ethics. That diatribe, like Ivan's poems, articles, and formulaic pronouncements, and like the novel itself, attempts to structure an essentially formless process, life. Where the narrative effort engages a healthy spirit, the result may be magnificent. But in Dostoevski's protagonists, the narrative urge finally reflects only formalized ressentiment and the failure to interact positively with other human beings.

Organic Mendacity and the Literary Act

Ivan Karamazov's condition of ressentiment parallels those of Ham-let and the Underground Man in that it is predicated on external circumstances, but aggravated by an internal predilection. In each case, this internal factor is legalistic in nature; it expresses itself as a tendency to resense and to restructure one's surroundings verbally and to seize control over life by recasting it into words. While they are not actually lawyers, these characters seek to impose a post-hoc, formalistic control over otherwise form-resisting people and situa-tions. Thus, Ivan's urge to write has grown in direct proportion to his disenchantment with social intercourse. As he has matured, and as the action of the novel bears out, his communication with others becomes limited to written forms. His "conversations" are better de-scribed as recitations of various texts, ranging from his articles (as in the confrontation with Father Zossima), to newspaper clippings[8] (as in his important discourse to Alyosha on the injustice of chil-dren's suffering), to his creative narratives (as when he relates the story "The Grand Inquisitor" to his younger brother). Conversely, Ivan cannot communicate at all in situations calling for an immedi-ate and spontaneous response. We have analyzed his impotence in the negative realms of hatred and revenge; even more important, perhaps, are his failures relating to the emotion of love and the ethic of justice. Both Lise and Katerina Ivanovna finally reject his cruel coldness to them. So does Dmitri, but only after Ivan's deceit-ful silence during the criminal process helps to send him to prison for a murder he has not committed.

Even before *The Brothers Karamazov*, Dostoevski had expressed the notion that human beings, to escape a negative stance toward others, must "love life more than the meaning of life." This maxim articulates what can justifiably be called his basic theme after 1861. Its message lends the spirit of Christianity a vibrancy sharply at odds with its historical practice in western Europe. Applied to the nov-els, the maxim serves to differentiate one type of Dostoevskian character from another; almost every one of his creations either "loves life" or fruitlessly seeks the rational "meaning of life." Ernest J. Simmons observes, in this vein, that Alyosha "is the only one of the three brothers who is able to love life more than the meaning of life," whereas Ivan, "unlike either of his brothers . . . is more concerned with the meaning of life than with life itself."[9] We can further associate with the "lovers of life" most of the "meek" figures of Dostoevski's great novels, and also many of the women and more than a few transgressors. The intellectuals, from the Underground Man through Raskolnikov, Stavrogin, the minor socialists or reformers, and Ivan, all fall under the opposite sign.

The short stories often employ an even more penetrating use of this theme. The puzzling "A Gentle Spirit" ("Kratkaya") may be partially interpreted in terms of an insoluble tension between the verbal, intellectualized narrator and his more instinctual, less literary wife. Their conflicting approaches eventually lead to her suicide and his crafting of the incident into a story. "The Dream of a Ridiculous Man" relates an individual odyssey from one perspective to the other. Its narrator learns from a small girl that his carefully structured approach to life has been fruitless. He describes this failed system as "knowledge being higher than feeling and the consciousness of life more important than life." In his ensuing fantasy, he creates a universe of innocents whom he proceeds (like the biblical serpent) to infect with consciousness; inspired by pure love, however, both he and they ultimately learn to surrender their newfound wills in the name of sympathy and godliness. The dream buttresses the comments of the little girl, and the narrator is able to conclude ecstatically:

It is an old truth, one that has been told and written a billion times, but which men still refuse to accept! "The consciousness of life is higher than life, the knowledge of the workings of happiness is higher than happiness"—this is what we have to fight against! And I shall! If only we all wanted it, everything could be arranged immediately![10]

To the opposing philosophies of Dostoevski's dichotomy, the late short stories add an intermediary possibility: the progression from "meaning of life" to "love of life itself" can be achieved through a stage of temporal experience. In Dostoevski's novels, this middle stage is represented by the figure of the great sinner, whose spiritual odyssey allows him eventually to aspire to earthly sainthood. The colorful description of Father Zossima's sinful and atheistic youth which fills many pages of The Brothers Karamazov indicates that ressentiment can be overcome only through an extreme commitment to experience and passionate human action. Love means nothing in the abstract; it must be earned.

Indeed, one of Zossima's few lengthy statements—his genius does not lie in language—explicitly describes the disease of organic mendacity and offers an antidote. As the only figure in the novel who has overcome ressentiment through experience and selfless love, Zossima gives the following advice to Fyodor, the paternal source of Karamazov negativity:

Above all, don't lie to yourself. The man who lies to himself and listens to his own lie comes to such a point that he cannot distinguish the truth within him, or around him, and so loses all respect for himself and for others. And having no respect he ceases to love. . . . The man who lies to himself can be more easily offended than anyone else. You know it is sometimes very pleasant to take offense, isn't it? A man may know that nobody has insulted him, but that he has invented the insult for himself, has lied and exaggerated to make it picturesque [kartinu sozdat'], has caught at a word and made a mountain out of a molehill—he knows that himself, yet he will be the first to take offense [obižaetsa] and will revel in his resentment till he feels great pleasure in it. And so he will pass to genuine vindictiveness. (p. 49)

Zossima's perfect comprehension of ressentiment comes not from books but from his personal struggle against it. A stage of complete action and immersion in human intercourse must, in Dostoevski's system, precede spiritual or intellectual maturity.[11] Thus, Dostoevski's dichotomy is actually a tautology; man *must* seek the meaning of life if he is ever to find that pure love of life which is the highest earthly condition. The painful process toward earthly reconciliation requires a plenitude of experience rather than a series of sterile formulations. It sometimes encompasses extremes of degradation, sin, and even serious crime,[12] but it is ultimately a divine process.

Dostoevski's novels appear, however, to identify at least one activity which can never aid in the achievement of a harmonious earthly existence—the consistently intellectualized enterprise of the literary artist. The novelist's urge to narrate reality stunts the growth toward life.[13]

The Novelistic Formulation as Meaning, Not Life

René Girard, a perceptive phenomenologist of the novel and a critic who seems to share Dostoevski's Christian world view, articulates well the antitheses described above. Girard observes that "the entire underground psychology strikes Dostoevski as an inverted reflection of the Christian structure, as precisely its double."[14] Girard concludes, however, that *The Brothers Karamazov*, unlike any earlier novel, achieves "the structure of incarnation" which "can only be born when the novelist begins to emerge from the underground; [the structure] can only attain its full development in full freedom" (p. 168).

While Girard never exactly defines "incarnation," he seems to propose that both Dostoevski and his work have, by *The Brothers Karamazov*, advanced from the search for life's meaning to the Christian love of life itself. Specifically, Girard sees the novelistic ending as the locus for a breakthrough to the essence of Christian truth. Thus, in *Deceit, Desire and the Novel* he says:

In all genuine novelistic conclusions, death as spirit is victoriously opposed to death of the spirit. . . . The conclusion is the site of the presence of truth, and therefore a place avoided by error. (pp. 305, 307; see chapter 2, n. 27, above)

As a corollary to this interesting axiom, he concludes that novelistic endings are usually banal and predictable, but that it is "the absolute banality of what is essential in Western civilization"—Christianity (p. 308).

While Girard's approach may suffer, ironically, from what the critic himself opposes in Freudian and sociological analyses of texts ("They only recognize a narrow and arbitrarily chosen part of reality"),[15] its application to the Christian writer Dostoevski, appears particularly fortuitous. But although it is true that there is a greater breadth in *The Brothers Karamazov* than in the earlier works, we need not necessarily conclude that the book achieves either an "incarnation" or a "serene vision."

Before I approach the final chapters of the novel with Girard's theory in mind, a look at several essential letters from this late period in Dostoevski's life may be in order, since they argue against placing too strong an emphasis upon a harmonious resolution in *The*

Brothers Karamazov. From its inception, the novel presented itself as a troubling task for the author; he writes to A. N. Maikov in 1870 that "my hero . . . is an atheist and a fanatic," and that the book will concern "a matter which has bothered me, consciously or unconsciously, during my entire life—the existence of God."[16] Although he was later to call Alyosha the hero of the work, Dostoevski never overcame his fascination with Ivan and the atheistic point of view. Thus, a decade or so later, as the work was being published, it remained a source of extreme doubt for the writer. His letters express disappointment at his continuing inability to convey religious faith through prose, whereas the chapters portraying Ivan's point of view, especially "Pro and Contra," "Interviews," and "Devil," he calls "the best in my book."[17]

Dostoevski's awareness of this paradox must have been particularly jarring since he had come to see his great novel as a means of self-salvation. As early as 1867, for example, he had written to his wife, promising her that he would "never, never, gamble again" and pointing out that "now the novel, only the novel will save us, if you only knew how dearly I hope for that!"[18] In an identical vein, he tells his friend Apollon Maykov in a letter of 10 September 1869, "On this second novel I pin all my hopes. Perhaps they will realize at last that I have not been writing a lot of rubbish all my life."[19] Dostoevski's "hopes" revolve around the portrait of the saintly Father Zossima, a portrait he intended as a sufficient response to the intellectuals, westernizers, and atheists.

Thus, perhaps the most poignant letter of all, which is worth quoting at length for its relevance to a discussion of narrative ressentiment in a religious writer, a full decade later explores Father Zossima's place in Dostoevski's masterpiece:

> But you raise an indispensable point: that an answer to all these atheistic statements [in *The Brothers Karamazov*] has not yet occurred to me, and it is necessary. This is now the cause of all my anxiety and my lack of peace [bespokoistvo].[20] For in answer to this whole *negative side* I would put forward that sixth book—*A Russian Monk*, which appears on 31 August. But why I tremble rests in this thought: will it be a *sufficient* answer?[21]

Again, the religious writer found it almost impossible to incorporate his most profound beliefs into his narrative. Somehow (and in a manner which Dostoevski himself did not fully understand) the spontaneity of true Christian faith seemed to defy formulaic, novelistic representation. Could it be that Dostoevski sensed the futility of this enterprise and transmitted his doubts and even his resentments to his articulate protagonists? Certainly the continuation of this important letter indicates a cosmic struggle between faith and narrative:

The answer is not a direct one, not to the position expressed [in "The Grand Inquisitor" and earlier chapters], that is, point by point, but it is an indirect answer. Here I present a kind of dispersed answer to the world view of those chapters but I present it not point by point but, so to speak, as an artistic picture. This is what unsettles [bespokoit] me, that is, will they understand me? Shall I accomplish even a part of my goal? And in addition there are still my responsibilities to artistic concepts: I had to present a modest and sublime character, while life is full of comedy and is only sublime in its internal feelings, so that against my will [ponevole], for the sake of artistic demands, it was necessary for me to introduce in the biography of my monk certain vulgar and banal aspects in order not to supercede artistic realism. Then there are several of the monk's sermons, which will produce cries that they are absurd, because they are too rapturous. Of course they are absurd in their ordinary sense, but in their inner meaning they seem to me to be just. The whole matter disquiets me [bespoko'us], and I would appreciate your advice.

The allegiance to a task which, by its very nature, rebels against one's "inner meaning" may produce a vindictive attitude toward that task, and toward the world in general. It does not seem to be a distortion to say that these remarkable letters imply a realization on Dostoevski's part that novel-writing substitutes "the meaning of life" for the "love of life itself." The scenes that propound beliefs wholly opposed to his own are, admittedly and troublingly, the most brilliant in *The Brothers Karamazov*. Just as the Underground Man reaches his verbal heights when espousing a viewpoint unsubstantiated by his own existence, just as Raskolnikov's article on the "Superman" contradicts his essential nature, so Ivan's essays and poems—and especially his devil—are among the most potent testaments to every concept Dostoevski abhorred.

The contention may be advanced, then, that the existence of ressentiment in the major artistic and intellectual protagonists of Dostoevski's works existentially reflects the author's own discomfort at being both a religious man and a driven narrative artist.[22] The choice of conjuring an imaginary and formalistic universe as salvation from the disappointments of life (in at least one letter, Dostoevski speaks of writing as "a temptation" which he should resist)[23] strikes the novelist as dubious.

Thus the absence of incarnation and serenity throughout the body of Dostoevski's works is not definitely overcome in his last novel. We would do well to look carefully at Girard's "locus of conclusion" in *The Brothers Karamazov*, where we may find a nonbanal, even a strikingly subtle, reiteration of narrative negativity.

Consistency in Conclusion: The Novel's Final Tableaux

It is always comforting to surmise that an artistic genius, at the close of his career, suddenly discovers a resolution to those conflicts which have suffused, and given power to, all of his earlier work. But it is more likely that, unlike conventional mortals, the artist struggles even more intensely as the end nears. As we shall see regarding *Billy Budd* and *The Fall*, two other final masterpieces, the artist of *The Brothers Karamazov* rearticulates, but with greater force than hitherto, the crushing tensions that often plague a genius' existence. We should not seek blissful banality in a novel's conclusion; we should only remark what is there.

The conclusion of *The Brothers Karamazov* resists even the semblance of a movement toward the exultation which is obvious in other "religious" masterpieces such as *The Divine Comedy*. The closing chapters on Ivan Karamazov, placed quite near the end of the novel, powerfully continue to invoke the theme of formalistic ressentiment. The lengthy courtroom scene and the scene of the child Ilyusha's burial—the two other major concluding sections of the book—also emphasize the negative structure of the whole.

As we have seen, the procurator Ippolit Kirillovich's ressentient condition—as well as the more than coincidental identity of their initials—ties him to Ivan Karamazov. Both consciously attempt to mold reality into a preconceived form. Both fail to arrive at an ultimate vision of truth because truth refuses to submit to that form. One of these artists loses his mind. The other, nine months after his "success" at the trial, dies of "rapid consumption." The trial scene's pervasive demonstration that words fail underscores the structural power of the late scenes involving Ivan's devil. These are followed, however, by a seemingly positive final scene in the epilogue. But even if the setting manages to evoke serenity, does what Professor Holdheim persuasively calls the "forced, weak and overly sentimentalized children's theme"[24] at young Ilyusha's funeral offset the thoroughly negative quality of Dostoevski's self-conscious statement articulated through Ivan and the lawyers?

In fact, the epilogue's atmosphere in no way attains Girard's "serene vision." Instead, it extends and reinforces the novel's underlying negativity. The first half, which takes place in Mitya's hospital room, ends on a note of dispute and, indeed, ressentiment. Katerina Ivanovna and Grushenka (who earlier says of her feelings for Mitya, "Perhaps I love only my ressentiment, not him") have a bitter argument that terminates not in redemptive forgiveness, but in Katerina's rushing out of the hospital, "eyes flashing with fierce resentment [zloboi]" (p. 693), and refusing to come to the boy's funeral. Structurally, then, Ivan's ressentient influence sets the atmosphere early in the epilogue.

Burdened with Katerina's resentment, Alyosha arrives late at the funeral. He ponders the many examples of bitterness and injustice which temporal existence seems to produce. Far from tranquil, the young monk can accept neither Mitya's unjust conviction for the parricide, nor Ilyusha's untimely death. At the outset of the scene, he refuses to countenance the youthful Kolya Krassotkin's enthusiastic statement that Mitya's innocent suffering is somehow justified and noble:

"The valet killed him, my brother is innocent," answered Alyosha. "That's what I said," cried [the boy] Smurov. "So he is an innocent victim!" exclaimed Kolya. "But even though he is ruined he is happy! I envy him!" "What do you mean? How can you? Why?" cried Alyosha, surprised. "Oh, if only I too could sacrifice myself some day for truth!" cried Kolya. "But not in such a cause, not with such disgrace and such horror!" said Alyosha. (pp. 693–94)

Alyosha's admirable (if essentially un-Christian) unwillingness to rationalize earthly injustice denies him any feigned acceptance of Ilyusha's needless death. In the end he has been "tempted" beyond human endurance by the overwhelming events which have destroyed his father and three brothers. These events, particularly Mitya's trial, the unseemly decay of Father Zossima's body, and finally this innocent boy's funeral, contrive to bolster and even to prove the skeptical position Ivan has articulated to his younger brother in the "Grand Inquisitor" discussion.

The end of Alyosha's youth, and the foreshadowing of his projected degradation,[25] are symbolized in the burial of his near-namesake Ilyusha. His incipient downfall is expressed even more significantly in the *form* of his concluding statement, a long narrative which fittingly closes the book. Never before has Alyosha been so wordy; his usual stance of saintly, tacit veracity, has always avoided the verbosity of the false formulators around him. Like the Christ of "The Grand Inquisitor," the silent, often inarticulate monk has moved many. His uncharacteristic garrulousness is thus a surer indication of the evil he foresees ("Perhaps we may even grow wicked later on," he says to the boys) than is the substance of his closing remarks. His two paragraphs of advice to the children represent Alyosha's first attempt to express "the meaning of life" rather than to seek "life itself." They mark his initial break with Father Zossima's teachings, his first step into the world of words.

A masterpiece remains so from beginning to end. Thus it is not surprising to discover these reflections of our thesis in its conclusion. Faith cannot be formulated or verbalized. A session at one's desk with pen and paper is a regression toward artificial structures antithetical to the religious experience. The act of writing reflects the downward movement of the Christian religion; its representative is the Grand Inquisitor, not the fullest flower of the faith, the utterly silent Nazarene. The modern Christian narrative courageously indicts its own procedures by generating a structure which undermines the verbal mode. Its implicit result, embodied in the condition of many of its characters, is negative. The word has failed, for it terminates in organic mendacity.

We have chosen to save the peace. But . . . we have mutilated friends. And without doubt, many among us were ready to risk their lives for the duties of friendship. Such persons feel a kind of shame. But if they had sacrificed peace, they would have felt the same shame. For then they should have sacrificed man; they should have accepted the irreparable destruction of the libraries, the cathedrals, the laboratories of Europe. . . . And this is why we wavered from one opinion to the other. When peace seemed threatened, we discovered the shame of war. When war was no longer a threat, we felt the shame of peace.

—Antoine de Saint-Exupéry on
the day the Nazis occupied Czechoslovakia;
quoted in Herbert R. Lottman, The Left Bank

PART 3 The Failure of the Heroic Narrative Vision: French Literature under Siege

5 The Revisionary Flaubert: *Salammbô*

FLAUBERT'S DILEMMA: WRONG TIME, WRONG PLACE, WRONG SEX

If Dostoevski articulates the modern novelist's ambivalent stance toward religious themes, Flaubert most powerfully conveys the narrative negativity of the modern artist in dialogue with heroic subjects. Long praising his devotion to "craftsmanship," critics have only relatively recently explored the negative implications of the relationship between his stylistic innovations and the themes that pervade his works. Sartre's mammoth endeavor, *L'Idiot de la famille* (see chapter 1, n. 17), epitomizes the "revisionist" trend, but elements of iconoclasm have entered into the analyses of Georg Lukacs, Victor Brombert, Jonathan Culler, and myself as well.[1] Recent criticism has tended to undermine the hitherto unending critical admiration for Flaubert's technical enterprise.

My approach to Flaubert emphasizes the implied relationship of author to legalistic protagonist. In this respect, Flaubert's novels invite comparison with Dostoevski's masterpieces, an invitation infrequently accepted by the critics even though the two men were also virtual contemporaries.[2] Flaubert, however, takes the Dostoevskian theme of legalistic ressentiment to new levels. Indeed, in Flaubert the phenomenon attains a stylistic sublimity unequaled among Continental writers. In few other contemporary artists do theme and aesthetic so perfectly reflect the process by which formalistic negativity becomes creative. And in none does the stylistic progression from priestly mendacity to legalistic mediocrity to authorial ressentiment develop so subtly.

As Harry Levin puts it, in an early reaction to Anglo-Saxon Flaubert criticism since Henry James:

Flaubert's own opinion [was] that he was "born lyrical" and had disciplined himself to prose. . . . It is possible to trace Flaubert's creative activity to the sublimation of the libido.[3]

Self-suppression informs every aspect of Flaubert's enterprise. In the first part of his career it explodes, resentfully, against exotic female protagonists. Later it fitfully manifests itself in prosaic male protagonists. But never does Flaubert's native lyricism produce a harmonic narrative vision. Was his conscious intention to abnegate his own inclinations either realizable or admirable? Contemporary bias, which may be gradually changing, to some extent finds in favor of the artist who stubbornly channels his native impulses into pure craftsmanship ("Art became his mistress," declares an admirer of Henry James);[4] voluntary enslavement to one's art is lauded. Thus Flaubert's lifelong flirtation with the lyrical and the exotic strikes us as nobly countered by his mature marriage to realistic prose. His peculiar form of repression is compared to martyrdom and associated with a vague sort of religious ecstasy, a sacrifice on the "altar of Art."[5]

In this view, predicated on the values of a specific critical milieu, Flaubert's most negative self-castigations become indices of a glorified existence. But such opponents of this cultural perspective as Nietzsche and Sartre have found little to admire in Flaubert. They see implicit in his enterprise the propagation, in the name of art, of personal and social repression and rancor.

How one feels about Flaubert's "sublimation of the libido" naturally affects the importance one assigns to the themes and symbols that run through his novels. Thus, while most critics would allow a healthy dose of biographical data in their approaches to such early stories as "Mémoires d'un fou" and "Novembre," their predominant thinking on the "realist" novels is that the author's experiences hardly inform those more mature works. Style, they would have us believe, eventually overcame instinct, emotion, and therefore autobiography in Flaubert. This axiom arises in no small degree from

Flaubert's own statements in his letters, where much of his aesthetic theory finds articulation. Erich Auerbach, for example, in his brief but well-known discussion of *Madame Bovary* in *Mimesis*, observes that

there occur in his letters, particularly of the years 1852–1854 during which he was writing *Madame Bovary* . . . many highly informative statements on the subject of his aim in art. They lead to a theory . . . of a self-forgetful absorption in the subjects of reality which transforms them (*par une chimie merveilleuse*) and permits them to develop to mature expression. In this fashion subjects completely fill the writer; he forgets himself, his heart no longer serves him save to feel the hearts of others. . . . Subjects are seen as God sees them, in their true essence. . . . The universe is a work of art produced without any taking of sides; the realistic artist must imitate the procedures of Creation.[6]

Auerbach's analysis may have relied upon Flaubert's:

Madame Bovary has no foundation in fact. It is an entirely invented story. I have added to it neither my own feelings nor my life. The illusion (if there is one) arises, on the contrary, from the *impersonality* of the work. This is one of my principles: one must not write oneself in. The artist must stand to his work as God to his creation, invisible and omniscient; he must be everywhere felt but nowhere seen.

   Art thus must rise above private proclivities and nervous inclinations. It is time to give it, by a pitiless method, the precision of the physical sciences.[7]

Auerbach's analysis appears to accept literally and sympathetically Flaubert's dictum of self-effacement and the possibility of achieving it throughout. In full, however, Flaubert's correspondence, like Dostoevski's, testifies to the writer's uncertainty about the act of writing and about the possibility for creative craftsmanship divorced from underlying subjective motivations.

   It is indeed quite unclear that Flaubert ever accepted absolutely the program for writing outlined in the 1857 letter. Five years earlier he had invoked objectivity while bemoaning his own frailty:

Passion does not make poetry; and the more personal you are, the weaker you will be. That has always been my sin; I have always put myself into everything I have done.[8]

Four years after the 1857 letter, he admitted:

A good subject for a novel is one that springs up fully formed, at a single spurt. It's the mother source from which everything else flows. One is certainly not free to write about any given subject. The public and the critics do not understand this. The secret of a masterpiece lies in *the conformity between the subject and the author's nature.*[9]

Three separate letters chosen from a correspondence comprising many volumes thus produce three contradictory observations about the craft of fiction. In the 1857 letter, Flaubert is writing about literature to an admirer whom he never actually met, which may explain its imposing tone and cast doubts on its remarks about writing. The 1852 letter, to his constant correspondent Louise Colet, is probably far more representative of Flaubert's felt beliefs.

In fact, the correspondence of the period which produced *Madame Bovary*, *Salammbô*, and *L'Education sentimentale* can be cited to support a variety of approaches to Flaubert's work. Even in the letters of a layman, after all, tone and content are likely to vary with mood, timing, and especially audience. In a professional writer's correspondence, one might expect at least that degree of variation. On balance, I believe that Flaubert's letters express his uneasiness in discovering a wide gap between the goal of "scientific" writing and the reality of extreme subjectivism. In the 1861 letter, for example, Flaubert seems to reject the notion of the novelist as deity; he sees his central enterprise not at all as objective, but rather as the predetermined result of his deepest *personal* conflicts. Other letters written between 1842 and 1862 suggest the dual obsession of his creative life: older and less intellectualized cultures, and Woman as the last repository of such cultures in nineteenth-century Europe.

Flaubert never stopped resenting the time, place, and even conditions of his birth; they were altogether too humdrum, bourgeois, and unheroic:

The soul is asleep now, drunk from *banal language*, but it will experience a frenetic awakening in which it will surrender to liberating joys, for nothing will remain to impede it, neither government nor religion, *no formula whatever*. . . . How I would love to have lived at least under Louis XIV . . . or in the time of Ronsard . . . or Nero? Have you never felt this at times, this shudder of history?[10]

Such words, whose equivalents flow from the lips of Flaubert's heroines Emma and Salammbô, express his constant theme of untimeliness; they display his general unwillingness to participate in the significant political and social battles of his era, which the writer, calling himself a "libéral enragé," chose to portray as banal.[11] Yet his native acuity allowed him to pierce the veil of his own historical envy. For, he humorously infers in another letter, he has no *lived basis* upon which to reject the present; he graphically admits that his "realism," if it exists at all, emerges from an underground spirit almost totally divorced from actual experience:

I am fundamentally what people call a *recluse* [*un ours*]. I live like a monk; sometimes (even in Paris) I stay inside for a week at a time. . . . As for what people call "society," I never enter into it. *I don't know* how to dance, nor to play any card game, nor even to make conversation in a salon, since everything they talk about there seems so inept.[12]

Flaubert, like some of Dostoevski's protagonists, assumed he was spiritually superior and so condemned social and political reality without ever having been engaged in it.[13] Flaubert's persuasion that he was "untimely born," together with his admitted lack of experience, produced the paradox of a "realist" writer with virtually no personal history. (Compare this to the opposite phenomenon in the politically active "romantics," such as Stendhal, Hugo, and Lamartine.) Indeed, the text of an 1846 letter to Louise Colet cogently expresses the condition which Scheler was later to attribute to resentful types in general. The letter also displays Flaubert's perennial preoccupation with the active heroism (and the vices) of earlier times:

Whenever I conjure up antiquity, a limitless sadness overtakes me in thinking of that period of magnificent and charming beauty, gone forever, of that vibrant world, filled with brilliance, so colorful and so pure, so simple, so varied. What wouldn't I give to see a victory, what wouldn't I sell to enter Subure one night when the torches were burning at the brothel's doors and the tambourines sounded in the taverns. As if we hadn't enough of our own past, we ruminate on [nous remâchons][14] that of humanity as a whole, and we delight in that voluptuous bitterness. So what if, after all, we can only live there—if it is only of that that we can think without disdain or pity![15]

In Flaubert, an idealization of a past age that did not redeem itself by offering inspiration for the present may well have brought on a significant resentment toward himself and others. More subtly, it seems to have elicited in him feelings of sexual ambivalence. (Ben-jamin Bart points out that the writer performed several acts of trans-vestism.[16] Perhaps more significant, evidence of sexual envy per-vades his narratives.) Woman, even in the nineteenth century, possessed the "vibrancy, color and simplicity" of the desired histori-cal period. Hence the feminine was for Flaubert the object of a fas-cination verging on identification:

If I could have been simply a beautiful woman dancer . . . how I should have wept, sighed, loved, sobbed.

There are days when one would like to be an athlete, and others when one longs to be a woman. In the first case it is because your muscles are aquiver; in the second, because your flesh is yearning and ablaze.[17]

Flaubert's travels seemed to confirm his intuition that only women and animals (and a few rare illiterate heroes such as Can-aris)[18] kept alive the marvelous worlds of the past. Even the East had become civilized, he lamented. Woman alone, he felt, tran-scended the deterioration which had gradually rendered banal the rest of Western civilization. Woman attained to the heroic mode by virtue of her sensuality and her moral indifference, the traits which elicited Flaubert's love of ancient civilizations.[19] To be a male in the nineteenth century was to be barred from the heroic condition.

Resentments begin in "powerless types of envy," Scheler re-minds us, and Flaubert envied two states of being which it was im-possible for him to achieve: a hero's existence of centuries earlier, and a woman's existence of 1857. Aware of the fruitlessness of his desire, he still refused to find suitable goals within the purview of historical actuality. In literature alone could he find solace:

Life is such a hideous thing that the only means to support it is to avoid it. And one avoids it in living through Art.[20]

Through writing, he might capture the two otherwise inaccessible ideals. Yet, at the same time, the twin fantasy was so bound up with action that the gap between it and the passive medium of words cre-ated an untenable paradox. Thus, in another letter, Flaubert com-plains about writing:

You will paint wine, love, women, glory, but always on the condition, old friend, that you will be neither drunk, nor lover, nor husband. . . . Once placed into life, one sees it poorly. . . . The artist, for me, is a monstrosity, something outside of nature.[21]

Flaubert seemed to believe that literature was a poor surrogate for life, especially that idealized life to which he aspired. Fixed on the identity of heroism and libido,[22] he could not help but resent the stringent demands, however self-imposed, of an art which denied the ego any expression. Nor could his desire to be a woman, once displaced onto narrative art, surface in other than negative fashion. He despised his female protagonists, for he allowed them every liberty which he denied himself; but their freedom, in turn, was a source of fascination and envy for him:

"Woman, what have I to do with thee?" seems to me to be more beautiful than all the vaunted utterings in Histories. . . . Only one poet, in my opinion, has understood the charming animals—the master of all masters, all-wise Shakespeare. Women are either *worse* or *better* than men. He has drawn them as overexalted beings, but never as rational creatures. That is why his female characters are so idealized and so lifelike at the same time.[23]

In an 1857 letter to Louise Colet, Flaubert speaks of being "man and woman at the same time, lover and mistress together" as he writes *Madame Bovary*.[24] Precisely this vicariousness led him to resent his fictional creatures, particularly the females, from the earliest prostitutes to the exotic Hérodias, from Emma Bovary's abused daughter, Berthe, to the last, pathetic "simple heart."

Dostoevski could not understand that those sections of *The Brothers Karamazov* given over to Ivan's skeptical theories were the strongest parts of his masterpiece. Ivan actually seems to have prevailed over the author's faith. So did the beautiful Salammbô (like Emma Bovary before her) challenge the will of her creator. But Flaubert managed to overwhelm his female protagonists, thereby succeeding for a time in repressing his essential self while fulfilling his godlike artistic responsibilities. The legalistic male protagonists of his later works were not to be so casually or so brutally destroyed.

DUAL RELATIONSHIPS IN THE CARTHAGINIAN EPIC

The tensions fostered by the phenomenon of ressentiment arise, in *Salammbô,* in an epic context which elevates them to a level of even greater significance than in *Madame Bovary*.[25] For in his later novel (*Salammbô* was published in 1862, five years after *Madame Bovary*),

Flaubert chose to replace the petty bourgeois figures of provincial France with heroic historical characters whose cosmic emotions and relationships reflect the development of human cultures. Yet on its most essential plane, *Salammbô* follows logically upon the earlier works. The identical motivations and interests that went into the creation of "Mémoires d'un Fou," "Novembre," and *Madame Bovary* were at work in Flaubert's "epic" novel.

Nonetheless, *Salammbô* has long been considered an aberration of sorts, an outpouring of Flaubert's undisciplined romantic instincts at the expense of his rational realism. Sainte-Beuve, chastising Flaubert for his "mania for depicting horrors," advised him gently to "cast aside down yonder on the African shore all his excess of fury and of avenging rage" and to produce "a strong, powerful, well-observed, living work" in a "vein that will please all." Henry James felt that Flaubert's "duality between the real and the romantic self has in its sharp operation placed *Madame Bovary* and *Sentimental Education* on one side together and placed together on the other *Salammbô* and the *Temptation*." Interestingly, however, the French critic saw *Salammbô* as a fantastic conglomeration of "sensations and abominations," while James perceived it as a medium in which Flaubert "could be frankly noble . . . whereas in *Bovary* and *Education* he could be but circuitously and insidiously so." Ironically, Sainte-Beuve's observation that "the soul [of *Salammbô* is] by preference and choice, malicious, vicious or frivolous" appears to ignore the identical factors at work in the earlier or later "realist" novels. James, on the contrary, praises the largeness of vision in *Salammbô* but also chooses to differentiate the work from those created by Flaubert's "real self."[26]

Two dominant thematic movements form the central thrust in *Salammbô*; but these same movements operate in all of Flaubert's works. His urge toward the heroic and the foreign, consistently epitomized by ancient civilizations or by Woman, is accompanied in all his works by the derivative implication that narrative is an essentially non-heroic and therefore unsatisfactory mode. The mutual contradiction of these two factors during the act of writing itself negates the primary urge and leads to ressentiment. On its deepest level of meaning, then, *Salammbô* rearticulates Flaubert's lifelong obsessions in a new setting; using epic figures instead of bourgeois ones.

There is nothing astonishing in this progression from the contemporary and familiar to the ancient and exotic, in a writer whose works and letters indicate such a preference. Even in light of his frequently articulated enchantment with Rome, Greece, and Egypt, however, we may still question Flaubert's choice of Carthage as the setting for his epic adventure. And why, as Sainte-Beuve complained, did he choose a relatively uninteresting Carthaginian generation?[27] Flaubert's depiction of a period and a people notable only for their impersonal violence and wholesale cruelty raises to a new level the tensions exhibited in his earlier works. In the Carthage of Hamilcar's time, Flaubert discovered a society in which "heroism" could be defined in terms of his own passive predilection for such figures as Nero and Sade: the unbridled expression of individual ego. As Lukacs puts it, the novelist's "deep hatred for modern society"[28] led him to establish a literary milieu in which brutality and atrocity became ends in themselves. In this way, the passivity and repression of Flaubert's middle-class existence were enabled to develop into their imaginative antitheses.

As Sainte-Beuve observed provocatively, Flaubert seems to have believed that "it is a proof of strength" to "appear inhuman in one's books," while remaining quite respectable in one's life. Thus the ressentient violence and arbitrary brutality inflicted essentially upon one character in *Madame Bovary*[29] extend, in *Salammbô*, to victimize thousands. It is as though Flaubert wished to annihilate an entire epoch because he envied its superiority over his own.

In her exotic mystery, Salammbô incorporates the enviable aspects of the earlier age. She captivates her creator, who deems her as worthy of intimate depiction as the females in "Novembre," *Madame Bovary*, and the later exotic text *Hérodias*. And, insofar as his mixed fascination with and hatred of her reflects his stance toward an entire civilization, it bears an unmistakable association with the previous novels and stories. Lukacs's view that the historical and political factors in the book swallow up the story's main characters may underestimate the breadth of its analogy between epical and personal developments.[30] For the predominant mood in *Salammbô*, one of extreme tension between uncomplex heroes and legalistic formulators, equally suffuses both the external and the internal, the visual and the psychological.

As is always true in the great novels of legalistic ressentiment, the first glimmer of the more profound emanation of the theme is a sign closer to the surface of the plot and the characters. In *Salammbô*, the essential structural negativity emerges first among the major personalities in the book. These, in turn, indicate the broader conflict between one kind of human behavior and another (a conflict requiring an epic tone). Thus Flaubert's characters give meaning to his atmospheric details and merit close attention.

Several important relationships in this seemingly idiosyncratic text resonate with mainstream nineteenth-century value inversion. The first of these gains prominence in the earliest chapters: Spendius, the wordy and deceptive slave, stays Matho's hand as the warrior instinctively seeks to avenge himself against Narr' Havas, the chieftain who had wounded him in the presence of Salammbô in chapter 1.[31]

Matho trembled. "Your sword!" he cried, "I want to kill him!" "Not yet!" Spendius replied, stopping him. (p. 703)

In the seconds while Matho hesitates a familiar psychological dependence arises between hero and slave, which is symbolically important to the theme of the novel. Having earlier attached himself to Matho by binding his wounds, and having seemingly attested to the latter's dominance by exclaiming, "I am yours! you are my master! Command!" Spendius now gradually reverses their relationship. He self-consciously insinuates his slavishness into Matho's mind and soul.

The Ivan-Smerdyakov relationship is here both inverted and intensified. The coward and weakling not only captivates the being of his master, but he also conceives and dictates the central act of the book, the incursion into Salammbô's palace to steal the sacred veil of Tanit. In both novels, a ressentient duality informs the motivating action of the story, but in *Salammbô* verbal dominance and intellectual creativity are vested in the *servant*, activity in the befuddled master. Matho's paradoxical subservience to his slave derives in part from his painful attraction to Salammbô. Separated from her, he regresses into a bitterness Flaubert specifically calls "ressentiment" (p. 741). Only contact with the exotic woman allows Matho a respite from the ressentient torpor which Spendius' influence otherwise causes. Because Salammbô's presence restores him to his natural condition of force and virility,[32] Matho desperately craves it. To the extent, however, that circumstances and the princess herself deny him possession of her, he retreats morbidly to the slavish stance inspired by Spendius. Once he is, so to speak, outside her magnetic field, this negative movement becomes quite explicit:

His impotence was torturing him. He was jealous of the Carthage which contained Salammbô as though it were a person who possessed her. If his nervousness were relieved, he would throw himself into a frenzy of reckless deeds. His cheeks on fire, his eyes reddened, his voice raucous, he would walk rapidly across the camp; or else, seated on the shore, he would scrub his huge sword with sand. He shot arrows at passing vultures. His heart overflowed in furious speech. (p. 711)

The chieftain's state of mind has all the familiar markings of ressentiment: the unresolvable envy, the victimizing of irrelevant objects, the consistent urge for futile gesturing, and, most important, the tendency to verbalize rather than to act. Matho thus obeys Spendius' advice: "Let your anger run free like a runaway chariot. Shout, blaspheme, ravage, and kill" (p. 711). Encouraged by the slave, Matho displaces his passion for Salammbô and his hatred of Narr' Havas into a plan to steal the most sacred object of Carthaginian ritual, the veil of Tanit.

Spendius stands as the primum mobile not only of his master's spiritual downfall but also of the novel's main action. His deliberately exorbitant demand to the Great Council of Carthage (that they give over aristocratic maidens to the barbarians) severs negotiations and leads directly to war. So, on the levels of both personal psychology and national politics, the slave verbally dominates his heroic antagonists. His power derives from language; he is a word-slinger among grand heroes and epic passions. The son of a Greek rhetorician and conversant in several languages. Spendius possesses the quickest tongue in the barbarian camp.[33] Reminiscent in his wordy cowardice of Thersites among the Greeks, Spendius nonetheless benefits from the implied sympathy of Flaubert, whereas his articulate epic ancestor received nothing but Homer's sharp derision. Thersites-Spendius reigns supreme in the modern epic. A character-type granted only several lines in the *Iliad*—a text Flaubert knew well—before he is ejected from the presence of noble warriors, he now saturates the page with vindictive verbosity.[34]

In a long letter to Sainte-Beuve in 1862, responding to many of the critic's negative comments about *Salammbô*, Flaubert emphasizes the importace of the Spendius-Matho relationship ("always in the foreground, and never lost sight of"); Spendius merits the following "defense":

You criticize me for not having introduced among the Greeks a philosopher, a thinker charged with the task of teaching us a moral lesson or performing good actions, a figure, indeed, who *thinks like us*. Come now! Is it possible? Aratus, whom you will recall, is precisely that figure upon whose model I created Spendius. A man of stealth and of ruses, who killed sentinels easily at night, but who had visions during the day.[35]

Aratus or Thersites, Spendius was created as the "us" of *Salammbô*, the penultimate author figure who manipulates the less literate, more purely passionate heroes of the novel. Introduced to the public only two years before Dostoevski's Underground Man, Flaubert's portrait of Spendius should receive more than the cursory glance afforded it by many critics.

Matho, in turn, fails to play Agamemnon to Spendius' Thersites. His slavishness follows the vogue for passivity. So the dichotomy between the heroic mode and the verbal, which might otherwise seem simplistic, is maintained consistently and on many levels throughout the novel. In his brilliant sketch of a coward's gradually dominating a warrior, Flaubert comments on the deterioration of the heroic mode in general and the subsequent emergence of verbal and hypocritical cultures such as his own. Perhaps the major indication of this intent is his marvelous portrayal of the corruption of the barbarians by their decadent enemies, the Carthaginians. The former, displayed in chapter 1 in a veritable orgy of animallike rejoicing, cannot at first fathom the casuistic bargaining of the city-dwellers:

They did not know how to answer such talk. These men, accustomed to war, grew weary of their stay in a city; they were easily swayed, and the people of Carthage observed their departure from the city walls. (p. 700)

The barbarians' instinct for revenge comes immediately to the fore when they realize that the Carthaginians, having convinced them to leave, intend never to pay them what they deserve (although Spendius' outrageous demands have been almost as responsible as Carthaginian mendacity for this impasse). But deprivation gradually teaches them to covet the enemy's comforts and to see Carthaginian civilization as a good. Their leaders, notably Spendius and Narr' Havas, exploit this envy by alternately repressing and reactivating their growing resentments.

The inhabitants of Carthage, on the other hand, show no such progression; they are depicted from the outset as a fearful and verbal group, acting "with exaggerated politeness and audacious hypocrisy." The deterioration of their civilization results in that relativization of previously absolute values which, as Nietzsche and Scheler observe, is the mark of ressentiment-prone cultures. Thus, religion as a dominant force has been hopelessly fragmented in Carthage;[36] the harmonious assimilation of religion into everyday life, still exemplified by Salammbô, has generally been reduced to superstition and heresy:

> They gave away their illness-repelling amulets; but they had first spat upon them three times to attract death [to the Barbarians], or, to make the recipients cowardly, they enclosed jackal-hair within. They invoked Melkarth's blessing aloud, but underneath their breath, invoked his curse. (p. 700)

Not surprisingly, for Flaubert consistently equates heroic behavior with the natural freedom of the animal world,[37] Carthage's degraded culture finds expression in its perverse attitude toward animals. Early in the novel, the barbarians watch in unbelieving horror as Carthaginians, in a fury of fear, destroy the most noble of all animals:[38]

> So this was the way Cathaginian peasants avenged themselves when they captured a wild beast; they hoped in so doing to terrify others. The barbarians, no longer laughing, relapsed into profound amazement. "What people is this," they thought, "who find amusement in crucifying lions!" (p. 702)

The peasants' unnatural deed finds its aristocratic complement in the acts of the Carthaginian council of elders, a group whose unheroic pragmatism is typified in the figure of Hannon. In the chapter bearing his name, this city leader demonstrates a capacity for bureaucracy which would have better suited him for a bourgeois than a heroic culture. Legalistic mediation had its place even in the ancient world and should be Hannon's forte; yet even as a mere verbal defender of his city he is a reprehensible failure and a coward, leaving others to die for his own inability to negotiate effectively.

Of all the male citizens of Carthage, only two substantially embody Flaubert's definition of a hero. The first of these, Giscon, stands as the polar opposite of Hannon. Flaubert portrays Giscon as strikingly as any other character in the novel, except perhaps Salammbô herself.

His large black mantle, held on his head by a gold mitre starred with precious stones, flowed around him and down to his horse's hooves; it seemed to blend into the color of night. Only his white beard could be perceived, together with the brilliance of his hair and the triple collar of blue medallions [plaques] which beat against his breast. (p. 696)

Introduced in this gorgeous array, Giscon soon displays a gift for leadership which more than matches his noble mien. Yet the aging hero is led to downfall and disgrace by the younger, resentful generation and is "abandoned by his own city" when he argues for a just agreement with the barbarians (who have, after all, helped Carthage repel the Roman enemy); it is he who "despite its ingratitude . . . would not dishonor" his country. Betrayed by Carthage, he finally falls to "vermin and filth" during his imprisonment by the barbarians, dying ignobly because his deteriorating city has seen fit to sacrifice him to its immediate political needs.

   The second heroic figure, Hamilcar Barca, is destined to survive the wars; he enters the novel in a manner befitting his stature as the father of Salammbô and Hannibal. Hamilcar returns to a city which is badly divided politically and tainted by the hypocritical pragmatism of advancing cultures. Resentments flare as the hero, by his very presence, reminds the council of elders of its own weakness. In a lengthy passage reminiscent of the council scenes in the early books of the *Iliad*, Hamilcar confronts his symbolic opposite, the physically repugnant and morally detestable Hannon. A living image of corruption, carefully opposed to the noble Giscon, the ressentient bureaucrat unsuccessfully challenges Hamilcar's leadership:

He had painted his face to cover its blemishes. But the gold powder from his hair had fallen on his shoulders like two brilliant medallions [plaques]. . . . Linens, saturated with a greasy perfume which trickled down to the ground, enveloped his hands, and his disease had evidently considerably progressed, or his eyes seemed to disappear into their lids. (p. 731)

The central confrontation parallels the opposition between ressentient values and heroic standards in the Matho-Spendius relationship. And even Hamilcar falls prey to the elder's politics of compromise and deception.

Flaubert meets the demands of his epic theme—the conflict not just of two men but of two modes of existence—by adopting an epic tone in this novel. But while the tone mimics that of the great epic poems of earlier Western civilization, the outcome of the conflict reverses the heroic victory that had been inevitable in classical literature. Like Melville in *Billy Budd, Sailor,* Flaubert here describes the vanquishing by ressentient characters of their heroic adversaries.

SALAMMBÔ AND SCHAHABARIM

In *Salammbô,* Spendius prevails over Matho, Hannon over Giscon, and the will of the legalistic elders over that of Hamilcar. But even these vital oppositions primarily reflect the text's central duality, that of heroine and priest. For the evolving tension between Schahabarim and Salammbô most fully reveals the implications of artistic ressentiment for Flaubert specifically, and the novelistic stance toward heroism in general.

Quite early in the book, Flaubert clearly associates the priests of Tanit with the realm of artistic expression. All the priests play musical instruments; all the religious rituals of the sect are accompanied by music with elaborate rhythms and melodies. Schahabarim, as high priest, not only epitomizes the musical aspects of art, but also shares with Spendius a verbal acumen and fine education which associate him with literature. Since "no one in Carthage was as learned as he," Schahabarim naturally assumes the role of Salammbô's companion and tutor. The central interest of the priest's latter years has been the care and upbringing of the princess. He has educated her according to his wishes and has had sole responsibility for the development of her personality and beliefs. The aristocratic maiden grows to maturity in the florid atmosphere of Schahabarim's words:

> But over the aridity of his life, Salammbô bloomed like a flower in the cleft of a sepulchre. Still, he was hard on her, sparing her neither penances nor bitter words. His condition established between them a kind of unisexual equality, and he less resented her his not being able to possess her than his finding her so beautiful and above all, so pure.

Strange words sometimes escaped him, and passed before Salammbô like broad flames illuminating abysses. (p. 753)

Although by no means his intellectual equal, the princess finds Schahabarim's theories and stories emotionally compelling. Indeed, the priest's mysterious vocabulary and fantastic imagination give him a sort of novelistic power over the impressionable girl, and she both loves and fears him. Schahabarim has carefully inspired and nurtured her romantic desires; but because he was long ago castrated in order to be made her high priest, he cannot effect more than a verbal arousal. Driven to rage at the sight of "the men who abandoned themselves to pleasure with the priestesses," Schahabarim contrives to instill in Salammbô the sexual desire which he himself can neither experience nor satisfy. He subtly stirs her latent passion for Matho, mingling it with a plan to recover the stolen veil. Just as Spendius has verbally incited the warrior to the theft, the articulate priest insinuates into the princess' spirit the idea of submitting to Matho in order to recover the holy object.

The priest's suggestive language at first produces a kind of lethargic dreaminess in the young girl, similar to that of Madame Bovary before she meets her various lovers. Her fear of both Schahabarim and her father (who has been ignoring her for his own political problems) contributes to a kind of catatonia. Yet, as the princess gazes at her serpent, she seems to intuit that the creature's languor, like her own, carries a potential for swift movement. Schahabarim's romantic words have nearly brought Salammbô to a stage of activity, but she still requires the presence of the revivified serpent, the image of virile force, to convince her of the power of her desire. The castrated priest may furnish the figurative "pen" in this process, but the reawakened serpent represents the "sword."

The narrative now approaches its dramatic climax. The priest continues to present the serpent to Salammbô, as though to irritate desires which only an outside force will be able to fulfill. Moving hypnotically to the rhythm of music and chanted prayers, she finally consummates her association with the mysterious reptile:

A fear of the cold, or a sense of modesty, perhaps, caused her at first to hesitate. But she recalled the orders of Schahabarim and went forward. . . . Salammbô panted under the heavy weight [of the serpent's body], her loins gave way; she felt she was dying, and the serpent struck her thighs gently with its tail; then, the music ceasing, it fell back. (p. 755)

Sainte-Beuve was embarrassed by this episode and evidently chose not to consider its intrinsic importance to Flaubert's narrative ambitions. But far from being gratuitous, its blatantly sexual nature is both intentional and logical, the realization of desires which Schahabarim had inspired through verbal innuendo. Without this preliminary incident, her sexual intercourse with Matho in his tent would never occur, the veil would not be recaptured, and the final battle would not come to pass. The centrality of this event— Salammbô's fusion with a dual symbol of masculinity and relig- ion—becomes even clearer as it calls to mind Emma Bovary's dy- ing physical union with the "homme-Dieu" on her crucifix. Just as Emma bestows upon her mystical object "le plus grand baiser d'amour qu'elle eût jamais donné," so the Carthaginian heroine achieves a peak of physicality with her serpent. Both women wish to escape the ordinary world of contemporary civilization, which has left their desires unfulfilled. Like all Flaubert's sensual heroines, both bring to their roles dreams of earlier, heroic places. And, un- like all of Flaubert's romantic male protagonists, both actively at- tempt to give meaning to their fantasies by seeking sensual and di- vine experiences. Thanks to Flaubert, however, neither protagonist fully succeeds in her attempt. Schahabarim, Spendius' equal in ar- ticulate expression, can merely instigate desire verbally—a magnifi- cent gift, but among the least personally satisfying. Only the female herself can physically perform the desired sexual act (just as only the warrior-hero can achieve the required act of daring); and she can only do so with a virile partner, not with a castrated story- teller.[39]

Flaubert, like his priest, resents Salammbô's sexuality, yet thrives on displaying it. He casts all his sensual female characters —from the prostitutes in "Mémoires" and "Novembre" to the fren- zied Hérodias—in the same mold with which Schahabarim shapes the Carthaginian princess. But the final deed belongs to the crea- tures; to the creators only the vicarious, frustrated pleasure of the voyeur.[40] Therefore, Schahabarim succumbs fully to ressentiment only *after* Salammbô carries out his orders. The twisted logic which we associate with this last state—organic mendacity—comes to the fore in this interesting passage:

With an inconceivable inconsistency, he did not forgive the girl for having followed his orders: Schahabarim had guessed everything, and the obses- sion with the idea revived the jealousies of his impotence. (p. 772)

In a larger sense, however, is not the "inconceivable inconsistency" of which the author here speaks really his own? Are not the presence of the laughing beggar at Emma's deathbed and of Giscon at Salammbô's union with Matho (both incredible coincidences) clear indices of Flaubert's ressentient revenge against heroines shaped by his own literary fantasies? "For the present, Salammbô no longer feared him," the priest surmises, with some justification; only Flaubert's gratuitous cruelty to her at the end of the novel redeems Schahabarim.

For Matho, too, little happiness is in store. Even his sexual union with Salammbô, whose imagery deliberately evokes the serpent's dance with the princess, contrives ultimately to destroy him. He surrenders both the barbarian's veil and further enjoyment of Salammbô. Like Flaubert's Marie abandoning the narrator of "Mémoires," Salammbô flees from her lover, leaving him enslaved to the female image. Symbolically tied by the same desire, Matho and Schahabarim actually encounter each other only once until the very end of the novel. In the midst of the epic carnage of chapter 13, the priest happens to perceive his virile rival and immediately begins to mouth insults which Matho at first refuses to acknowledge. When the warrior finally does become enraged, he throws his axe at his wordy adversary. As always, however, Flaubert protects the representative of his art, and somehow Schahabarim survives the onslaught—survives, indeed, most of the book's heroic figures; he is protected by a benevolent creator who paticipates in the sublime revenge of their mutual artistry.[41] So it comes to pass that Narr' Havas, not Matho, is given Salammbô in marriage, despite the former's treachery to Carthage and to his own camp. In the final chapter, Matho is exposed to the brutality of the Carthaginian hordes, the degenerate remnant of a great civilization. The priests, not the people, perform the coup de grace upon Matho; significantly, Schahabarim himself, in the closing scene, grasps Matho's still-beating heart and presents it as a symbolic offering to the life-supporting sun.

Matho is never a hero in the Greek manner; Spendius' domination bars that path. As a hero of any sort, however, he is anathema to Schahabarim, the artist-priest. But while Flaubert allows the priest to annihilate the warrior, he preserves for himself the obliteration of his heroine. Horrified by the sight of the common herd de-

stroying her unique lover and with him the virile and religious qualities which he, like the serpent, has embodied, Salammbô swoons
and, astonishingly, dies.

The author, like the priest, uses language to attack what both
fascinates and repels him; Flaubert's female protagonists always disappear or die before his novels end. (Is it mere coincidence that
most of the central male figures in Flaubert, from Homais to Frédéric Moreau and Bouvard and Pécuchet, survive the end of their
stories?) We cannot help but find the youthful Salammbô's sudden
demise somewhat gratuitous; the brief explanation afforded by the
final sentence, that she dies "for having touched the veil of Tanit,"
seems less convincing than an analysis based on an awareness of
author-character tension.

Any reader of *Salammbô* will note the violent deaths of numer-
ous figures, great and small. But in Flaubert the heroic mode (represented either by ancient heroes or exotic women) always suffers
unique annihilation, frequently leaving behind as implicit victors a
ressentient caste of articulate, artistic characters. The cleverness of
verbal forms, then, an almost supersaturating element in Flaubert as
in Dostoevski, manages to prevail on the literary page against even
the professed wishes of the novelist. Whether he is avowedly religious, like Dostoevski, or praises heroism, like Flaubert, the great
modern novelist ultimately rejects his absolutist vision in favor of
the overwhelming negativity of his verbally ressentient characters.
From this "exotic" text, fully consistent with Flaubert's central
oeuvre, it is not so long a step to the realistic lawyers of his later
masterpiece, *L'Education sentimentale*.

6   Lawyers and Liars: *L'Education sentimentale*

THE APPEARANCE OF RESOLUTION: TEMPORALITY IN LIEU OF CHARACTER

To the synthetic sensitivity of a reader fresh from Flaubert's earlier work, *L'Education sentimentale* poses a dilemma. It cannot, as I have suggested in the preceding chapter, easily be placed beside *Madame Bovary*, for all Sainte-Beuve's applauding its "return" to a contemporary French setting;[1] nor do even its more exotic and elaborate passages evoke fully the atmosphere of *Salammbô*. Perhaps, as Lukacs seems to believe, *L'Education sentimentale* is sui generis, the perfect novel of disillusionment, *the* nineteenth-century text.[2]

Surely there are signs of progression in this book toward the objectivity which Auerbach, perhaps too literally, believed to be at work in *Madame Bovary*.[3] The author's resentment of his protagonist seems diminished here, and the centrality of time itself—the unmediated flow of external events—implies a resolution of Flaubert's dual obsession.[4] For temporality, as Lukacs has shown, is displayed dispassionately, as it could never have been when situated within the span either of an unhappy woman's life or of a failed ancient generation; and Woman loses her piquancy when dispersed to the four corners of an essentially historical novel.

The earlier, ressentient reaction of author to character is lacking almost completely. The clearest sign of this apparently positive metamorphosis is the successful deletion of the female protagonist; she has been replaced here by a mediocre young man. Furthermore, the setting is vibrant with activity, no longer the static boredom of the provinces or the decay of a dying civilization. Flaubert seems to have overcome, in destroying Emma and Salammbô, the element of his desire which lured him toward the "exotic woman." By violently crushing an earlier culture with several strokes of his bourgeois *porte-plume*, he may also have assuaged his sense of historical untimeliness.

There are passages in *L'Education sentimentale* which could not have appeared, given their lack of competitive tension between author and protagonist, in earlier novels such as *Madame Bovary*. It is worth comparing and explicating two representative texts in order to grasp the authorial progression from self-involved ressentiment to indifferent social satire. First, from *Madame Bovary:*

Elle se rappela tous ses instincts de luxe, toutes les privations de son âme, les bassesses du mariage, du ménage, ses rêves tombant bans la boue comme des hirondelles blessées, tout ce qu'elle avait désiré, tout ce qu'elle s'était refusé, tout ce qu'elle aurait pu avoir. Et pourquoi? pourquoi? (p. 637)

Emma's gnawing memories, the conditionalizing of her sense of failure and shattered potential, bind her to Flaubert. The ornithological simile sensitizes the reader to a wounded view of reality which emanates from the author's own negative self-awareness. External life disappoints constantly. The rage within Emma is fired by that of her creator.

The narrative stance toward Frédéric Moreau in *L'Education sentimentale* differs considerably:

Alors, il fut saisi par un de ces frissons de l'âme où il vous semble qu'on est transporté dans un monde supérieur. Une faculté extraordinaire, dont il ne savait pas l'objet, lui était venue. Il se demanda, sérieusement, s'il serait un grande peintre ou un grand poète; et il se décida pour la peinture, car les exigences de ce métier le rapprocheraient de Mme Arnoux. Il avait donc trouvé sa vocation. Le but de son existence était clair maintenant, et l'avenir infaillable.[5]

While we may observe that Frédéric's thoughts express an optimism about the future, and Emma's a depressed resensing of past failures, this difference is in itself indicative of the development from a ressentient to a nonressentient authorial stance. The male protagonist consistently manages to glamorize his existence, but his ambitions are absurdly out of keeping with his potential. (Like Emma, Frédéric reads Walter Scott, but unlike her, he casts himself fantastically in Scott's role, not in those of his adventurous characters.) Yet he exhibits a conceit which constantly forestalls any ephemeral doubts or lingering resentments.

Thanks to Frédéric's transparent, self-satisfied mediocrity,[6] Flaubert situates himself incontestably above his protagonist; he accomplishes this through style. Whereas Emma's resentments and his own coincide in an unspoken mutuality which his style supports by avoiding explicit commentary, Frédéric's ebullience is so ludicrous that it can be safely satirized from without. No adverb dares to modify the passage that relates the mystery of Emma's spiritual processes. But the use of the word "sérieusement" in the passage describing Frédéric's aspirations immediately eliminates the danger that the reader will confuse them with the writer's personal motives. Frédéric's absurd dual ambition may thus quite easily be mocked by the Olympian author, who is not in competition with his newer hero. So, too, does the objectifying phrase "où il vous semble" serve to remove any semblance of sincerity from Frédéric's "frisson de l'âme." This is the type of direct communication with the reader which Flaubert spitefully refuses to conduct during his privileged associations with female protagonists.

Emma's soul, like those of Salammbô and of the heroines of the earliest stories, is revealed in the internally logical uniqueness and completeness of its expression. Frédéric's thoughts are instantly satirized by their banality, revealed by the style in which Flaubert presents them. Emma at her most passionately resentful resists even gentle narrative irony; her drives emerge from the same fierce negativity which Flaubert attempted, in writing novels, to transfer to her. Frédéric, on the contrary, is inspired by no single ideal or emotion, only by the passing stimuli of the external moment. His decision to become a painter instead of a poet, for example, is a caprice springing from an episode with Mme Arnoux; once it passes, it is never alluded to again.

Emma's imagination, as indicated in this passage, thrusts forward from ambition to action, from failure to venom and back to ambition again. The verbs are active and (except for the re-sensing verb *se rappela*) fully transitive. But Frédéric's soul, like his milieu, receives and reacts; it does not create and move ahead. The verbs in the second passage imply this passivity ("il fut saisi"; "lui était ve-nue"); the world works *upon* Frederic, who virtually disappears ex-cept as an object of seemingly detached satire.

A happy lack of realizable ambition leads Frédéric from woman to woman. He will never suffer the extremes of desire which so fas-cinated Flaubert in his females, because he will always have Rosan-ette when Mme Arnoux is reticent, Mme Dambreuse when Rosan-ette angrily departs, and either the innocent Louise or the universal prostitute when all else fails. His affairs, like his promiscuous politi-cal associations, leave no vindictive scar. Frédéric, unlike the care-fully schooled Emma and Salammbô, simply makes no demands upon the haphazard flow of people and events.

The history of a period thus lives through Frédéric (as Sainte-Beuve justifiably claimed it could not through Salammbô) because no single significant factor dominates the tabula rasa of his mind. His brief periods of bitterness (e.g., "Frédéric, whose pride was sick," says to himself that "to take his revenge" against the unrecep-tive Mme Arnoux, he will treat Louise badly in her stead) never progress to a state of mind because there is always something new to arouse his undemanding curiosity, and never time for a profound feeling of any sort. This unreflectiveness has its advantages, espe-cially from the point of view of a spirit encumbered, as I shall dis-cuss, with legal training. But spontaneity sits poorly on a figure like Frédéric, who has neither the charm nor the talent to take advan-tage of it.

Through the juvenile ups and downs of Frédéric's sentimental and political behavior, Flaubert manages to depict a protagonist who is impossible to resent. Yet, like a lingering cancer after a nearly successful operation, Flaubert's virulence survives and finally pervades even this most objective of texts. We have noted Flau-bert's seeming resolution through Frédéric of his unattainable de-sires to live in heroic times and to be a woman. We find, however, that the choice of Frédéric as protagonist expunges that much of the ressentiment toward his characters which Flaubert had exhibited when they were women or heroes; it exacerbates, as if seizing upon what had before only been immanent, the still more torturous *hatred of self* which comes from treating a virtually autobiographical pro-tagonist. The females and the ancient heroes, carrying with them the best of Flaubert's ambitions, could be casually destroyed. What remains is Frédéric-Flaubert, inept in love and revolution, qualified only to receive the imprint of time and events and to write about them retrospectively.

The unhealthy cells of the old resentments reappear as we analyze Flaubert's formation of Frédéric's character. First, rather than create a woman in order to despise and destroy her, Flaubert endows Frédéric with a moderate but consistent misogyny. Perhaps this quality itself accounts for Frédéric's endless procrastination in consummating his emotion for any of the women to whom he is attracted. Surely much of Flaubert's venom seeps into Frédéric's thoughts about Mme Arnoux; imagining scenarios and rejections where none exist, he spends most of the book wavering between apathy and rage. When Mme Arnoux, who is busy with her sick child, fails to answer Frédéric's messages, he lashes out: "Her insolence had gone too far! A prideful anger seized him. He swore to himself never again to have even a desire; and like a leaf swept away by a hurricane, his love disappeared. He experienced a sense of consolation [il en ressentit un soulagement], of stoic joy, then a need for violent activity; and he ran aimlessly through the streets" (p. 111). For Mme Dambreuse, Frédéric feels "an inexplicable hatred [une malveillance inexplicable]" (p. 96), and the pliant Rosanette he rewards by deceiving her just after the birth of their child and by abandoning her after its death.

Just as Flaubert's envy of women is objectified but not resolved through a protagonist who shares rather than challenges it, his perennial fascination with and avoidance of heroism are also passed on to Frédéric, whose dismal lack of personal inspiration robs him of the potential for heroic as well as romantic fulfillment. Frédéric frequently finds himself at the heart of the Parisian rebellions of those years. As revolutionary masses surround him during the uprising at the Pantheon, Frédéric spouts clichés about the "sublimity of the people" and then runs off to Mme Arnoux at precisely the instant when action is called for; he leaves a secondary character, Dussardier, to fight and shed blood for a cause. This pattern is repeated as he flees from the February 1848 revolution to write of it "in a lyrical style" (p. 114). Frédéric's unwillingness to act during moments of historical crisis mirrors Flaubert's lifelong hesitancy to participate in the political movements of his day, even though he never ceased to criticize society in his writings. In an important letter of 1871, Flaubert, who so often imagined heroic action and even deeds of barbarous brutality, expressed his wish to escape from the real confrontations of revolutionary Paris. "Oh! if I could only escape to a place where there are no more uniforms . . . where no one speaks of violence," he moaned, "where you wouldn't have to be involved! But the world's too small for us poor mandarins."[7] In *L'Education sentimentale,* he smugly observes that nothing is "more amusing" than Paris during the first days of the revolution. That Frédéric's fickleness in political allegiances is supposed to satirize (from above) the constant shifting of bourgeois loyalties from Louis Philippe to Napoleon to the Republicans cannot eradicate the underlying authorial malaise.

Even though the novelist seems to maintain a bemused stance in *L'Education sentimentale* which would have been impossible earlier, the structure of the text thus is neither more allied to pure temporality nor less based on subjective elements than the prior works. A close analysis of character once again allays the temptation to discover artistic resolution where none exists. For it is not only Flaubert's continued bitterness in works written after *L'Education sentimentale* which implies the absence of resolution here; it is also the choice of profession made by both Frédéric and his closest confidant and rival, Charles Deslauriers.

FROM HERO TO LAWYER: THE PROTOTYPE

Lukacs believes that, in the absence of tension between internalized hero and externalized culture, time becomes the only real subject of *L'Education sentimentale.* "J'ai tâché de faire un livre sur rien," after all, was Flaubert's blueprint for his mature novels, and the flow of politics in Paris from 1840 to 1851 does appear to limit any profound attempt at characterization or psychology within this text. Frédéric holds our interest not in his own right but as a conduit for the passage of historical time. The resulting effect is curious, because Flaubert places in Frédéric's quite ordinary mind thoughts worthy of Goethe's Werther or Chateaubriand's René; he is not insusceptible to the *impression* of love (Mme Arnoux) or natural beauty (promenades with Rosanette near Versailles), yet we know that he cannot emotionally progress beyond impressionability to true feeling. Somehow, in Flaubert's masterpiece, the centrality of sincere emotion—seen in French literature even as late as in Stendhal's Fabrice—gives way to abstract, almost unidimensional mediocrity.

Paradoxically, Frédéric holds center stage almost throughout the text. As we have observed, he yields his place only occasionally, and then usually to his close confidants or lovers. It is as though Flaubert, cleaving to his protagonist, chooses not to impair temporal developments with any abundantly rich human optic. To grasp this, one need only compare the effect of the novel to that of Henry James' The Ambassadors.[8] While Frédéric's "love" for Mme Arnoux consistently distracts him from any significant relationship (even with her!) which might impede the flow of external events, Lambert Strether's increasing emotion for Mme de Vionnet enriches his, and through him the reader's, subjective appreciation of everything he sees. Both characters, by substituting a form of complexity for a relatively simple reality, fail to consummate their desires, but in Strether this complexity is romantic—even poetic —while in Frédéric it is contrived and, ultimately, legalistic.

Flaubert's most fully conceived male protagonist is, in fact, a lawyer. Just as the clash of civilizations in Salammbô is reflected with precision in the relationships between individual characters, so here the bankruptcy of a culture is captured within the profession of the protagonist.[9] This innovative use of character reached its fullest development eighty-seven years later, with Camus' Jean-Baptiste Clamence.

Frédéric Moreau's role as a kind of trampolene upon which bounces, in a constant rhythm of appearance and disappearance, the events of a historical period, requires a modicum of definition. We can assume that the most important attribute of this receptive, resilient protagonist is his profession, since the narrative devotes far more space to it than to the details of his childhood or even to the description of his physical features. There may well be an uncertainty, at the end of this novel, as to what Frédéric looks like, or even whether he has made love to a woman before he sleeps with Rosanette toward the end of the book.[10] We cannot preserve equal ignorance as to his chosen field. The text virtually begins with the discussions leading to his decision to go to law school, treats the legal education in detail, and takes us through his examinations and his flirtation with practice. Deslauriers, his best friend and the next most important character, is constantly discussing his own legal career with Frédéric. Flaubert wanted to make law a part of his protagonist, so that the nature of the epoch could emerge under the microscope of a single mediating perspective.

There are at least three possible reasons for this point of clarity in Frédéric's otherwise amorphous essence. Perhaps Flaubert needed to work through his own real experience in law school, having until then elaborated through narrative only his fantasies; perhaps he felt that a lawyer, because of his mediating function, could best act as a conduit for the passions and thoughts of others; or perhaps he associated the legal profession with the essence of contemporary French culture.

These three elements recur and eventually concur in a thematic of personal and cultural reaction and passivity. Only glossed with learning and ambition, Frédéric is no more destined to be an effective lawyer than to be a wonderful storyteller or a passionate revolutionary. As with Flaubert (who lodges his protagonist in the rue Saint-Hyacinthe, now the rue Paillet—his own residence during law school), Frédéric's first days at the law school bode poorly for his subsequent career:

Carrying a brand new blotter under his arm, he went to the opening lecture at the Law School. Three hundred bare-headed youths sat in an amphitheatre listening to an old man in a red gown whose voice droned on to the accompaniment of the scratching of pens on paper. This lecture-hall reminded Frédéric of the classrooms at school, with the same dusty smell, the same sort of chair, the same boredom. He attended lectures regularly for a fortnight. But he dropped the Civil Code before they got to Article 3, and he abandoned the Institutes of Justinian at the *Summa Divisio personarum.* [11]

Alienated but, like his creator, lacking the force of character either to quit his studies or to excel at them, [12] Frédéric endures a humiliating series of examinations, which the knowledgeable Flaubert describes in detail. Passages like these differ from the rest of the text; they interrupt the sheer flow of temporality and force the reader to focus on the protagonist in his singularity:

Finally the time came when he had to give answers on Procedure. He was asked about third-party complaints. The professor, shocked to hear theories opposed to his own, asked him harshly: "Is that what you think, sir?

How can you reconcile Section 1351 of the Code with your peculiar approach?" Frédéric had such a headache, not having slept at all the night before. A beam of light struck his face through a slat in the window. Standing behind his chair, he slouched and pulled at his moustache. "I'm still waiting!" said the man in the fancy robe. And, probably annoyed by Frédéric's movements: "You won't find the answer in your beard!" This sarcasm produced laughter among the gathering. (p. 30)

Through law, Flaubert manages to interject into his masterpiece both autobiography and social satire. A failure at law himself, he similarly debilitates his hero; a procrastinator at physical love, he so creates Frédéric; personally averse to political action, he depicts the protagonist and his student friends likewise.[13] None of the lawyers in this text, Deslauriers included, finishes his self-appointed tasks, in either political or sentimental matters.[14] The mediocre contemporary male finally gains three-dimensionality in *L'Education sentimentale*, and his formation is in the legal sciences.

I will resist the temptation to analyse Frédéric's use of language in detail, a procedure better applied to his collegial successor, Camus' Clamence. It would be wrong to subject Frédéric's spoken or written language to such *explications*, because Flaubert does not endow him with a verbal intelligence analogous to that of, say, the priest Schahabarim or the slave Spendius. Frédéric is crafted to conduct, not to create, values. Yet it must be observed that his consistent reaction to political events is verbal; whether at the Pantheon early in his law school career, or at the Tuileries during the 1848 uprising, he retreats into language. His journalistic "élucubration" (p. 116) and eventual scorn for "l'émeute" (p. 127) define his participation (as they had, in a sense, Flaubert's).[15] It is left to less educated types like Dussardier to fight and die for an ideal.

Frédéric's sentimental universe, like that of Camus' more gifted lawyers almost a century later, contains little of essence within language and nothing outside it. His sentimental education is ultimately less successful than even his legal schooling, with which, ultimately, it is bound up:

He pictured himself in an assize court, on a winter's evening, making the closing speech for the defence; the jury was pale, the breathless audience was almost bursting the partition of the courtroom; he had been speaking for four hours now, and was recapitulating his arguments, finding new ones, and feeling that every phrase, every word, every gesture was lifting

the blade of the guillotine suspended behind him. Then he was at the trib-
une in the chamber, an orator carrying the safety of an entire people on
his lips, overwhelming his opponents with his eloquence or crushing them
with his repartee, speaking with thunder and music in his voice, ironic, pathetic, passionate, sublime.[16]

No finer slant on the progression from *Madame Bovary* and
Salammbô to the later novel can be found than within this passage.
Flaubert's women read (or are read to), dream, act, and then die.
Flaubert's men dream, but of nothing more heroic than themselves
as lawyers, fail to act, and survive. Yet survival brings to the two
lawyers at the end of this novel (foreshadowing, as we shall see, the
two lawyers who conclude *The Fall*), only a further flight from that
dream-within-a-dream. Their closing words evoke the sum and substance of their sentiments, the loss of something that never happened anyway, the absence of an absence, the airiness of sheer
language:

One Sunday late in the afternoon, Frédéric and Deslauriers, newly coiffed,
picked some flowers in Mme Moreau's garden, then headed over to "the
Turque," still carrying their large bouquets.

Frédéric handed his [to one of the girls], as though to his fiancée. But
the heat, a fear of the unknown, a kind of remorse, and even the pleasure
of seeing so many women at his disposal, moved him so much that he got
quite pale and stood still, saying nothing. Everyone was laughing, enjoying
his uneasiness; thinking they were teasing him, he fled; and, since Frédéric
had the money, Deslauriers was forced to follow him.

People saw them leave. It made for a good story which was still re-
membered three years later.

They told it to each other at great length [prolixement], each refining
the other's memories; and, when they were finished: "That's the best we
ever had!" said Frédéric. "You think so? That's the best we ever had!" said
Deslauriers.

7 Literary Legality during the Holocaust: Camus' Variations on the Nineteenth-Century Theme

HISTORY AND INFLUENCE

In the Europe of 1942, *The Stranger*'s Europe,[1] institutions of intellect and culture were flocking to the Nazi cause. Our brief look at French law books of the period hinted at the extent to which the formally complex methods of European legalism contributed to Nazi oppression.[2] No wonder Camus makes *The Fall*'s protagonist a lawyer; Clamence's verbal complexity renders him an easy victim of moral relativism and passivity, not only during the central moments of his personal life, but also during the central years of twentieth-century French history, the Occupation.

Like Dostoevski and Flaubert, whose models he frequently followed,[3] Camus expounded his deepest self-critical awareness through the medium of legal characters and situations. But unlike those earlier writers, Camus had within his actual field of experience the harrowing realization of his fears. European intellectual culture (legal, literary, and even religious) had been no match for its beast within. Ressentient passivity, sentimentality, intellectualized formulations—these had somehow vanquished the urge for effective, active resistance against barbaric force.[4]

In retrospect, Camus' first and last masterpieces both endure as eminent elaborations of the nineteenth-century novel's great themes of negativity: ressentiment and legality. But, in their precise context of historical conflagration, *The Stranger* and *The Fall* stand even more powerfully as reminders of the massive evil which intellectuals endure when they allow formal structures to replace their native sense of justice.

LEGALISTIC DISTORTIONS OF THE NONAESTHETICIZED WORLD VIEW IN *THE STRANGER*

The same breed of legalism which leads to substantive error in the case of Mitya Karamazov leads to another kind of falsehood in *The Stranger*.[5] Once again, inquisitor (*juge d'instruction*) and procurator (*procureur*) extrapolate from the stuff of legal testimony a verbal formula which they impose upon the otherwise elusive nature of a criminal defendant. Once again, the legalistic theme requires the reader to recollect the first part of the novel while he is in the midst of the second, in order accurately to perceive the novelistic vision of criminal investigation. And once again, the legalistic mode is revealed to be passionately self-interested and value-attuned, predicated on a combination of pseudo moralism and imposed behaviorism, rejecting spontaneity and all that resists intellectualized formulation.

Clearly, the legal procedure's conclusion that the protagonist is a "moral monster" derives from the deliberate exaggeration of incidents which were wholly unrelated to the actual crime and more or less innocuous in their original form. As has been noted, Continental criminal procedure, particularly through the examining magistrate, aims to articulate a vision of the defendant; personality is far more at issue in every Continental criminal investigation than would, or could, be the case in England or America.[6] But Camus, like Dostoevski, painstakingly reveals to the structurally attuned reader that idiosyncratic distortions are endemic to any enterprise which seeks to invest a given reality with narrative significance. The inquisitor, as he toys with the suspect by alternating protestations of friendship with horrifying barrages of verbal abuse, plays the part of the novelist; he recognizes and then elevates to language only those elements of his subject which serve his peculiar ends. Following Dostoevski's example in another way, too, Camus creates a protagonist whose basically nonverbal (*renfermé*), sensual nature, like that of Mitya, estranges him from the universe of legal reasoning. If, indeed, the protagonist is the "foreigner" implied in the novel's title, his alienation from institutions is nowhere more pronounced than in his confrontation with the law (or, ironically, in his stance toward organized religion—Dostoevski and, later, Melville and Camus emphasize that the most rational-seeming element in society, law, has in fact much in common with religion, which appears least so).[7]

The protagonist, whose name is Meursault, uses words sparingly and relatively simply. No lawyer he, and no Underground Man, he displays in the first part of this story an easygoing sensuality bordering on recklessness if not immorality. But as he wins the affections of the pretty Marie and the friendship of a variety of lowlives and eccentrics, and as he enjoys the sun and pleasures of Algeria, Meursault's essentially sound, harmonious nature breaks through. He is a working man, straightforward and mildly intelligent. His main defects are an inability to use words in a socially acceptable way and a concomitant susceptibility to purely naturalistic influences.

If this man neglects to mouth homilies at his mother's funeral or sleeps with Marie the very next day; if he turns down his boss' offer of a job in Paris or agrees to listen to the complaints of a friend who happens to be a pimp—what harm has been done? As the remarkable present-tense narrative of part 1 proceeds toward the crime which concludes it, we find no moral aberration. Meursault may be a bit "bizarre"—Marie's affectionate label for his casual views about marriage, and his own sobriquet for the "robotic woman" whom he watches while at Céleste's cafe—but only in the sense that he fails to answer our need for verbal complexity in a protagonist. He stands leagues apart from the priests, intellectuals, and lawyers who populate the novels of Flaubert. Mitya Karamazov aside, Meursault is the only male character studied here who experiences sensual pleasure, wins the love of a woman, and interacts normally with colleagues and friends. But, like Mitya, he is doomed to condemnation and banishment from polite society.

The reader notes Meursault's estrangement from institutional realities during his interviews with both the inquisitor and his own defense attorney in part 2. The attorney, who is privy to the findings of the inquisitor,[8] informs his client that the preliminary investigation into the murder of an Arab on a hot Algerian beach has revealed "indications of insensitivity" in Meursault on the day of his mother's funeral. Meursault's response is typically straightforward, and thus dramatically inapposite to his role as criminal defendant:

I'm sure I loved my mother, but that didn't mean anything. All healthy creatures have more or less desired the death of those they love. (p. 96)

Similar to the "fantastic" statements of Mitya and Raskolnikov during their interrogations, this remark outrages the defense counsel, not so much because it expounds an intellectually untenable theory, but rather because it defies the concept of "reasonableness" required by the law. The attorney quite correctly advises his client "never to say that at the trial, nor in front of the inquisitor." Yet Meursault manages to add with characteristic honesty (which some might call simplicity) that his "physical needs sometimes would affect" his emotions, and that the heat on the day of the funeral caused his seeming indifference to his mother's memory. Since "the sun" ultimately becomes Meursault's only articulated defense for the homicide (p. 146), the conflict between his sensate, unsentimental, and nonverbal nature and a moralistic, intellectualized, and cognitive written legal procedure heightens throughout the investigation. As his lawyer puts it, Meursault's remarks amply illustrate that the defendant "had never had anything to do with criminal justice before."

With this as background, Meursault embarks on his most interesting interview with the inquisitor himself. The latter, "a tall man with fine features," adopts the literary lawyer's traditional mix of friendship and attack. Like Porfiry befriending Raskolnikov, he takes Meursault into his confidence: "What interests me is you," he observes amicably. But this personal curiosity expresses itself first as a procedural demand that Meursault retell "what I had already told him" about the events on the beach. The European codes of criminal procedure, which foster a heavily narrative approach to uncovering reality, allow the inquisitor to demand that the suspect recount not once, but several times, what occurred, in the hope that these various accounts will illuminate the case.[9]

Unable to elicit such a clue from the rigorously nonverbal Meursault, the inquisitor "suddenly asked me in an out-of-context way if I loved my mother. I said, 'Yes, everybody does,' and the clerk, who had been typing away, must have missed a key since he became confused and was obliged to back up a bit" (p. 99).[10] Unlike his clerk, the inquisitor cleverly betrays none of the "reasonable man's" surprise at Meursault's casual remark about the universality, and hence the banality, of filial affection, but rather switches "again without apparent logic" to the essential issue of why Meursault had shot the Arab four additional times after he fell to the sand. Meursault has no answer for this; he would have to be a Camus, rather than his antithesis, to find the words to narrate the amazing cacophony of sensations which we, as readers, have experienced with him on the beach at the end of part 1.

The seasoned lawyer now begins to recognize that Meursault's nonconformity may well transform the humdrum murder of an Arab into a case with fascinating possibilities.[11] Continuing his tactic of disequilibrating shifts in tone and subject, the inquisitor suddenly pulls a crucifix out of a file cabinet:

And in a completely altered voice, almost trembling, he exclaimed: "Do you recognize this?" I said, "Of course." Then he said quickly and in a passionate way that he believed in God; that he was persuaded [sa conviction était] that no man was so guilty that God would not forgive him, as long as that man would become like a child through repentance, a child whose soul was open, and ready to accept everything. (pp. 100–01)

Meursault, who, like Billy Budd in a similar situation, neither needs nor seeks any metaphysical mainstay, "really didn't follow his reasoning too well because I was warm and there were big flies in the office which were landing on my face, and also because he frightened me" (p. 101). He finally admits to the inquisitor that he does not believe in God.

We have already seen in Dostoevski's inquisitors and Flaubert's intellectuals and priests an existential fascination with the less verbal and more direct individuals whose lives they have come to control. Nineteenth-century fiction recognized well that the intellectual superiority and professional expertise such types display mask an intense personal involvement in the dialogue. In this wonderful scene, Camus develops this thematic ironically. The inquisitor, whose life-and-death pronouncement on Meursault should theoretically derive from a perfectly balanced outlook, cannot conduct himself in a flawlessly reasonable manner. His religious fanaticism, even if it merely serves as a ploy in the traditional strategy of seeking a confession, reveals the articulate figure's fundamental subjectivity. Reality and perhaps even justice here seem subservient at best to the institutionalization as law of a personal world view.

Camus' depiction of the inquisitor reiterates the Dostoevskian statement that the Continental law disguises with seeming rationality an arbitrary value system, refusing to countenance the explanations, however internally logical, of those who cannot conform:

> He said to me that this was impossible, that all men believe in God, even those who turn their faces away. This was his persuasion [sa conviction] and, if he ever had to doubt it, his life would no longer have any meaning. "Do you wish," he shouted at me, "that my life have no meaning?" (p. 102)

The inquisitor seems to pass over into a legally irrelevant and even irrational realm of inquiry. Meursault articulates his view that such an issue "is none of my business," but the inquisitor concludes from this remark that he "had never seen such a hardened soul."

In subsequent interviews, always in the presence of the defense attorney,[12] the inquisitor invariably affects a friendly tone with the protagonist. "He never spoke to me again about God, and I never again saw him as excited as he was that first day. . . . I must say that at the close of the eleven months of inquiry,[13] I was surprised to find myself enjoying only those rare moments when the inquisitor took me to the door of his office and patted me on the shoulder, while saying cordially, 'That's all for today, Mr. Antichrist'" (pp. 101–02).

What Meursault fails to realize is that his earlier dramatic confrontation with the inquisitor has been sufficient to inspire in the latter a particular narrative approach to his case. Having failed the double-barrelled test of crucifix and filial love, Meursault may be pigeonholed as an "Antichrist," like a caricatured secondary figure in a novel, and so treated with bland friendliness. The lawyer has conjured up an effective label which will soon gain fatal reinforcement. For at the trial, which Camus describes with an obsession for legal precision that recalls Dostoevski and Flaubert, the procurator brings to verbal fruition the analysis of Meursault's morally repugnant character first conceived during the preliminary inquiry. Turning to the jury,[14] the procurator observes, in a style reminiscent of Ippolit Kirillovich:

Did he at least express regret? Never, gentlemen. Not one time in the course of the preliminary investigation has this man seemed moved by his abominable transgression. . . .

. . . And if, in the course of my long career, I have had to ask for the supreme penalty, I have never felt that lamentable duty so amply repaid, justified, and enlightened by the conscience of a compelling and sacred precept, and by the horror which I relive [que je ressens] before a human face in which I read nothing but monstrousness. (pp. 147, 150)

The procurator's eloquent formulation confirms as official a portrait of an individual existence that would otherwise seem unremarkable. He builds upon the inquisitor's theme and gives it the persuasive voice of legal artistry. Like the novelist, the lawyer concentrates on "given cases," which he renders lastingly significant by his verbal gift.

But Camus, like Dostoevski, subtly indicates through his descriptions of legal procedure the pitfalls of verbal formulation. The legal enterprise, beginning with the preliminary investigation, manages to distort the human subject it analyzes. A series of tiny mistakes by witnesses, sifted by the inquisitor's imagination and articulated at the trial by the procurator, leads to graver error. For whatever flaws Meursault does possess, moral monstrousness, like "knowing the value of words" (another prosecutorial assessment of Meursault, p. 147), is not one of them. Indeed, each chapter in part 1 builds a portrait of a man with his own system of what are, on balance, positive values. Meursault stands, as an individual, for the total rejection of verbal sentimentality. As such, he partakes of the free flow of human existence with honesty, if not perfect Cartesian rationality. He enjoys sensuousness (Marie), and, by turns, compassion (Salamano), loyalty, however misplaced (Raymond), and even everyday labor. His "system" prior to the crime finds anything formulaic to be "bizarre," a characterization it later applies to the legal process and its practitioners.[15]

Yet each of the eight witnesses at the trial, like each of the witnesses at Mitya's trial, fails to convey the benignity of the defendant's moral system. The director and concierge of the funeral home distort or misstate the events and conversations originally narrated in chapter 1 of part 1. Both report that Meursault "didn't want to see his mother" (pp. 131–32), but the earlier narrative reveals that Meursault asked the concierge "to see my mother immediately" (p.

9), and that he tacitly conveyed this desire to the director as well (p. 10). A close review of the original rendition of the funeral scene reveals that after Meursault has expressed his desire to view the body, the concierge suggests the repulsive possibility that decomposition—caused quickly by the Algerian heat—has already begun (p. 14).[16] Only then does Meursault shy away from having the coffin opened, a decision which he immediately regrets but, with typical honesty, refuses to reverse. Meursault *does* want to see his mother at first, as any grieving son would; but the natural fear of seeing her decomposed body (a fear instilled by the concierge's anecdote) prevails, in Meursault's straightforward system, over the formalistic gesture of having the coffin opened.

The incident, a paradigm of Meursault's consistent spontaneity, becomes objectionable only when viewed through the legal microscope. Similarly, when the director testifies that one of his employees discovered at the funeral that Meursault did not even know his mother's age (p. 132), he is isolating for legal consumption a brief and innocuous moment of a spontaneous conversation first narrated in chapter 1 (p. 26).[17] After all, it is part of Meursault's unarticulated system to deemphasize sentimental irrelevancies such as remembering someone's age, and then to refuse to lie about lacking such knowledge. But during the legal process, Meursault's nonmalicious and even admirable economy of sentiment is transformed into a serialized portrait of a "monstrous" individual. No wonder Marie, who is forced to tell the court of the origins of her affair with the defendant at the Fernandel film the day after the funeral, leaves the witness stand sobbing that "they forced her to say the opposite of what she was thinking" (p. 139), and that there was no way for her to convey Meursault's true personality.

Only we, who as readers have traversed the narrative with Meursault, can judge the efficacy of the investigatory mode. When the defendant declares that "the sun" produced the homicide, we know that within a system based on openness to sensual experience, the natural environment on the day of the murder—coupled with his slight drunkenness from the luncheon wine (p. 79), a condition never revealed by the legal ratiocination—did in effect rob him of free will. Indeed, in an American court, Meursault's lack of real premeditation (pp. 86–88) would have formed the basis of a viable defense; with the "personality" issue virtually inadmissible there as well, Meursault might have received a relatively light sentence for manslaughter. But the European novelist, ensconced in the legal traditions of the Continent, realizes the dramatic intent of narrative-oriented criminal procedure. The European trial, as some commentators have inferred, is no more than a representation in dramatic and linguistic form of a view of the defendant created by the inquisitor from the data of the preliminary inquiry.[18] From the moment he refuses to play the inquisitor's game with the crucifix, Meursault exchanges his fluid and indefinable essence for a static portrayal as a hardened criminal.

The protagonist's capital offense, then, is his being-against-the-law, not his act against the Arab. Meursault is a "stranger," not to human love (whether filial or sexual), but to regimentation of any kind. Thus the word *bizarre* recurs no fewer than four times in part 2, describing the mutual abhorrence of Meursault and the legal system; for him, legal formulations share the mechanical unnaturalness of the robot-woman at Céleste's. Conversely, the law regards his free-flowing unsentimentality with a disbelief which differs from Marie's finding it "bizarre" (p. 65) only in that its curiosity about his character stems from legal necessity rather than passionate attraction.

Just as artistic legality refuses to comprehend vitalistic individual world views, so may the novelist indicate his alienation from many of the subjects to which he applies his mimetic genius. In *The Stranger*, Camus follows Dostoevski and Flaubert by making it clear that the behavior most foreign to his own narrative mode is the same free-flowing sensuousness which he theoretically attempts to capture in writing. *Lawyer and author understand each other.* If the Meursault of part 1 is a stranger to anyone at all, it is to his verbally gifted creator, whose bizarre task consists of presenting human spontaneity within the confines of an artificial and formalized literary genre. So even Camus, whose mimetic gift allowed him marvellously to capture a nonnarrative personality in part 1, insists on transforming it in part 2. By the end of the novel, Meursault, has become an articulate advocate; he terminates the narrative with an uncharacteristically lengthy discourse on the benignity of natural forces. Has his participation in the trial, which he styles more as an observation of it, changed Meursault for the better? The wordy closing, reminiscent of Alyosha's jarring verbosity at the end of *The*

Brothers Karamazov,[19] cannot be taken as a clear affirmation of the protagonist's growth. Meursault's verbal "maturation" in the final moments of his life brings him closer to Camus, not necessarily to truth.[20]

THE LITERARY LAWYER AND FASCIST POWER: *THE FALL* OF A CIVILIZATION

> *Quand on n'a pas de caractère, il faut bien se donner une méthode.*
> —Clamence *in* The Fall

Were they thrown together in the same unit of the French Foreign Legion, the narrators of *The Stranger* and *The Fall* would probably prefer a month alone in the harsh desert sun and sands to a moment in each other's presence. At first glance, it might appear that so thorough an opposition in personalities would foreclose discourse between them forever. Their common native tongue is used by each for such different aims that this mutuality becomes, ironically, the most obvious distinction between them. The carefully wrought grammar and syntax and the clever puns of Jean Baptiste Clamence would fall on unappreciative ears if the unidentified audience for his long monologue turned out to be a Meursault.

But instead Clamence's auditors are you and I, readers of complex literary texts; thus even our decision to peruse the pages of *The Fall*[21] indicates alliance with its verbose narrator, just as the very act of reading implies estrangement from the taciturn Meursault. Camus contrives to make the identity as telling as possible by associating the reader's presumed affinity to Clamence with the assumptions of another literate and liberal profession. In the last paragraph of *The Fall*, Clamence "discovers" that his patient listener, like himself, has been trained as a lawyer.

Clamence's profession, a sign of the insuperable breach between him and Meursault, produces his effective style and increases his power over his listener. Whereas the narrator of *The Stranger* abrogates his implicit control over the reader's sympathies, Clamence carefully "files a brief" in his own behalf, using the tools of his trade and appealing to his audience's evident collegiality. Indeed, when Clamence confides to his listener, about the proprietor of the Mexico City Bar, that "his silence is deafening, like that of primitive forests," or when he speaks of the man's "frankly natural simplicity," he could as easily be conversing with a fellow attorney about Meursault's attitude as a defendant. Interestingly, Clamence confesses as a first example of his own essential mendacity that he respectfully attended the funeral of his concierge, a man whom he detested.

Insofar as Meursault and Clamence are deliberately contrasted, both in self-expression and in general outlook, the reader probably sides with the intellectual lawyer, rather than the nonverbal sensualist; immersed in the difficult task of deciphering these novels, we are inclined to appreciate Clamence's constant, self-absorbed, and complex inquiry into the relationship between language and meaning. As the "confession's"[22] final paragraphs confirm, the narrative displays the strengths and foibles of reader and narrator alike. Flaubert ends his masterpiece with Frédéric Moreau and Charles Deslauriers, lawyers both; this duality is replicated at the end of *The Fall*. But now it is the reader who stands as a mirror image to the protagonist as lawyer.

In his former life as a Parisian attorney, Clamence had gained temporary peace of mind. Respected for his professional talents and forcefulness, he had the good fortune to consider himself a genuine altruist. His humane concern for the suspected criminals who required his legal services extended to the blind man crossing the street, and to the motorist whose car had gone dead. But behind the charity, and the sense of "harmony" which it produced in Clamence, lay the aloofness implicit in his trade. "My profession . . . relieved within me any sense of bitterness about my neighbor, who was always in my debt without me ever owing him anything." A detached condescension toward his clients, as well as toward the women who amused him from time to time, was the "sole cause of my interest in others."

How tenuous the moral complacency of modern man! For Clamence, whose retreat to watery Amsterdam adds to his image as the new Underground Man, loses his equilibrium through a mere handful of negative events. Like Dostoevski's intellectual and legal protagonists, an unresolved sense of insult derived from one or two situations sends Clamence into a self-imposed exile, the better to deploy his true gift: stylized verbosity. Only in his own good time does Clamence manage to tell us about his failures, weaving them subtly into the fabric not so much of a confession as a legal brief.

Organizing carefully his narration of the original troubling circum-stances, he begins by telling us the more innocuous ones, only in the fateful final chapter revealing the collaborative cowardices which more than match the private ones. Each incident, however, points to the basic Clamence, to an essentially passive and overly verbal nature which resists engagement and ends in mendacity.

The "investigation" in *The Fall* thus brings to logical fruition the theme that originated with Dostoevski's inquisitors. The dis-junction of lawyer and suspect, never absolute (think of Porfiry and Raskolnikov), fittingly ceases to exist. Clamence, the "juge-pénitent," brings them together in one character. It follows that the sole object of his investigation, which is still a *criminal* procedure as we shall see, is himself, and the sole medium, a tortured, highly for-mulated, and essentially literary discourse. We are compelled to fol-low his ironic communication, as both judge and suspect, for his story is ours as well.

Clamence tells his auditor, as they stroll together along the quays of Amsterdam, of the mysterious laughter which had under-mined the lawyer's smug sense of power years earlier on the Pont des Arts (p. 47). In part, surely, the laugh reminded Clamence of his failure on an earlier occasion to leap from another Parisian bridge into the Seine to prevent an attempted suicide (pp. 81–82). But in its anonymity, the laugh stood as an indictment of Clamence's en-tire existence. Disembodied, it reverberated with his own detach-ment; its tittering overtones mimicked the tenor of a life led falsely, affecting outward joy while masking the inner grotesqueness of ver-bose insensitivity. Like Ivan Karamazov's devil, Clamence's "uni-versal laugh" articulated and embodied his disjointed inner state.[23]

The laugh, then, represents Clamence's self-indictment for the excessive admiration with which he had previously viewed his pro-fessional and personal achievements. Its ironic validity is borne out by an incident involving a motorcycle, an event Clamence specifi-cally places under the sign of "ressentiment" (p. 64). The classic symptoms of that peculiar literary malaise emerged in him when, sitting in his car behind a stalled motorcycle during a Paris traffic jam, he decided to create a scene and assert his power; instead, he became an object of ridicule, receiving an almost paradigmatic box on the ears from a passerby and slouching back to his car to the hoots of the crowd. Clamence, like the Underground Man, can never forget such "indignities," however trivial to the normal mind. Even as he relates it in Amsterdam, he "plays it over" endlessly in his mind. Strongly allusive of the Zverkov party scene in *Notes from Underground*, the motorcycle incident both exacerbates Clamence's evolving sense of insecurity and drives him further into the last outlet for his romantic self-admiration, the area of elaborate verbal structures, fortified in exile.

Ostensibly, the Clamence we meet in Amsterdam is a witty eccentric, enjoying a premature and literate dotage. A combination of latter-day Ancient Mariner and modern nihilist, whose healthy irony mitigates the solemnity of his observations about human behavior, he buttonholes lonely tourists. In fact, however, Clamence's parodying of the overly self-conscious model established by nineteenth-century ressentient protagonists is a deception as dangerous as it is disarming. Still practicing his former profession in the mock consultations he offers to the patrons of the Mexico City bar, he raises the Dostoevskian combination of social negativity and verbal complexity to a self-satisfied ethos in which, even more explicitly than in Frédéric Moreau's system, falsehood is a primary assumption:

And don't lies finally put us on the road to truth? And my stories, true or false, don't they tend toward the same aim, don't they have the same meaning? So, does it really matter whether they are true or false, if, in either case, they are indicative of what I've been and of what I am? We sometimes see more clearly into a person who lies than one who tells the truth. (p. 140)

Like the intellectual philosophers (the Underground Man and Ivan Karamazov), and the legal philosophers (Porfiry Petrovich and Ippolit Kirillovich), Clamence here waves away all viewpoints opposed to his own. And like the artist-priest (Schahabarim) and the mediocre lawyer (Frédéric), he is able to embellish his arguments and make them almost enticing.

For is not Clamence's intellectual nihilism a playful yet realistic approach to Camus' world, which has formally rejected absolutes such as "truth"? Camus rearticulates the problem of nineteenth-century intellectual and legalistic deception in the context of twentieth-century absurdism and loss of values. Here, Clamence's lies

wield a charm which would be overpowering (especially for the protagonist's implicitly identical auditor) were it not for Camus' deliberate invocation of the historical event which perhaps contributed
most to that loss of values. Recall what we have hypothesized about
the structural effect of the novelistic approach to legal investigations. *Truth*, established by the original narration of events, pre-
dates their subsequent ratiocination under the legal microscope.
Clamence's investigation of himself, fraught with deceit, is even
less able to oppose an anterior vision of truth than were the earlier
legal inquiries we have analyzed.

It is not insignificant that Clamence's "confession" takes place
in the context of European fascism and its aftermath; Camus is in-
voking the broader reality of contemporary history. The type of
falsehood that informed the personal destructiveness of the nineteenth century's intellectual protagonists, and even the institutional injustice of its lawyers, takes on a new dimension when it is
made to confront cosmic historical dilemmas such as the Nazi presence in Europe. And, although his listener notes that the usually
prolix but always lawyerlike narrator "passes quickly over these
meaningful details" (p. 143), Clamence does admit that

> I was tempted by the Resistance. . . . I arrived in the unoccupied zone
> with the intention of finding out about the Resistance. But once I did that,
> I hesitated. The idea began to seem a little crazy and, to be frank, roman-
> tic. I think, above all, that underground action simply went poorly with
> my personality. . . . I admired those who gave themselves over to this hero-
> ism of the depths, but I could not imitate them. (pp. 141–42)

How many Frenchmen, how many cultured Europeans, perceived
their situations as Clamence did his! Joseph Haennig, the first literary lawyer discussed in the present study (see introduction) was after
all only a French attorney practicing in wartime who could not
quite motivate himself to face grotesque realities squarely. His 1943
essay on the racial statutes (see the appendix, below) probably permitted him to retain a modicum of self-respect; he, too, avoided the
"heroism of the depths." Specificity, the concretizing of both history and form, drives Camus' meaning home. Clamence's professional and personal "fall" indicts a particular system of values—that
of modern European culture.

The verbal protagonist says of the Nazis what may likewise be said of him: "If you don't have a character, then you must give yourself a method" (p. 16); his method is codified falsehood. Having participated, through passive acceptance, in bestial injustice, Clamence tries to translate his personal failure into wordy philosophy. For Clamence's ressentient passivity, duplicated by millions like him, has had fatal consequences in the context of twentieth-century history. Self-confessed or ironic mendacity may be better than unknowing or hypocritical falsehood, but irony and complexity in the absence of deep-rooted values lead the passive observer inexcusably to accept whatever external reality happens to impose itself.

Clamence's "fall" is that of a full generation of Europeans. Literary, legal, and Christian institutions were, at best, inept to suppress the beast in their midst. And when the unprecedented systematic massacre of innocents was over, that culture still stood, like Clamence, in a stance of ridiculous self-affirmation. His error, like those of many postwar "existentialists," is to accept only half of Nietzsche's system, his seeming nihilism, and even to extend that into an absurdist vision of the universe. Failing to conceive the positive, ethical value system which must replace the rotten present code, Clamence has learned nothing from his articulate self-investigation.[24]

Ironic absurdism as a modern version of Christian passivity is subjected to a critical self-appraisal in this tale. Like the Pope,[25] whose position Clamence briefly assumes by proxy during the war, and like all great European institutional figures, Clamence fails to find the courage to say, "This far you can go, but no further." So Clamence's auditor, if he is to benefit from the protagonist's long and treacherous discourse, must adopt the protagonist as a negative model, and not as a clever and sophisticated word-slinger whose nihilistic vision of the universe should be emulated by all intelligent readers. We need not accept Clamence's invitation at the end of his elaborate narrative to slink away from the next person who needs our help on a Parisian bridge.

Camus' courageous last work provides an explicit historical setting within which the literary-legalistic mode of investigation has utterly failed. Not only has the lawyer become a criminal; he has brought to criminology a full-blown self-congratulatory construct.

His original failure to act earned the ironic laugh which marked his downfall, but the failure to have learned from the experience is doubly damnable. So, too, European religion, law, scholarship, and literature, once safe harbors for such clever Clamences, may have rationalized their own values out of existence.

In this world of lies, Truth is forced to fly like a scared white doe in the woodlands; and only by glimpses will she reveal herself, as in Shakespeare and other masters of the great Art of telling the truth—even though it be covertly and by snatches.

—Melville, Moby Dick

PART 4 The Creative Use of Statutes for Subjective Ends: The Case of *Billy Budd, Sailor*

8 Narrative Plot and Legalistic Dimension

ENTERING THE HOLY OF HOLIES

Billy Budd, Sailor—the title resounds magically within the spirit of anyone who has grappled with the intricacies of Melville's final tale. As with a biblical story,[1] each sentence, even a single word, produces new questions for the interpreter and inspires passionate partisanship among the exegetes. The story's narrative tone contributes deliberately to its mystery; the narrator frequently claims he is unable to describe central characters (he says of John Claggart, "His portrait I essay, but shall never hit it"), and he intersperses the "primary" sections of the story with a series of extremely difficult self-confessed "digressions."

The text itself poses problems. Melville wrote the novella over a six-year period (1885–91), adding and deleting entire sections and characters and rearranging many of the incidents. He died in the midst of his effort, and the story was not published until 1924. We now have, fortunately, a good idea of the form he ultimately intended for the tale, thanks to a relatively recent edition by Harrison Hayford and Merton Sealts.[2] In my analysis, I generally assume a holistic text, while trying not to lose sight of its occasionally confusing genealogy.

No work is more central to my theme than *Billy Budd, Sailor*. Fascinated by the law, Melville follows a schema by now familiar to us: a series of creative verbalizers organize criminal proceedings against a nonverbal defendant whose moral system differs from their own. Foreshadowed by the more benign "Bartleby the Scrivener" (1853), which anticipates many legalistic aspects of *Billy Budd, Sailor*, Melville's final novella goes beyond the treatment of law to portray a conflict between organized Christianity and more just and natural behavioral modes.

Indeed, the story is rich with complexities that appear to defy a unified interpretation, yet never fail to elicit a variety of doctrinaire responses from readers, including even some ostensibly dispassionate professional critics.[3] My hope is that the comparative methodology of this study will shed light on the legal and ethical elements in the tale. That aim accomplished, my analysis need only be considered one of the many responses to an incredibly evocative story.

MELVILLE'S LEGAL BACKGROUND

As Melville labored over his final masterpiece, at least four law-related factors played on his imagination. First, he had a distinguished lawyer in his family; his father-in-law, Lemuel Shaw, was chief judge of the Massachusetts Supreme Court. In this capacity, Shaw tried some difficult cases under the conscience-jarring provisions of the Fugitive Slave Act. As Robert Cover has observed, Shaw may have been a model for Captain Vere, another adjudicator who seems forced to apply a given statute to morally innocent defendants.[4] Second, Melville, like Camus, directed his attention to a specific body of laws which he integrated into his stories. The Mutiny Act, the Articles of War, and their English equivalents Melville knew well, not only because of his lifelong fascination with sailors, but also as a result of his having served on a naval vessel upon which the Articles were read in full at frequent intervals.[5] Third, like his near contemporary Dostoevski, Melville sharpened his legal competence in those areas which particularly interested him by following actual cases in great detail. One of these, the widely publicized *Somers* case of 1842 (in which Melville's first cousin Guert Gansevoort was a principal), merits a significant paragraph of analysis in *Billy Budd, Sailor*, written more than forty years after the trial took place.[6] And while some have argued that the *Somers* affair would not have been sufficiently alive in Melville's memory to provide direct inspiration for his final story,[7] the fact remains that James Fenimore Cooper's full transcript and analysis of the case kept it in the public consciousness until as late as the 1880s.[8] Newspaper and magazine accounts of the *Somers* are often highly literary, a fact which must be kept in mind as we read Melville's "inside" account of the trial on the *Bellipotent*.

Finally, like Flaubert and many other novelists, Melville maintained an active interest in current as well as past legal matters. The infamous Haymarket trials, which were publicly conducted in 1887, resulted in the execution of four anarchist leaders on what some considered dubious evidence. They may well have given Melville additional inspiration to treat the essential moral issues so frequently encapsulated in courtroom dramas.[9]

For all these reasons, Melville's awareness of the influence of law was very much alive as he wrote *Billy Budd*, and he ultimately arranged his tale to center on a trial, a statute, and a lawyer figure. The latter is Captain Edward Fairfax Vere, the apparent voice of disinterest, reason, and formality, and as lawyerlike a naval officer as one finds in literature. Just as Camus' Clamence realizes his practical talents and moral nature during his superlative performances as a defense attorney, so Vere can only allow his personality full sway during his adjudicatory arguments in the case of Billy Budd. Indeed, if the comparison between Vere and Clamence be allowed, we may also see a link between Camus' Meursault and the happily uncomplicated foretopman whose fate Vere comes to control. Billy and Meursault, who tend to participate freely in unstructured reality, suddenly find themselves harnessed by legal forms totally alien to their nonverbal natures. Like Bartleby, they too would "prefer not to" participate. But unlike Bartleby, who has violated no criminal statute, they must.

PLOTS AND DIGRESSIONS

The perfect fit of form and content in *Billy Budd, Sailor* proves that the action of a novel or short story cannot be adequately described by an Aristotelian recitation of the bare plot line. Rather, as Victor Shklovski reminds us, a novelistic plot is "the fashioning of the subject of the story as produced by the introduction of interrupting digressions."[10] The use of legalistic structures, as I have indicated throughout, perfectly fits the digressive tendencies of the novelistic form, forcing the reader to stop and start, backtrack, and focus on details, rather than make smooth temporal progress. Novelistic meaning, these texts teach us, eludes Aristotelian expectations! And certainly no one who has entered into the studied complexity of Melville's final work would easily swallow any schematic attempt to describe its "plot." Such efforts by filmmakers, librettists, and some literary critics[11] only deplete the narrative subtlety which is the story's essence. Yet a kind of recasting of the story, loyal to its digressions, is both possible and necessary to our purposes here.

The tale, subtitled *An Inside Narrative*, is brief—approximately ninety pages. It begins with the description of a certain type—the "Handsome Sailor," of which the title hero is a fine, albeit flawed, example. The essence of this type is set forth in the following passage:

It was strength and beauty. Tales of his prowess were recited. Ashore he was the champion; afloat the spokesman; on every suitable occasion always foremost. Close-reefing topsails in a gale, there he was, astride the weather yardarm-end, foot in the Flemish horse as stirrup, both hands tugging at the earing as at a bridle, in very much the attitude of young Alexander curbing the fiery Bucephalus. A superb figure, tossed up as by the horns of Taurus against the thunderous sky, cheerily hallooing to the strenuous file along the spar.

The moral nature was seldom out of keeping with the physical make. . . .

Such a cynosure, at least in aspect, and something such too in nature, though with important variations made apparent as the story proceeds, was welkin-eyed Bill Budd—or Baby Budd, as more familiarly, under circumstances hereafter to be given, he at last came to be called—aged twenty-one, a foretopman of the British fleet toward the close of the last decade of the eighteenth century. (p. 44)

Billy Budd brings the overt values of his type to the specific historical environment of this novella. His fate is unraveled not in an allegorical locus of anytime and anywhere, but rather in the period of the great revolutions and mutinies which threatened the stability of the British navy. "It was the summer of 1797," we are told. Billy is impressed from a merchant ship, the *Rights of Man*, onto Captain Vere's naval vessel, the action-bound *Bellipotent*. The cheerful Billy accepts his fate. Resentment and "double meanings and insinuations of any sort [being] quite foreign to his nature," he departs the homeward-bound ship, leaving on the *Rights* only the memory of "the jewel" of its crew, whose popularity and natural esteem among his fellow sailors he now brings to the *Bellipotent.*

Further to inform his reader of the story's historical context, Melville moves from Billy to the general subject of mutinies, and to the specific and majestic subject of Admiral Nelson, the contemporary and colleague of the *Bellipotent*'s fictional Captain, Vere (who has not yet been mentioned). Nelson, Melville reminds us, quoting Tennyson, is "the greatest sailor since our world began" (p. 58). He becomes the subject of chapters 4 and 5, is mentioned twice again later in the text, and is strongly alluded to at Vere's death (pp. 63, 69, and 129). Nelson appears here as a kind of Handsome Sailor himself, for on the troubled ship the *Theseus* (like Billy on the *Rights*), he has quashed an incipient mutiny, his method "not indeed to terrorize the crew into base subjection, but to win them, by force of his mere presence and heroic personality, back to an allegiance if not as enthusiastic as his own yet as true" (p. 59).

As the narrative winds through ironically self-proclaimed "by-paths" to the exposition of its central actions, Captain Vere is finally introduced. A good, if somewhat pedantic, bookish, overly conservative and prudent officer, he bears the nickname "Starry Vere" partly because he is occasionally seen gazing absently at the heavens but also because of Andrew Marvell's poem about his ancestor "Starry Vere," who was noted for his "discipline severe."

Chapter 8 introduces the last of the tale's principal players, the *Bellipotent*'s master-at-arms, John Claggart. His portrait, the narrator admits, only approximates reality, for, like Vere (and unlike Billy), Claggart is twice described as "exceptional" (pp. 74, 76).[12] Both figures stand out on board a ship because their verbal gifts and complex intelligence oppose them to the usual sailor type. Billy, never described as exceptional, is simply a fine example of that type, whose traits are clearly distinguished from those of Vere and Claggart:

> And what could Billy know of man except of man as a mere sailor? And the old-fashioned sailor, the veritable man before the mast, the sailor from boyhood up, he, though indeed of the same species as a landsman, is in some respects singularly distinct from him. The sailor is frankness, the landsman is finesse. Life is not a game with the sailor, demanding the long head—no intricate game of chess where few moves are made in straightfor-wardness and ends are attained by indirection, an oblique, tedious, barren

game hardly worth that poor candle burnt out in playing it. Yes, as a class, sailors are in character a juvenile race. (pp. 86–87)

Claggart, like Vere, is "finesse," particularly finesse with language, with verbal obfuscation and with achieving ends through "indirection." These traits, unexceptionable on land, clash with the simplicity of men at sea.

Claggart, whose daily dealings with the sailors heightens his dialectical sense, suffers from an animus his captain does not share. He is obsessed with Billy Budd. This passion, "never declared," is treated in a vitally important passage, which I cite in part here, saving the complete text for analysis in the next chapter:

> But the thing which in eminent instances signalizes so exceptional a nature is this: Though the man's even temper and discreet bearing would seem to intimate a mind peculiarly subject to the law of reason, not the less in heart he would seem to riot in complete exemption from that law, having apparently little to do with reason further than to employ it as an ambidexter implement for effecting the irrational. That is to say: Toward the accomplishment of an aim which in wantonness of atrocity would seem to partake of the insane, he will direct a cool judgment sagacious and sound. (p. 76)

Why does Claggart have it in for Billy? We do not completely know. But as the narrative proceeds, it affords us some hints. Billy and Claggart are types in opposition. It has become a critical commonplace to think of this opposition in terms of good and evil, or in terms of heart versus head, but these are reductive analyses, unworthy of the text in its wholeness.[13] The real opposition here, as indicated in the passage, is between the Handsome Sailor's innate joyful openness and the intelligent master-at-arms' "ingratiating" indirectness, or, as I shall call the dialectic here, between *overtness* and *covertness*.

Since, as Melville tells us, "in this matter of writing, resolve as one may to keep to the main road, some bypaths have an enticement not readily to be withstood" (p. 56),[14] let us backtrack a bit to explore the matter of overtness and covertness. Earlier in the text, in establishing the tale's historical background, Melville provides his reader with an invaluable clue to the story's meaning. In chapter 3 he describes the manner in which British historians related the Nore mutiny to the public back home:

Such an episode in the Island's grand naval story her naval historians naturally abridge, one of them (William James) candidly acknowledging that fain would he pass it over did not "impartiality forbid fastidiousness." And yet his mention is less a narration than a reference, having to do hardly at all with details. Nor are these readily to be found in the libraries. Like some other events in every age befalling states everywhere, including America, the Great Mutiny was of such character that national pride along with views of policy would fain shade it off into the historical background. Such events cannot be ignored, but there is a *considerate* way of historically treating them. If a well-constituted individual refrains from blazoning aught amiss or calamitous in his family, a nation in the like circumstance may without reproach be equally discreet. (p. 55, emphasis mine)

People in positions of authority, Melville tells us, should not simply declare outright everything they know or believe. Interested audiences must be treated with consideration. Some truths, directly conveyed, are too upsetting.

What is here posited nonpejoratively as a mode of "considerate" communication becomes questionable when exercised by a John Claggart. Claggart proves himself a master at considerateness, as well as arms, during the famous mess-hall episode in chapter 10. Billy accidentally spills some soup (the "greasy liquid" understandably beloved of Freudian interpreters of the novella)[15] in Claggart's path. About to strike Billy, the master-at-arms quickly restrains himself. His stern expression immediately alters; he smiles and says merely, "Handsomely done, my lad! And handsome is as handsome did it, too!" Not a sailor in the mess hall now believes that Claggart has anything against Billy. But as he removes himself from the men's view, Claggart vents his resentful rage on a drummer boy, who perhaps has something of Billy's natural gait and spontaneity and happens to be passing by. Melville thus establishes a *model* for covert communication (a species of the Nore historians' "considerate" communication) which we will have occasion to recall further in our analysis.

Meanwhile, Claggart's antipathy to Billy evolves into a strategy. He sends out several deputies to tempt the young foretopman to mutiny, but Billy, always the loyal counterpart to Nelson, throws them out. Finally, in chapter 18, Claggart takes a fateful step. He accuses Billy, before Captain Vere, of conspiracy to mutiny. With customary indirectness, he induces the reluctant and angrily unbelieving Vere to call Billy to defend himself against the charge. Billy's stutter (his only flaw) prevents him from framing a coherent answer. "Speak, man!," the captain repeatedly implores. But the handsome sailor, never a talker, responds otherwise. His essential harmony of outward form and inner nature compels him to express nonverbally his aversion to an unjust attack. Billy strikes, and Claggart falls to the cabin floor. Vere, moved by these events to a wholly uncharacteristic and almost cathartic show of emotion, cries, "Struck dead by an angel of God! Yet the angel must hang!" The ship's surgeon, amazed to see the usually calm captain so passionate, confirms Claggart's death. Vere immediately summons a drumhead court, although the surgeon and other officers privately deem it more "dictated by usage" to refer the matter "to the admiral" (p. 101).[16]

Chapter 21, the longest in the text, describes the trial of Billy Budd for striking a senior officer in time of war (no other charge, as we shall see, is fully mounted by Vere during the arguments). A handpicked court, listening to its captain as sole nonparty witness, prosecutor, and fellow adjudicator all in one,[17] overcomes its initial misgivings and sentences Billy to hang.

Before an awe-struck crew, the very next day, Billy is executed. Directing the men quickly back to work, Vere appeases his fellow officer's fear that the men may mutiny on seeing their favorite so disposed of by counselling the dampening influence of "forms, measured forms" upon the crew. They docilely return to their duties; indeed, as we learned earlier in the tale, on the *Bellipotent* "very little in the manner of men . . . would have suggested to an ordinary observer that the great mutiny was a recent event" (pp. 59–60). The crew is perhaps partly satisfied by the ever-loyal and finally articulate Billy's last words, "God bless Captain Vere!" (p. 123).

The event stands thus, unremarked until this narrative by any but the men who were present and, curiously, by the readers of an official naval chronicle of the time called *News from the Mediterranean*. Its "long ago superannuated and forgotten" account, given in chapter 29, inverts values and confuses facts. Claggart is described as an upstanding model of loyalty and Billy as a depraved foreigner who vindictively stabbed him to the heart. The Nore historians' form of "considerate communication" has been adopted in the authoritative report, designed to appease its audience and to teach a lesson in patriotism. Only Melville's "inside narrative" sets the record straight.

Vere himself, shattered undoubtedly by the choice he says the law compelled him to make, never really recovers. Wounded in an insignificant battle prior to the renowned episodes at the Nile and Trafalgar, Vere, "the spirit that 'spite its philosophic austerity may yet have indulged in the most secret of all passions, ambition, never attained to the fullness of fame." He dies mumbling "Billy Budd, Billy Budd," a phrase well understood by those who witnessed the extraordinary events on the *Bellipotent*. Indeed, the officer of marines, the member of Billy's court-martial who was "the most reluctant to condemn," comprehends the centrality of Billy's trial and execution to Vere's existence and understands why Vere is preoccupied with the incident at his death. But, like most of Vere's subordinates, he "kept the knowledge to himself" (p. 129).

The tale ends on its least ambiguous and most lyrical note. For the crew—the straightforward, overt, and uncomplicated sailors—have composed a ballad called "Billy in the Darbies." Its strikingly simple verses speak of the heroic Billy at death, the "jewel" of the ship who can only observe, without bitterness,

> —O, tis me, not the
> sentence they'll suspend. (p. 132)

THE TRIAL SCENE: BEYOND THE DILEMMA OF RIGHTEOUSNESS

Earlier Critical Approaches to the Law of the Case

The centerpiece of this amazing story is the trial scene in chapter 21, which stands to the whole as a microcosm of its meaning, just as trial scenes in the other literary masterpieces we have examined frequently bring forth the fullest sense of the larger text.[18] Captain Vere, as "co-adjutor," sole witness, and statutory interpreter, is its focus of attention. Initially, and explicitly, the trial scene attempts to provide the reader with the "evidence" needed to judge not so much Billy as Captain Vere. Perhaps the novella's most puzzling character, Vere has won the admiration of the vast majority of critics, who seem to accept his statements during this scene as unambiguous.[19] In the late 1940s and 1950s negative perceptions of Vere were virtually nonexistent in America; when expressed, they were greeted with serious professional antipathy.[20] Even legal analysts of Vere's position, writing during the antiauthoritarian 1960s, were likely to show respect for Vere's dilemma and full faith in his veracity. Thus the eventual "drop-out" Charles Reich claims:

The chief agent of the law is Captain Vere. . . . Melville allows Vere no choice within the terms of the law itself: if the law is obeyed, Billy must hang. . . . We may perhaps criticize the law, but not the officer whose "vowed responsibility" is to "adhere to it and administer it." . . .

Clearly, then, *Billy Budd* is designed to give us a case where compromise is impossible, and where Vere, and we, are forced to confront the imperatives of law. As Melville presents the case, there is no escape for Vere. It is in this light that we must appreciate Vere's reactions.[21]

In the 1970s, Robert Cover, whose use of the story as a crucial analytical tool in his exceptional *Justice Accused: Antislavery and the Judicial Process* ought richly to be appreciated, noted with admiration Vere's "righteousness" under the circumstances (p. 4). Comparing Vere to Melville's father-in-law, Chief Judge Lemuel Shaw, Cover asks the necessary question: "What deep urge leads a man to . . . embrace, personally, the opportunity to do an impersonal, distasteful task?" (p. 4).[22] But Cover's historical approach to Shaw not surprisingly forestalled a more intensive analysis of Vere and resulted in a view of the fictional adjudicator essentially in agreement with Reich's.

It was left, paradoxically, to a small minority of literary critics to begin the slow process of challenging the basis upon which Vere's "righteousness" must lie: the validity of his assertion that the positive law *compelled* the court to sentence and execute Billy. In the midst of the McCarthy era, Leonard Casper wrote an article provocatively entitled "The Case Against Captain Vere."[23] Effectively incorporating the *Somers* affair of 1842, Casper notes an allusion to the case in Melville's earlier *White Jacket*: "Three men, in a time of peace, were then hung at the yard-arm, merely because, in the captain's judgment, it became necessary to hang them,"[24] and wonders if Vere needed to hang Billy. Casper's approach pointed to an opening in the story for the legal analyst. "Vere's behavior," he went on, anticipating Cover, "demands explanation because of its unnaturalness" (p. 151). Where Reich saw Vere as nobly applying the dictates of an unnatural law, Casper went one step toward saying the converse:

By refusing all natural considerations, Vere makes his verdict unnatural, a perversion as serious as Claggart's. By shifting responsibility for his decision to the King, Vere denies that he is a free agent with an individual sense of discrimination and judgment. (p. 151)

Casper's article forms a meritorious but too pithy basis for a full-fledged inquiry into the legal meaning of the story. He uses no legal materials. His hint that Vere and Claggart are afflicted with a similar spiritual disease is not elaborated. Three critics in the 1960s, C. B. Ives, Merlin Bowen, and E. A. Dryden, take these hints a bit further, partly through the use of some related legal data.

Merlin Bowen, a lifelong Melville specialist, illuminated this text primarily through his path-breaking willingness to compare Captain Vere (thought to be a "good" character) to John Claggart (clearly the novella's villain.) Taking account of Melville's evident knowledge of naval law in his analysis, Bowen became one of the first to intuit the author's subtler meaning. He is worth citing at length:

Such an estimate of Vere is, of course, not the most common one to-day. There has been for many years a tendency to see in *Billy Budd* Melville's last "testament of acceptance," his long-delayed recognition of necessity—almost, as it were, the death-bed recantation of his "absolutist" errors. . . . In such a view, at any rate, Captain Vere commonly assumes the stature of a tragic hero. He is seen as a brooding and compassionate Lincoln, courageously facing up to the hard necessities of action and responsibility, as a sort of latter-day Abraham "resolutely offering [young Isaac] up in obedience to the exacting behest." What somehow goes unnoticed is that the action of hanging Billy is undertaken in clear opposition to Vere's own conscience and in obedience to "the exacting behest" not of God but of social expediency.

Surely, though, it must come as a shock to any reader of Melville to find him here at the end of a long and deeply considered life with nothing more to show for it than this sorry wisdom of resignation to a forced complicity in evil. Nothing in the earlier writing—certainly not in *Clarel*—could have led one to predict so complete a reversal of attitude. And when one remembers the motto—"Keep true to the dreams of thy youth"—glued to the inside of the writing box on which *Billy Budd* was composed, one's doubts of such an interpretation grow.

Fortunately, there is no need to rely upon external probabilities in disputing such a view. The pages of *Billy Budd* themselves contain sufficient evidence upon which to base quite a different estimate of Captain Vere. . . . And when the simple and loyal-hearted sailor, Billy Budd, left speechless by Claggart's accusation of treason, impulsively knocks the liar down and so kills him, the practical Vere knows his duty at once and resolutely proceeds to hang, for the greatest good of the greatest number, a man innocent in all but the most technical sense of the word. . . .

Billy Budd will appear as a much more coherent, though still puzzling, work of art if regarded as a study in the possible consequences of a commitment to a fixed and theoretic pattern rather than to patternless life itself with all its contradictions, crosscurrents, and inescapable risks.

In the book's central opposition of civilization and nature, head and heart, there can be no real question where Captain the Honorable Edward Fairfax Vere stands: quite clearly, and despite his own instinctive feelings in the matter, he stands with Claggart and against Billy. By both temperament and training, he is much closer to the petty officer he despises than to the young foretopman he admires.[25]

C. B. Ives, writing in 1962, dealt with some of the technical legal material generated by the story. Ives' contribution, however, lay even more in his insistence that an understanding of the story begins with the real events to which Melville was responding and not necessarily with the tale's allegorical or metaphysical levels of meaning. Those meanings, Ives posited, must come only after we have explored the tangible data which Melville himself knew so well:

Did Melville make his captain's case so strong that the problem disappeared?—so strong that every reasonable captain would have acted as he did? If so, the story has lost some of its realistic appeal. Vere's position was exactly that; he said that he had no choice and that, in fact, he was faced with no problem at all. I believe that the reader is mistaken if he accepts Vere's position at face value.[26]

Ives goes on to an accurate, if brief, presentation of the actual British statutes Vere invokes, examining them with care because he believed the text mandated such research. He notes several procedural defects in Vere's approach, several substantive oddities, and some details of legal history and custom which cast into doubt, he felt, the court's harsh decision to hang Billy.[27] But Ives only began the process I hope to complete here; more significantly, he also refused to draw conclusions from his data about Melville's perceptions of law, moral choice, and society generally. Rather, Ives (compellingly, it must be said) saw Vere's rush to hang Billy as idiosyncratic, "a sacrificial gesture, born of a kind of self-punishment that had become habitual in Vere's life," for

the customs of the sea did not require it; and the Articles of War provided only a deceptive excuse for the exercise of Vere's extraordinary "priestly motive," which, as Melville suggests at the beginning of Chapter [21], may well have contained the elements of true insanity. (p. 38)

Finally, but again too cryptically, E. A. Dryden's epilogue to his *Melville's Thematics of Form* challenged assumptions about Vere. Alluding briefly to the distorted *News from the Mediterranean* (chapter 29 of the tale), Dryden emphasizes Melville's antipathy to "authorized" formal versions of reality, which deceitfully smoothed over truth's "ragged edges." "The Articles of War," he goes on, without elaboration, "merely cover with an official mask the same irrational forces which are found undisguised 'across the channel.'"[28]

Ives, Bowen, Dryden, and a handful of others tried to move the focus of *Billy Budd* analysis off the dead center of Vere's supposed lack of choice. Yet the view retains its force, for no integrated alternative hypothesis has yet been articulated.

The Framework for Adjudication: Vere's Possible "Insanity"

As we have seen, most analysts of Captain Vere's actions and arguments during the trial have both accepted his articulated dichotomy of moral innocence and legal guilt in the case and rejected the narrative's invitation to question his interpretation of the law. The captain argues that the law's strict forms must prevail, even, or especially, over a situation that inspires admiration for the defendant and repugnance for the required outcome. Vere claims that, despite the moral innocence of Billy, the external, positive law absolutely mandates his execution. Not to endorse this statement of the issues might appear to lessen the force of the story; in general, critics have preferred to discuss it in terms not so explicitly evoked by the narrative: innocence versus maturity, absolutism versus relativism, individual versus communal needs, or, of course, good versus evil.[29]

If it can be textually demonstrated, however, that Vere deliberately distorts the operative law in the case in order to arrive at a verdict and a sentence harmonious with his deepest *private* urges, then the central problematic reverses itself. Instead of the dilemma of a righteous man forced, against the dictates of his conscience, to apply an unambiguous positive law, we have an inquiry into the uses of external forms to justify intense subjective urges. If adjudicatory "insanity" is present in Captain Vere, then Melville's statements about law are raised to an even greater level of significance, one likely to enhance our understanding of the tale as a whole.

We should recall that the lengthy trial scene begins in a strange way. In the short preceding chapter and on into the first paragraph of chapter 21, Vere's behavior and state of mind, not the law of Billy's case, are the subject of narrative scrutiny. By dwelling upon the surgeon's misgivings (shared by the other junior officers who hear of the incident) about the captain's rush to judge Billy, and then reinvoking the insanity motif from the passage describing Claggart's "exceptional" nature (p. 76), the narrator indicates that the adjudicator, as much as the accused, now stands trial. He advises the reader to make his own decision about Vere, however, based on "such light as this narrative may afford" (p. 102), and returns to the scene of the drumhead court. The phrase begs the reader to be as scrupulous and alert as possible in attempting to understand Vere. The narrative provides ample hints, but no clear answers; the reader must work at an understanding.

We should not minimize the aesthetic importance of these allusions at the very moment we enter into the trial scene. The surgeon's fears that his captain may have become "unhinged" (p. 102) because of something in this case are now raised to the level of a legitimate narrative question. At the end of the chapter, the question is reiterated, in a passage frequently misread as a clear endorsement of Vere's behavior:[30]

Not unlikely [the court was] brought to something more or less akin to that harassed frame of mind which in the year 1842 actuated the commander of the U.S. brig-of-war *Somers* to resolve, under the so-called Articles of

War, Articles modeled upon the English Mutiny Act, to resolve upon the execution at sea of a midshipman and two sailors as mutineers designing the seizure of the brig. Which resolution was carried out though in a time of peace and within not many days' sail of home. An act vindicated by a naval court of inquiry subsequently convened ashore. History, and here cited without comment. True, the circumstances on board the *Somers* were different from those on board the *Bellipotent*. But the urgency felt, well-warranted or otherwise, was much the same. (pp. 113–14)

The surgeon's misgivings, the mention of insanity, and the *Somers* reference establish a framework around the trial itself. It is an "urgency felt" by the adjudicator, and not necessarily a reality, which leads to the capital sentence. Furthermore, Vere's apprehension is stated to be less warranted than that of the *Somers'* officers.[31] After all, the fictional captain knows well that the sailor sentenced to death is not a mutineer. Whether or not the *Somers'* officers, including Melville's cousin Gansevoort, actually believed in the guilt of their three sailors, their dilemma at least appeared to produce a genuine crisis of command. No observer on the *Bellipotent*, Vere excepted, perceives any general threat of mutiny on the quiet ship. Billy's actionable crime is not conspiracy but the striking of one of the most hated figures on board. Was the supreme penalty necessary? Only Vere seems to think so. Thus, on the *Somers*, several officers joined the captain in endorsing the hangings, whereas we already know that no other officer privy to the incident shares Vere's sense of imminent danger.

Vere's courtroom pronouncements are matter for careful analysis. The outward forms of legal argument must be rigorously dissected to discover the essential Vere. In doing so, we learn not only about the story, but about modern literature's sense of justice as well. For if Camus' Clamence is the modern novel's quintessential lawyer, the trial scene in *Billy Budd* is its paradigmatic statement on how acts of judgment are rendered, how statutes and precedents are read, and how authoritative communicators deceive through clever speech.

Vere's Procedural Errors

As with the insanity motif, Melville uses legal technicalities in this last story to alert the careful reader to profound but hidden themes in the text. Chapter 20, a short but significant bridge between Billy's fatal act and its lengthy legal ratiocination, explicitly raises doubts about Vere's concept of legal procedure in the case. The surgeon, the careful officer whom Vere summons to confirm Claggart's death, cannot fathom the captain's behavior:

As to the drumhead court, it struck the surgeon as impolitic, if nothing more. The thing to do, he thought, was to place Billy Budd in confinement, and in a way dictated by usage, and postpone further action in so extraordinary a case to such time as they should rejoin the squadron, and then refer it to the admiral. He recalled the unwonted agitation of Captain Vere and his excited exclamations, so at variance with his normal manner. Was he unhinged?

But assuming that he is, it is not so susceptible of proof. What then can the surgeon do? No more trying situation is conceivable than that of an officer subordinate under a captain whom he suspects to be not mad, indeed, but yet not quite unaffected in his intellects. To argue his order to him would be insolence. To resist him would be mutiny.

In obedience to Captain Vere, he communicated what had happened to the lieutenants and captain of the marines, saying nothing as to the captain's state. They fully shared his own surprise and concern. Like him too, they seemed to think that such a matter should be referred to the admiral. (p. 102)

The junior officers' skepticism indicates that Melville, who knew the relevant law well,[32] intended the legal aspects of this case to be examined. The characters' fear that their captain's procedures are not "dictated by usage" further suggests—as Vere confirms at the trial—that the substantive law of the case was identifiable and accessible to all in the Articles of War of 1749.[33] Melville's own experience on a naval vessel taught him that the Articles were publicly recited, and with amazing frequency, on warships.[34] Thus the officers certainly knew that, in the twenty-second paragraph of the Articles' second section, the following provision was to be found:

If any officer, mariner, soldier, or other person in the fleet, shall strike any of his superior officers, or draw, or offer to draw, or lift up any weapon against him, being in the execution of his office, on any pretence whatsoever, every such person being convicted of any such offence, by the sentence of a court-martial, shall suffer death.

Indeed, in the midst of the highly confusing admixture of substantive legal theories which he offers to the court, Vere does emphasize this part of the Articles as operative in the case. "To steady us a bit," he declares, "let us recur to the facts. In wartime at sea a man-of-war's man strikes his superior in grade, and the blow kills. Apart from its effect the blow itself is, according to the Articles of War, a capital crime" (p. 111).

Yet, given this substantive law, Vere's junior officers immediately recognize a *procedural* scheme that must also come into play. The Articles of War of 1749 mandate a series of guidelines whose protective effect (in a military setting) would be surprising if one were not aware of at least a century of British naval precedent for such safeguards.[35] As they stand, those same Articles which offer Vere his best arguments in favor of convicting and executing Billy also indicate that the captain commits no fewer than eight procedural errors.

NECESSITY TO REGAIN THE FLEET FOR THE TRIAL. The surgeon and his equally discomfited fellow officers have two main fears about Vere's decision to assemble a drumhead court immediately. First, they feel that they should "postpone further action in so extraordinary a case to such time as they should rejoin the squadron" (p. 101). On this point, their fears are grounded in their recall of the sixth through eleventh provisions of the Articles, which specifically grant court-martial commissions only to fleet or squadron commanders, not to individual commanders; indeed, captains could only be so commissioned when their ships were docked in Great Britain or Ireland, and then only if expediency dictated departure from the usual procedures.

RECOURSE TO THE ADMIRAL. The officers' second expectation, also based on the statute and naval tradition, is that the case "should be referred to the admiral" (p. 102). Every educated man on the *Bellipotent* (and probably a good number of ordinary sailors) would have known that, under the Articles, capital crimes must be brought quickly to the lord high admiral's attention. The admiral's jurisdictional interest in such matters commenced, according to the Articles, at the earliest stages of the proceedings:

XXIII. Provided always, and be it further enacted, That no person or persons not flying from justice, shall be tried or punished by any court-martial for any offence to be committed against this act, unless the complaint of such offence be made in writing to the lord high admiral, or the

commissioners for executing the office of lord high admiral for the time being, or any commander in chief of his Majesty's squadrons or ships impow-
ered to hold courts-martial, or unless a court-martial to try such offender
shall be ordered by the said lord high admiral, or the said commissioners, or
the said commander-in-chief, either within three years after such offence
shall be committed, or within one year after the return of the ship, or of
the squadron, to which such offender shall belong, into any of the ports of
Great Britain or Ireland; or within one year after the return of such offender into Great Britain or Ireland.

And the admiral's interest extended—here by long naval tradition—to the stage beyond conviction, in which the admiral was to
have full review powers.[36] Indeed, the parliamentary debates on
the Articles emphasized what the statute then made explicit: that
only for trials concerning mutiny might the admiralty be avoided prior
to sentence and execution.[37] Billy was neither a deserter nor (despite Vere's extremely clever use of the *idea* of mutiny during the
trial) a mutineer, so this jurisdictional power of the admiralty
clearly should have applied under the Articles to Billy's case.

REQUISITE NUMBER OF JUDGES. Once the proceedings commence, Vere's assembly of the court raises other technical issues.
Articles 12 through 14, and long naval custom, both in England
and the United States required at least five (and no more than
thirteen) members on any legitimate court.[38] Since the trial was to
take place only when the fleet or squadron had been rejoined, normally these judges were all at or above the rank of port captain. But
Vere, while placing Billy's substantive crime under the rubric of the
Articles of War, decides that the number of judges should be determined by procedures applicable to "summary" courts; he handpicks
only three officers, one of whom is not even a naval officer. The
choice of the marine officer, who later gains prominence at Vere's
deathbed, again indicates Vere's land-oriented personality, and so
subtly heightens the irony of his procedural techniques.[39]

INAVAILABILITY OF "SUMMARY" MEASURES. In sanctioning the
use of three instead of five judges, and in failing to return to the
squadron and seek out the admiral's jurisdiction, did Vere correctly
employ his so-called summary powers? None, after all, are granted
in the text of the Articles of War, and a review of the British authorities (and Americans commenting on customs largely derived

from the British) indicates that "summary" proceedings would have been inappropriate in a case like Billy's. John McArthur, writing of this general period of English naval law, observes:

A captain or commander of any of his majesty's ships or vessels, has the power of inflicting punishment upon a seaman in a summary manner for any faults or offences committed, contrary to the rules of discipline and obedience established in the navy: this power the framers of our naval articles and orders wisely considered preferable to establishing inferior courts-martial for trying trivial offences, as calculated less to obstruct his majesty's service at sea, and as carrying more promptly into execution the rules and articles laid down for its regulation.

Moreover, the prompt punishment of trivial offences is attended with salutary effects in the discipline of a ship, and from the public example makes a great impression on seamen's minds, thereby deterring them from committing greater crimes.

By the 4th article of the Old Printed Instructions, a captain was not authorized to punish a seaman beyond 12 lashes upon his bare back, with a cat-of-nine-tails; but, if the fault should deserve a greater punishment, he was directed to apply for a court-martial. (pp. 67–68)

Summary procedure was geared for trivial offenses, not major crimes. Vere should have followed the procedures outlined by the Articles of War. His arbitrary three-man court cannot be justified by a simple reference to "summary" proceedings.

VERE'S MULTIPLE ROLES. Vere's peculiar behavior during Billy's trial flies in the face of the entire thrust of naval procedure. The captain, perhaps sensing that even his docile court might wonder about his active role in the proceedings, takes pains to quell their apparent apprehensions:

What he said was to this effect: "Hitherto I have been but the witness, little more; and I should hardly think now to take another tone, that of your co-adjutor for the time, did I not perceive in you—at the crisis too—a troubled hesitancy, proceeding, I doubt not, from the clash of military duty with moral scruple—scruple vitalized by compassion. For the compassion, how can I otherwise than share it? But, mindful of paramount obligations, I strive against scruples that may tend to enervate decision. (pp. 109–10)

Yet the Articles of 1749 reversed earlier practice by prohibiting commanders-in-chief from presiding over courts-martial.[40] Even

Vere clearly doubted his propriety in assuming the roles of sole witness and implicit accuser as well as presiding officer.

TRADITIONAL LENIENCY IN SUCH CASES. Cowed by the articulate captain who chose them, Billy's judges still manage, however
hesitatingly, to urge leniency. "Can we not convict," one of them
falteringly inquires of Vere, "and yet mitigate the penalty?" Vere
promptly quashes this last attempt at independence on the court's
part by implying that leniency might not be "clearly lawful for us
under the circumstances" (p. 112).

Oddly, Vere has some justification in this one instance. The
terms of the first branch of section II, paragraph 22 of the Articles,
which addresses Billy's offense, do not allow for any penalty except
death. Some capital crimes under the Articles, such as the rest enu-
merated there, are punishable by "death, or such other punishment
as a court-martial shall think fit." But whatever the wording of the
provision, its legislative and practical history indicate a strong actual bias against execution.[41] Furthermore, leniency in the enforce-
ment phase was traditional regarding all the Articles. Speaking of
the "Cromwellian" naval Articles of 1649, an authority observes,
for example, that "while severe in their terms, these articles were
enforced with discretion." There is no known instance of the death
penalty being executed during the period of the Commonwealth.
Indeed, even for the incendiary offense of mutiny, few if any commanders found it necessary to rush through to a hanging.[42]

EXECUTION IMPERMISSIBLE WITHOUT REVIEW. If any point in
procedures, general or summary, was clear, it was that the convener
of a court-martial could not execute a capital sentence prior to review on the highest level:

XIX. And it is hereby further enacted, That from and after the
twenty-fifth day of December, one thousand seven hundred and forty-nine,
no sentence of death given by any court-martial held within the narrow
seas (except in cases of mutiny) shall be put in execution till after the report of the proceedings of the said court shall have been made to the lord
high admiral, or the commissioners for executing the office of lord high admiral, and his or their directions shall have been given therein; and if the
said court shall have been held beyond the narrow seas, then such sentence
of death shall not be carried into execution but by order of the commander
of the fleet or squadron wherein sentence of death shall be passed in any

squadron, detached from any other fleet or squadron upon a separate service, then such sentence of death (except in cases of mutiny) shall not be put in execution, but by order of the commander of the fleet or squadron from which such detachment shall have been made, or of the lord high admiral; and in cases where sentence of death shall be passed in any court-martial held by the senior officer of five or more of his Majesty's ships, which shall happen to meet together in foreign parts pursuant to the power herein before given, then such sentence of death (except in cases of mutiny) shall not be carried into execution but by order of the lord high admiral, or commissioners for executing the office of lord high admiral.

So strict was this view that, in the *Somers* case, mentioned in the novella, several American naval officers were court-martialed for having hanged three sailors who may well have been engaged in a mutiny. But Billy, we must always recall, was not even accused of mutiny; Vere would have known that, in the British navy, a sentence exceeding twelve lashes for a summary conviction (mutiny cases arguably aside) could not lawfully be carried out by a mere ship's captain.[43] Even if he felt that his court satisfied all the other procedural exigencies of the Articles of War or of a summary proceeding, he had no right to execute its severe sentence.

CONCEALED NATURE OF PROCEEDINGS. Vere's implied awareness of his officers' doubts about his procedural approach leads him to his most characteristic procedural breach: he conducts Billy's trial in the utmost secrecy. Ives quotes authoritative texts to the effect that "courts-martial shall always be held in the Forenoon, and in the most public place of the ship, where all, who will, may be present."[44] A 1917 American naval handbook, for further example, continued to emphasize that "the sessions of courts-martial shall be public."[45] In precise opposition to this long custom, Vere proceeds covertly, an approach which arouses subsequent controversy and criticism among the officers. We will return to this breach later, for it, like some of the others, is evocative of the larger significance of both Vere's personality and Melville's feelings about the law.

Vere's Curious Use of Substantive Law

Along with the surgeon and other junior officers, we begin to see how quickly an intelligent individual can muster "cool, outer forms" to serve formless, subjective ends. "Struck dead by an angel of God!" is Vere's response to Billy's violent deed. "Yet the angel must hang!" All his procedural breaches desperately seek to fulfill this single, intuitive vow. The powerful adjudicator knows the value of "forms, measured forms." He begins to use and abuse them as soon as he has articulated this basic desire.

Once Vere neglects custom and refuses to refer the matter to the admiral, he remains master of himself and of the situation. The form of the trial is maintained. Orchestrating brilliantly, the authoritative "co-adjutor" picks the weather side of the ship, the loftiest perch from which to observe his appointed court. Procedural safeguards set aside, he can write his own transcript, picking and choosing from among the laws, statutes, and jurisprudential theories which further the sentence he has ordained. Like a lawyer with a weak case, Vere moves beyond the Articles of War during the trial, attempting to substitute a quantity of legal data for the quality of argument he knows his case to lack. But unlike such a lawyer, Vere fears no critique of his artful brief. He has no adversary, and the jury is in his pocket; they will not disobey the "pitiless logic" of his multifaceted substantive pleading. So if he cleverly alludes to "martial law," "plain homicide," or "the Mutiny Act," they have neither the authority, the skill, nor the temerity to complain.

Why does Vere obfuscate? Once procedure has been overridden, does not section 2, paragraph 22 of the Articles of War provide ample support for the hanging? Yet it speaks of striking a superior officer "being in the execution of his office." Is Claggart acting within his office when Billy strikes him? Is lying to one's captain about a fellow sailor's loyalty part of a master-at-arms' job? Is not Claggart culpable, at the very moment his duplicitous speech agitates Billy to violence, of another offense under the Articles? Vere surely knows that section 2, paragraph 23 indicts anyone using "reproachful or provoking speeches or gestures, tending to make any quarrel or disturbance." Claggart's indirect provocation of Billy's violence is the quintessential act of resentment, not at all the duty of a master-at-arms. Furthermore, had Vere not set himself firmly against mitigation, his inquiry might have revealed yet another breach of the Articles by the insinuating Claggart. The unsuccessful attempt by Claggart and his henchmen to incite Billy to mutiny, acts amounting to a violation of section 2, paragraph 19, would have emerged, had it been subjected to the light of day.

If any person in or belonging to the fleet shall make or endeavor to make any mutinous assembly upon any pretence whatsoever, every person offending herein, and being convicted thereof by the sentence of the court-martial, shall suffer death: and if any person in or belonging to the fleet shall utter any words of sedition or mutiny, he shall suffer death, or such other punishment as a court-martial shall deem him to deserve.

Billy's sole offense under the Articles of War, striking an officer, is thus mediated by Claggart's anterior lawbreaking.

With supreme irony, Melville indicates Vere's skewed sense of the real sources of "mutiny" on board his ship. In the name of preserving the "good of the whole," an innocent man is sacrificed. Yet the full story, had it been revealed to the men, would have damped down any mutinous sentiments better than the summary execution of an innocent. But Vere, as shall be shown, does not want the full story to be known; in some ways, he does not even wish to know it himself. As we dissect it with the analytical tools the narrative mandates, Vere's behavior becomes more and more evocative. Although he stands as Melville's representative of adjudication here, he is forced to rely on the tactics of a litigator: the use of any marginally applicable theory to gain the support of the court.

The first deviation from a substantive argument strictly based on the Articles is Vere's sudden appeal to "martial law." "But for us here, acting not as casuists or moralists, it is a case practical, and under martial law practically to be dealt with" (p. 110). Repeating the ominous term a few minutes later, Vere answers the marine officer's emotional defense of Billy's motives: "And before a court less arbitrary and more merciful than a martial one, that plea would largely extenuate. At the last Assizes, it shall acquit. But how here?" In these two parallel arguments, Vere appears to remind the court of its legal, as opposed to moral, jurisdiction over the case. In rhetorical terms, this statement duplicates the device used by Vere in the famous passage from the same lengthy speech:

Well, the heart here, sometimes the feminine in man, is as that piteous woman, and hard though it be, she must here be ruled out. (p. 111)

General usage confirms Vere's rhetorical invocation of the phrase "martial law," since the court obviously derives its jurisdiction from the applicable military law, and not from any ethical or philosophical code. But a further irony pervades Vere's dialectic once his own gross violations of that law are understood! If Vere's invocation of "martial law" intends to stress the court's obligation to strictly legal authenticity, then his own covert illegality in the matter becomes reprehensible.

In Vere's behalf, it must be observed that there is a second meaning of "martial law" which might have provided his best argument for the hastiness of the procedure. Contrary to the first sense of the phrase, the alternate meaning calls for the *abrogation* of established law in favor of what one commentator calls "the will of a military commander operating without any restraint, save his judgement, upon the lives, upon the property, upon the entire social and individual condition of all over whom this law extends."[46] The essential feature of this use of the term is its invocation of *necessity*. Covered by "the haze of uncertainty [surrounding] it,"[47] this meaning of "martial law" would appear to be applicable only at a time of great urgency; furthermore, it usually applies to civilian populations placed under military rule due to some crisis necessitating extraordinary measures. In Britain, the executive agency declaring martial law during the period of the story would probably have been the Crown, Parliament, a governor, perhaps the admiral of the Fleet, but rarely if ever a single ship's captain. If he did, extraordinarily, invoke it, "his judgment would be subject to review by his military superiors," a stipulation not imposed upon higher-ranking executive authorities.[48]

If Vere meant to invoke the alternate sense of "martial law," he should have done so only if the situation fully warranted a fear of insurrection on the ship. As Ives observes, "A captain might hang the mutineers as a matter of necessity, in disregard of the Articles of War. In such cases it was normal to secure the advice and judgment of his officers in a summary court. . . . But Billy Budd was not a mutineer. . . . Vere's stated reasons for the hanging were that Billy had struck his superior and that there was *danger* of mutiny by some other members of the crew" (p. 33). Such dubious grounds for a declaration of martial law, resulting in a capital sentence without possibility of appeal, would normally require a broadly felt sense of impending crisis. As we have seen, the other officers privy to the incident have no such apprehension, nor were there frequent calls to martial law in the historical period of the story.[49] Certainly it was a period of war, and of a "crisis for Christendom," too;[50] but far more inflammatory shipboard situations had been defused that year without violence and on the *Bellipotent*, above all, as the narrative explicitly states, mutiny was not in the air (see p. 59). Vere's utter control over the court demonstrates the docility of his men (even the surgeon never attempts to voice his procedural concerns to the captain); compared to Claggart's, Billy's relationship to the crew would have rendered more popular, and less conducive to mutiny, a decision to follow usage and to imprison Billy until the ship rejoined the fleet.

The captain's best argument—although his position of power makes it unnecessary for him to articulate it fully—that "martial law" calls for an abridgement of proper procedures, thus appears unjustified in Melville's carefully sketched setting. If this is true, we are faced with yet another telling aspect of Melville's view of the law in this text. "Beware of those leaders who counsel moral breaches in the name of form or formal breaches in the name of necessity," he seems to tell us. "Their 'needs' may be quite different from ours."

Frederick Wiener, an authority on military law, observes:

It is because an appreciation of the importance of necessity as the underlying justification is so essential to an understanding of the principles of martial law that the point is so strongly emphasized here. As a distinguished soldier-jurist [Holmes] has said, "We need education in the obvious more than investigation of the obscure." Now, viewed in the light of the principle of necessity, martial law is nothing more and nothing less than an application of the common law doctrine that force, to whatever degree necessary, may be used to repress illegal force.[51]

Was Billy, by the time of the trial, in any way a purveyor of "illegal force"? Holmes' "education in the obvious," applied to Billy's case, would have led to no more than imprisonment until the fleet was rejoined; only Vere's verbal dominance and clever use of the "obscure" convince crew and reader alike that a hanging is "necessary" in this case.

Cognizant of his flimsy substantive argument, Vere invokes the Mutiny Act, another name in his statutory litany. But as Ives and Hayford and Sealts point out, the Mutiny Act applied only to land forces, and Vere's double invocation of the statute (pp. 111–12) appears inapposite, indeed quite surprising.[52] After all, the use of the phrase "martial law" serves his rhetorical purposes sufficiently, albeit unorthodoxly. But why does Melville burden Vere with an egregious legal error serving little or no argumentative purpose? The mistake may, of course, be Melville's, but the *Somers* passage implies his awareness of the distinctions between various military acts. Moreover, Vere's gaffe does help to integrate his overall disposition. As we shall observe, Vere's attraction to land-oriented law, which is also evinced by his plea that the court adopt the wholly inapplicable model of a judge "[a]shore in a criminal case" (p. 111), can be effectively juxtaposed to his resemblance to a "King's envoy" and his generally unsailorlike demeanor. His inappropriate mention of the Mutiny Act, like his appointment of the marine to the court, indicates Vere's emulation of "certain men of the world," his virtual fascination with the landsman's mode of behavior. The latter, consistently equated in the tale with the use of verbal indirection, bears as little relationship to life at sea as the Mutiny Act does to Billy's case.

But Vere goes further in relying on land-oriented law. His response to the sailing master's plea that the penalty be mitigated adds yet another substantive body of laws to his arsenal:

No, to the people the foretopman's deed, however it be worded in the announcement, will be plain homicide committed in a flagrant act of mutiny." (p. 112)

Implausible as well as inaccurate, the theory of "plain homicide" crumbles because there is nothing "plain" about Billy's act if it is analyzed as a homicide. Dozens of questions, having to do with Billy's intent, the degree of premeditation, the defenses of provocation or of temporary insanity, and so on, would have to be raised under any criminal code (including the Articles)[53] if the charge were homicide instead of striking a superior officer. And if an impartial judge would see these complexities, how can Vere casually assume that men already favorably disposed to Billy would attribute to him homicidal and mutinous motives? In the tradition of manipulative communicators, Vere here states the precise opposite of what he means. By the phrase "however it be worded in the announcement," Vere can only mean "as I intend to word it in the announcement." For unless he places Billy's act in the worst possible light (as did the *News from the Mediterranean*), "the people" had rather see their Handsome Sailor alive and well than hung up on the yardarm.

So in violation of each of the laws and statutes he mentions to his impressionable court, Vere accomplishes Claggart's passionate aim. Billy is destroyed. Yet the dual skepticism of the surgeon and the narrator as to the appropriateness of Vere's behavior before and during the trial is fully sustained by a legal analysis of the situation. With piquant irony, Melville carefully suggests that one who calls loudest for a purely formal analysis of a phenomenon may be one who most subtly conceals some private animus. Thus, it is worth our while to go on to explore the nature—and the narrative mode —of Vere's not so peculiar "insanity."

9 "Considerate" Communication and Vere's Hidden Motive

VERE AND NELSON

James Fenimore Cooper said of Captain Mackenzie's fatal command on board the *Somers*:

> The act was, unquestionably, one of high moral courage, one of the basest cowardice, one of deep guilt, or one of lamentable deficiency of judgment.[1]

The legal errors committed by Captain Vere cast into odd perspective the recognition that, of Cooper's four possible views of Mackenzie's decision, only the first has been fully explored with respect to the behavior and significance of the fictional captain. Most critical commentary on Vere disregards the various negative attributes clearly indicated in the story in favor of accepting the character's own assessment of his dilemma. But once it is perceived that Vere acts as a virtual outlaw during the trial of Billy Budd, his lofty verbalizations can be viewed with some intellectual distance. The rest of the tale can be incorporated into a search for the fundamental causes of his "unhinged" behavior.

Thus, as in other great legal novels I have discussed, a trial scene brings to fruition the superb interplay of detail, digression, and tone in the work as a whole. Cast as a comparative thematic, the image of an adjudicator endowing his covert resentments with the force of law is by no means unique. We need only recall the examining magistrates, prosecutors, and defense attorneys in Dostoevski and Camus. But while firmly grounded in this tradition, Melville's tale takes it a step further. For Vere does not dislike the defendant; if he resented Billy, his rush to judgment would correspond more obviously with Ippolit Kirillovich's resentful prosecution of Dmitri, or the pious French prosecutor's attacks on the iconoclastic Meursault.

Instead, Melville complicates matters within his "considerate" narrative. To the extent that he has noticed it at all, Billy's presence on the Bellipotent strikes Vere as a "King's bargain" (p. 95); the captain even deems him an intelligent enough sailor to be considered for a promotion to the "captaincy of the mizzentop."[2] Unlike Claggart, Vere shows an easy admiration of the foretopman's popularity and pleasing looks.

Why, then, does Vere single-mindedly and illegally press for Billy's execution? A possible link between the captain's "insanity" at the trial and Claggart's textbook ressentiment toward Billy suggests itself; the object of Vere's covert rage, however, is revealed to be far more considerable. For Vere shares with Claggart two essential attributes: a prudent dissembling of underlying obsessions, and a burning envy of sublime embodiments of the heroic, sailorlike mode. The first aspect of the duality—the ability to mask inner drives behind politic outward displays—heightens our awareness of the "considerate" nature of communication in the story. If we recall the passage in chapter 3 on the Nore historians, we can see Vere's verbal stance at the trial as perfectly exemplifying the notion that delicate matters must be presented carefully to impressionable audiences; his final legal argument (the "plain homicide" theory) both reiterates the considerate communicator's motto and partly reveals the true object of his own deepest feelings. In answer to the sailing master's request for a lenient sentence, Vere delivers this remarkable utterance:

Gentlemen, were that clearly lawful for us under the circumstances, consider the consequences of such clemency. The people (meaning the ship's company) have native sense; most of them are familiar with our naval usage and tradition; and how would they take it? Even could you explain to them—which our official position forbids—they, long molded by arbitrary discipline, have not that kind of intelligent responsiveness that might qualify them to comprehend and discriminate. No, to the people the foretopman's deed, however it be worded in the announcement, will be plain homicide committed in a flagrant act of mutiny. What penalty for that should follow, they know. But it does not follow. *Why?* They will ruminate. You know what sailors are. Will they not revert to the recent outbreak at the Nore? Ay. They know the well-founded alarm—the panic it struck throughout England. Your clement sentence they would account pusillanimous. They would think that we flinch, that we are afraid of them—afraid of practicing a lawful rigor singularly demanded at this juncture, lest it should provoke new troubles. What shame to us, such a conjecture on their part, and how deadly to discipline. You see then, whither, prompted by duty and the law, I steadfastly drive. But I beseech you, my friends, do not take me amiss. I feel as you do for this unfortunate boy. But did he know our hearts, I take him to be of that generous nature that he would feel even for us on whom in this military necessity so heavy a compulsion is laid. (pp. 112–13)

Essential to an understanding of Vere's motives, this statement argues for the supremacy of appearance over substance, even when a man's life is at stake. Vere justifies the hanging by saying that it is the only means of communication which "the people" will understand. Desperately afraid that his tortuous legal arguments are failing, he resorts to a political one. And the court responds, with a unanimity until now virtually matched by Melville's readers; the same critical audience which commends Hamlet for his unwillingness to kill a villain paradoxically applauds Vere for his orchestrated hanging of a joyful innocent.

Why does one act of violence appeal to the reader and another, far more justified one seem rightly delayed? Vere supplies a possible answer in this very speech. For while he openly urges the court to hang Billy as a form of considerate communication to the crew, he subtly brings considerate communication to bear upon that very court. Vere's assumption that only a hanging will satisfy the crew is nonsense, but so persuasive is his rhetoric that neither the court nor most readers question it. However, as has been indicated, the complexity of Billy's case might have generated various "official" communications to the crew. For example, the officers need only have indicated that the foretopman had been imprisoned pending further inquiry into the matter. Or, if dissimulation as to that complexity were deemed in order, Vere needed only to have the announcement slanted in Billy's favor. The crew undoubtedly would have responded with less talk of mutiny to any finding that would keep their Handsome Sailor alive than to one which implicitly grants the hated Claggart the legal status of victim. This Vere later realizes when he, like Mackenzie, insists that "forms, measured forms" (p. 128) must be applied *after* the hanging to keep the men from reacting violently to the death of their hero.

Thus Vere, in his final argument to the court, exercises over it the same form of deception which he advises them to use on "the people." His ruse succeeds, but at what cost! For his covert methodology, in the service of his deeper, unstated desires, demands the sacrifice of the crew's favorite, the embodiment of the mode opposite Vere's own. Billy, second only to Nelson as the story's model of sailorlike "frankness," dies not for any of the many articulated legal or diplomatic reasons Vere's landsmanlike "finesse" suggests (p. 86), but because he unwittingly stands in place of the envied, magnificently overt Admiral Nelson.

The opposition between sailor and landsman, between the overt and the covert, ultimately underlies Vere's urge to have Billy hanged. Insofar as he emblematizes Nelson's heroic personality, Billy provides an avenue for Vere's hitherto frustrated vengeance. So when the captain arranges a violent sacrifice to lessen the threat of mutiny, it helps to recall the actual historical example of Nelson in a similar circumstance, which is related early in the tale:

In the same year with this story, Nelson, then Rear Admiral Sir Horatio, being with the fleet off the Spanish coast, was directed by the admiral in command to shift his pennant from the *Captain* to the *Theseus*; and for this reason: that the latter ship having newly arrived on the station from home, where it had taken part in the Great Mutiny, danger was apprehended from the temper of the men; and it was thought that an officer like Nelson was the one, not indeed to terrorize the crew into base subjection, but to win them, by force of his mere presence and heroic personality, back to an allegiance if not as enthusiastic as his own yet as true. (p. 59)

While Nelson by his mere presence was able to subdue an ascertainable threat of mutiny on the *Theseus*,[3] Vere fabricates from the stuff of Billy's deed a crisis that would not otherwise have come into being and proceeds to destroy the jewel of his crew, as though resentfully to invert Nelson's bloodless procedure.

Claggart's complex envy of Billy attains fuller thematic elaboration in Vere's analogous approach to Nelson. Indeed, Claggart and Vere share a variety of characteristics, culminating in their tendency toward considerate communication on the one hand, and toward envy of more popular and overt types on the other. Both men's natures are called "exceptional" in the narrative, precisely because their covert "finesse" so thoroughly differs from sailorlike directness. In nostalgically positing his "old fashioned sailor" and "man before the mast" (p. 86), Melville reveals something of the tired, older figure who has himself been playing the landsman's "intricate game of chess" for too long; but this dichotomy also reveals the basis of Claggart's rage against Billy, and Vere's against Nelson: the complex individual's strange mixture of attraction to and hatred for the straightforward, essentially nonverbal hero.[4]

The "exceptional" man, however, (like his underground precursor), never proceeds directly to his aim. And if, in the face of overt types whose health and joy stand as insults to their more sallow and crafty sensibilities, Claggart and Vere remain temporarily impassive, it is because they both possess that "uncommon prudence . . . habitual with the subtler depravity, for it has everything to hide" (p. 80). Like Claggart, Vere's aims are "never declared" (pp. 76, 96, 112); the master-at-arms' personality is "hidden" (p. 76), while Vere's is "undemonstrative," "not conspicuous," and "discreet" (p. 60). While Claggart "has shown considerable tact in his function" (p. 94), Vere tends to "guard as much as possible against publicity" (p. 103). And while the captain at one point orders Claggart to "be direct, man" (p. 92), the uncharacteristic inconsiderateness of the remark bespeaks less a man who opposes verbal dissemblance in general (immediately after, he commands Claggart never to mention the Nore mutiny) as one who recognizes the sophistic tactics of a colleague in covertness.

Claggart's clinical form of envy defies explicit denomination by the narrator, but, like Vere, he employs in its service a covert methodology discernible at least to wizened sailors like the Dansker, a veteran of one of Nelson's crews. That old salt tells Billy twice that "Jemmy Legs is down on you" (pp. 71, 85), a prophecy about Claggart which Billy fails to understand. Yet who but this seasoned "cynic" could intuit the depths of a negative spirit combining what the narrator tentatively calls "envy and antipathy" (p. 77), a mixture we might call ressentiment? A consummate dissimulator, Claggart fools everyone else when, in the soup-spilling incident in chapter 10 which deliberately foreshadows Vere's covert arguments during the trial, he masks his true reactions to Billy. Repressing his spontaneous impulse, he responds instead with: "Handsomely done, my lad! And handsome is as handsome did it, too!" While the remark exemplifies the covert communicator's tendency to reveal subtly his true emotions, its far greater effect, as Claggart wishes, is to distract all onlookers to the incident. His wisecrack succeeds in hiding his villainous motives from the "tickled" foretopman and from such observers as Billy's friend Donald, both of whom thereafter disbelieve the Dansker's analysis of Claggart.

Perhaps still more important to the steady convergence of Vere and Claggart in the narrative is the master-at-arms' subsequent attack on the unfortunate drummer-boy, which epitomizes the "considerate" man's tendency to lash out at surrogates (the ressentient man's "innocent victims"). Unwilling as yet to chastise publicly the real object of his bitterness, the master-at-arms instead assaults another youthful sailor during his "less guarded" exit from the mess hall (p. 72). Only someone who had taken the trouble to watch Claggart depart and also grasped the interpretive principle of "parallelism" could have correctly deduced that the implied object of Claggart's rattan-lashing was Billy Budd himself. The reader should recall this lesson during the trial scene: the verbally manipulative man shows his true colors only when his audience is sufficiently distracted not to notice them.

Melville's relatively late decision[5] to include the surgeon's uneasiness about his captain's behavior gives further play to the juxtaposition of Claggart and Vere. (It also clearly indicates Melville's intention to underscore Vere's legal errors.) The surgeon is the first to call attention to Vere's subjective motivation, just as the Dansker manages early on to pierce Claggart's veil of politic outward behavior. The narrative indirectly supports the prophetic misgivings of both characters in two remarkably similar passages, which we have already alluded to but now quote in full. First are the opening paragraphs of the trial scene:

Who in the rainbow can draw the line where the violet tint ends and the orange tint begins? Distinctly we see the difference of the colors, but where exactly does the one first blendingly enter into the other? So with sanity and insanity. In pronounced cases there is no question about them. But in some supposed cases, in various degrees supposedly less pronounced, to draw the exact line of demarcation few will undertake, though for a fee be-coming considerate some professional experts will. There is nothing nam-able but that some men will, or undertake to, do it for pay.

Whether Captain Vere, as the surgeon professionally and privately surmised, was really the sudden victim of any degree of aberration, every one must determine for himself by such light as this narrative may afford. (p. 102)

Readers alert to the developing comparison of Claggart and Vere will notice that this passage evokes an earlier section, in which the narrator employs "a certain X" to help explain, indirectly, the res-sentient complexities of the master-at-arms:

But the thing which in eminent instances signalizes so exceptional a nature is this: Though the man's even temper and discreet bearing would seem to intimate a mind peculiarly subject to the law of reason, not the less in heart he would seem to riot in complete exemption from that law, having appar-ently little to do with reason further than to employ it as an ambidexter im-plement for effecting the irrational. That is to say: Toward the accomplish-ment of an aim which in wantonness of atrocity would seem to partake of the insane, he will direct a cool judgment, sagacious and sound. These men are madmen, and of the most dangerous sort, for their lunacy is not contin-uous, but occasional, evoked by some special object; it is protectively secre-tive, which is as much as to say it is self-contained, so that when, more-over, most active it is to the average mind not distinguishable from sanity, and for the reason above suggested: that whatever its aims may be—and the aim is never declared—the method and the outward proceeding are al-ways perfectly rational. (p. 76)

These two passages profit by comparison, particularly in light of the narrative interest in deceptive communication. Both deal with "exceptional men," and both point to the tendency of covert individuals to mask insanely destructive passions with perfectly ra-tional formal discourse. The passage about "X" applies fully to Vere's later arguments during the trial, which exemplify the notion that an apparently rational "outward proceeding" may conceal a wanton "atrocity." As in other great literary depictions of the legal process, the trial of Billy Budd parodies the seeming orderliness of criminal law by revealing it to be an instrument in the service of the "protectively secretive" passion of the prosecuting authority.

When exceptional figures inflicted with burning resentments

are provoked, they almost instinctively disguise their passions from curious onlookers. The first principle of their behavior at such times—"the aim is never declared"—cannot be violated, but substitutes for the envied object may be overtly attacked. For Vere, Billy stands to Nelson as, for Claggart, the drummer-boy stands to Billy: a surrogate evocative of the true source of frustrated rage.

From Vere's imaginative perspective, Billy conjures the great Horatio. After all, both Billy and Nelson are introduced as variations of the "Handsome Sailor," the type in which "the moral nature was seldom out of keeping with the physical make" (p. 44). They are stamped by a consistent harmony of inner and outer man and an almost organic rejection of hypocrisy and covertness.[6] Most critics would correctly associate Billy's openness with his overall simplicity. But Melville's equation of Billy and Nelson in the tale's opening chapters may be meant to emphasize in addition that Nelson represents simplicity and sailorlike honesty on the highest level. Each epitomizes the sailor's harmonic mode. Just as the foretopman is "a superior figure of their own class" (p. 43), so Nelson has been called, as the narrative's invocation of Tennyson reminds us, "the greatest sailor since our world began" (p. 58). In this light, Vere's complexity is united with Claggart's, no longer as a virtue, but as the antithesis of the sailorlike condition. Vere gazes at Billy without Claggart's venom; but when Billy strikes the captain's implied ally, all Vere's subtle envy of Nelson erupts in a violent urge to narrative vengeance. Of course, this "aim is never declared" openly.[7]

To fathom Vere's unarticulated rage toward Nelson, one need only consider the dilemma of a man whose ample talents might have garnered him a glorious reputation in any other historical period, but whose career is instead constantly dwarfed by that of his colleague of the Nile, the *Theseus*, and Trafalgar. Indeed, Vere may realize that some of his peers do in fact compare the two, and to his own detriment. These fellow captains might remark that only "the queer streak of the pedantic running through" Vere (p. 63) has kept him from deserving the fame bestowed by "the gazettes" upon Sir Horatio Nelson.

Comparative envy, as Max Scheler has reminded us, is the most pernicious, and it has a long professional tradition. Melville's brilliant depiction of Vere's failed emulation has naval precedent in

Whetstone's 1585 report of Essex's intellectualized envy of the honors granted Lord Admiral Howard:

He took it likewise very heinously, that *Charles Howard*, the Lord-Admiral, was advanced, during his absence, to the Earl of *Nottingham*. . . . All this *Essex* conceived as a Diminution of that Honour which he thought to be the Right of his own peculiar Desert.[8]

And let us not forget that other spurned Elizabethan, the articulate Iago!

Watching Billy strike out at Claggart, Vere feels within his soul the excitement of potential vengeance against the envied Nelson. Billy will die in Horatio's stead, hanged after a trial orchestrated by his emotional antagonist and antithesis, Vere. Like the Grand Inquisitor, or "the man of sorrows" (p. 88), Vere can see the beauty of this alternate moral nature, yet at the same time wish to destroy it.

Critic Ralph Willett puts it well, seeing Vere as "the negation of . . . Melville's great man," Nelson, who is "the modern counterpart of the pagan gentleman,"[9] and who manifests the Handsome Sailor type at the most significant level of naval accomplishment. Nelson's every expression embodies his inner essence, from the form of his ship to the quality of his writing (pp. 57–58). Vere, on the other hand, typifies the complexity of "certain men of the world." Without his uniform, "scarce anyone would have taken him for a sailor" (p. 60); he seems better attuned to the life of a "discreet" lawyer than that of a naval captain, in whom "personal prudence . . . surely is no special virtue" (pp. 58, 60). His career at sea appears to have reached its zenith during the West Indian cruise which won him his promotion, but the present dramatic moment in history calls for a Nelson, not a bookish pragmatist.

Vere cannot achieve fame because his spirit is out of joint with the times and with the element in which it must operate. Ironically, the military career in which he might have excelled is dominated by Wellington and by the great soldier whose name he bears, Lord Fairfax. Andrew Marvell's poem, cited in the story, reveals that the army, not the navy, is Vere's heritage.[10] His actions at the trial, as we have seen, indicate a desire to rely on land-oriented law, as though he were attempting to change the venue of the proceedings to the more circumspect medium of courts on land. Vere's name and the allusion to Marvell's poem further indicate a literary aspect of the captain's personality that helps to undermine the heroic mode. Vere's surname, and his nickname, "Starry," descend to him from Anna Vere, whose "discipline severe" is mentioned in the poem and in the story (p. 61). As Maxine Turnage notes in a stimulating article on the aesthetic symbolism embodied in the story's characters, Vere's inheritance from Marvell's Starry Vere, and the "serenity of a world like that of the poem . . . make him irreparably a stranger to the man-of-war's world in which he must confront and manipulate the strife generated by his subordinates' condition."[11]

Unable to respond to his men with Nelson's (or Billy's) naturalness, Vere implicitly adopts the precedent of his "starry" ancestor: imaginative discipline. As the central events unfold, he attempts to create a narrative form which will enable him to destroy the representation of overt naval simplicity, the Nelson in Billy. But like the asymmetrical European ironclads compared to the "frame incorruptible" of Nelson's *Victory* (p. 57), Vere's aberrant aesthetic also degrades his chosen artistic mode.

Carefully crafting his statement, Vere communicates the sentence to both Billy and the crew in the hermetic medium of the narrative artist. The words *closed, concealed, seldom . . . revealed, privacy, covers, absence, blotted, shadows, refrained,* and *tactic* cast a deliberate pall of secrecy over Vere's below-decks meeting with the doomed sailor. Even the captain's artistic equal, the narrator, absents himself from much of Vere's communication after the trial.[12] And while genuine compassion has often been imputed to Vere as he tells Billy of his fate, the narrative hints at continuing forms of skillful maneuvering by the captain. After all, Billy's open nature has at least twice before been imperiled by "closeted interviews,"[13] and the brief text of chapter 23, in which the interview with the doomed man and the explanation to the crew are discussed, is ominously freighted with negative words and phrases. How perfect a capstone to Vere's scenario to have Billy call God's blessing upon him at the moment of execution! And how unlikely that the irreligious stutterer, uncoached, would think of such an elegant denouement!

Vere's death shortly after these events requires that he be judged by his actions at the trial, his only real attempt to fulfill "the most secret of all passions, ambition" (p. 129). Even in death, how-

ever, he remains true to his characteristic covertness. For in pro-
nouncing Billy Budd's name, the dying man fittingly invokes the
overt, heroic mode epitomized by Nelson, the rival he could neither
destroy nor emulate. The utterance also illuminates the considerable section of narrative which extends beyond the deaths of its
three major characters.

THE PENULTIMATE WORD: MELVILLE VERSUS HOMER

> *Entering the cabin, the officer paused at the
> threshold, for Nelson was on his knees writing.
> The words, the last that he ever penned, were
> written in the private diary he habitually kept, in
> which were noted observations and reflections
> upon passing occurrences, mingled with occa-
> sional self-communings. They followed now,
> without break of space, or paragraph, upon the
> last incident recorded—"At seven the enemy
> wearing in succession"—and they ran thus:—*
>
> *"May the Great God, whom I worship,
> grant to my Country, and for the benefit of
> Europe in general, a great and glorious victory;
> and may no misconduct in any one tarnish it; and
> may humanity after victory be the predominant
> feature in the British fleet. For myself, individu-
> ally, I commit my life to Him who made me, and
> may His blessing light upon my endeavors for
> serving my Country faithfully. To Him I resign
> myself and the just cause which is entrusted to me
> to defend. Amen. Amen. Amen."*
>
> —A. T. Mahan, The Life of Nelson:
> The Embodiment of the Sea Power
> of Great Britain (1897)

As an example of narrative fiction *Billy Budd, Sailor* probably
should not be considered a "tragedy," although the term frequently
appears in analyses of the tale. Rather, as we have seen, it is a
highly self-conscious literary work in which no character's fate pre-
dominates over the centrality of narrative structure. Melville demonstrates the nontragic, non-Aristotelian nature of his narrative (as
does Flaubert, in, say, *Madame Bovary*)[14] by placing some of the
richest elements in his tale either before or after the elaboration of
his central characters' destinies. Recalling other personages mentioned earlier in the story, the novella's concluding pages reinforce

the dominant movement in the work, which is the downfall not of any one figure, but of the author's verbal mode.

The heroism and overtness that were elaborated in Billy survive him through the mention of Nelson's subsequent career, and through the folkloric and lyrical poem "Billy in the Darbies." Pragmatism and covertness survive Claggart and Vere in the distorted journalistic account of the events on the *Bellipotent*, and in the implied convergence of Vere and narrator. Both display the complex narrative genius which contrives to destroy Billy and deliberately to arouse ambivalent responses in the audience as to the necessity for such destruction. As if to extend Vere's fascination with the heroic beyond his death, just as Vere had carried on Claggart's ressentient battle against Billy, the narrator mentions Nelson's great victories in the paragraph describing Vere's demise (p. 129). Our discerning memory of Nelson's earlier role in the tale thus evoked, we cannot help but recall the narrator's treatment of the admiral's far more awesome demise:

At Trafalgar Nelson on the brink of opening the fight sat down and wrote his last brief will and testament. If under the presentiment of the most magnificent of all victories to be crowned by his own glorious death, a sort of priestly motive led him to dress his person in the jewelled vouchers of his own shining deeds; if thus to have adorned himself for the altar and the sacrifice were indeed vainglory, then affectation and fustian is each more heroic line in the great epics and dramas, since in such lines the poet but embodies in verse those exaltations of sentiment that a nature like Nelson, the opportunity being given, vitalizes into acts. (p. 58)

We have truly entered the holy of holies.[15] The mystery of this paragraph remains with us long after we have forgotten the details of the trial scene, but some of its meaning is unlocked only there. Indeed, Richard Chase's perception that actual artists are, by implication, characters in *Billy Budd, Sailor* (p. 238) gains credibility from the association of this paragraph with the trial; both hint at an even higher level of structural opposition in the tale. Ethical action and writing, we learn here, have not always been dissociated phenomena; Nelson embodied the symmetry of art and heroism. Only ressentient modern-day verbalizers see alienation from heroic activity as a sine qua non for the verbally expressive life.

The passage on Nelson at Trafalgar associates "the great epics and dramas" with Nelson's narrative act before battle. Melville, recognizing the development from the heroic epic into narratives such as his own, self-critically perceives the contemporary degradation of the form. For the great epic writers like Homer, as for the rare, almost superannuated modern individual, Nelson, heroic action and narrative art were inextricably linked.[16] One arm acted, the other wrote. The match of outer form with inner man achieved artistic harmony in such figures.

Melville appears in this paragraph to deny the inevitability of the contemporary disjunction between artist and polity. Yet he confesses himself to belong to the line of overly self-aware and complex literary types, beginning emblematically with Hamlet, who do not participate in the classical unity of literature and action. Writing during a late Christian epoch, he adopts "the considerate way" of self-expression, a culturally compelled choice which places him with Vere and Claggart, against Nelson and Billy.

Melville figuratively joins with Vere as landsmen destined to deal with the sea in their own peculiar way, by constructing tortuous verbal patterns around, instead of forthrightly admiring, the heroes in their midst. For both, form has come to replace, rather than embody, meaning.[17] But while Vere's use of language furthers an irrational personal vendetta against the heroic naval mode, Melville's is poignantly courageous, reminding us of James Fenimore Cooper's words about Mackenzie. Instead of destructively flailing out, he seeks meaning. Yet he knows, with Nietzsche, that the first, painful step in growth is to give up the worst in ourselves.

Small wonder, then, that Melville continues in this final narrative to ponder Christianity, against whose antinaturalistic and overly complex tendencies he had always struggled. His lifelong "quarrel with God"[18] points to the ultimate level of meaning in the tale, a message far too delicate to reveal in any but a considerate way. To grasp this meaning it is necessary to extend our methodology to the very symbolism of Claggart's plot against Billy, an enmity which rarely arouses critical controversy.[19] Even otherwise conflicting analyses of the story still manage to agree that Billy is a Christlike figure, and Claggart a satanic one, or an antichrist. Yet of the eighty or so narrative epithets about Billy, about two-thirds convey clear pagan, classical, or Judaic overtones, and only ten even imply Christianity.[20] Nor do the epithets tend more toward the Christian at the end of the story, as many have contended;[21] on the contrary, the word "barbarian" is emphatically associated with Billy twice as he approaches death (p. 120), and the chaplain's attempt to save the condemned man elicits a surprisingly strong rejection from this supposedly Christlike figure, reminiscent of Meursault's scornful treatment of the prison chaplain. The clouds on the day of the hanging are compared to "the fleece of the Lamb of God," but Billy's soul departs with a quintessentially Homeric metaphor: "ascending [it] took the full rose of the dawn."[22] In line with his character and central act in the story, Billy's attitude at death spiritually negates the teachings of Christ and of Christianity. His overt joyfulness and stutter, and the twice-stated association of him with Rome (pp. 53, 120), make Billy more representative of classical civilization in decline, perhaps at the birth of Christianity. He is far more Nietzsche's "noble kind of man" than a *figura Christi*.

Turning to Claggart, the reader must be struck by the descriptions (approximately twenty) linking him with the serpent. Interestingly, however, the next most frequent descriptive emphases are upon Claggart's deference to governmental authority and fine physical features (fourteen and nine instances, respectively). While Claggart clearly represents evil, his covert scheming is masked by a delicate and almost beautiful countenance and an awareness of how best to ingratiate himself with authority.

The text also contains a series of puzzling allusions which combine with those discussed to produce an allegorical message quite opposed to the traditional interpretation. This message links Claggart to Christianity, both at the founding of the religion and as it developed. The narrative data establishing this relationship is so simple that critics have passed over it; but our analysis is grounded in Melville's suggestion that great truths are only revealed plainly when the audience has been distracted. First there is the matter of John Claggart's initials; then his narrative epithet "the man of sorrows" (p. 88); and finally the association of Claggart with "a certain X" (p. 74), whom the narrator explicitly employs to explain "through indirection" his enigmatic master-at-arms.[23] This patent evidence of a Claggart-Christ association is bolstered by the tone the narrative takes on when dealing with Claggart. The narrator prefaces his description of the master-at-arms by admitting failure in the face of such a subject: "His portrait I essay but shall never hit it" (p. 64). The far less covert epic poets Milton and Dante use this formula about divine—not satanic—figures in their works, to emphasize the need for extreme caution in depicting the Trinity.[24] The modern novelist, who seeks even greater indirection, enjoins himself against overtly citing any authority "tinctured with the Biblical element" (p. 75). Hence, he will only suggest, never propound, a new religious vision.

The meager biographical data which the narrator supplies about Claggart reveal that his age at death is around thirty-five (p. 64), as was Christ's. The "dearth of exact knowledge" (p. 65) about his ancestry and even nationality, which is grist for his enemies' mill, matches the general ignorance about Claggart's early career. There is a rumor that he had once been arrested. Like Christ, he has risen quickly, through hard work. His "passion," like Christ's, is ultimately vindicated after his death by sympathetic governmental officials; Vere, more a Constantine than a Pontius Pilate or an Abraham, bestows legal and institutional acceptance on the new system of values. Finally, both figures are transformed into heroes by authoritative accounts that favorably depict their roles in the central events of their times; *News from the Mediterranean* clearly alludes to the Gospels.[25]

Considering Claggart's role in the tale, that of a figure who succeeds in undermining the values that have prevailed on a ship (which are Billy's essentially overt ones), the evidence implicating him as a Christ figure need not seem shocking. Into the pagan spontaneity of Billy's world steps his moral antipode, who generates there, through perhaps misunderstood words and actions, a new and covert mode of behavior. This "too fair-spoken man" (p. 88) uses his verbal skills to bring these new values to the attention of a definitive authority figure, who initially resists them. But the representative of classical man in decline lashes out at the new force in a last effort to preserve his heroic integrity. Pagan Rome, bearer of the overt values condoned by Melville's narrator from the beginning of the tale, crucifies the newcomer, whose mode Melville subtly condemns through his association of Claggart-Christ with overwhelmingly negative epithets and actions.

In the end, however, the newcomer manages to prevail. As Nietzsche puts it, Rome, the "strongest and most noble people who ever lived . . . without a doubt has capitulated" (see the introduction, above). For Vere-Constantine "veers"[26] from established values and chooses to accept and perpetuate those of Claggart-Christ. Beyond his wildest hopes, Claggart succeeds posthumously in destroying everything Billy stands for, through an institutional injustice that carries out the violent scheme he has initiated. The Mediterranean *News* formalizes Vere-Constantine's choice in a written account—"all that hitherto has stood in human record to attest that manner of men" who confronted each other on the *Bellipotent*—which falsely identifies Billy-Rome as vindictive murderer and Claggart-Christ as victimized hero.

Melville seeks to correct the inversion of values created by those covert, ancient Mediterranean reporters. His story, written at a moment of "crisis for Christendom," considerately communicates quite a new outlook on the Crucifixion. It depicts Christianity as the initiator into Western civilization of ressentient values that substituted narrative falsehoods for overt justice. This trespass of obscure, private motives into the area of public values eventually extended from law to literature itself.

All his life, Melville struggled with the Christian values of his day and felt a repeated attraction to non-Christian alternatives. But he also knew of the difficulty of relating profound beliefs: "In this world of lies, Truth is forced to fly like a scared white doe in the woodlands; and only by cunning glimpses will she reveal herself, as in Shakespeare and other masters of the great Art of telling the truth—even though it be covertly and by snatches."[27] Indeed, most great artists, because they capture life with extraordinary fullness, cannot be understood by their contemporaries, whose function in furthering the everyday aims of ordered society requires a converse narrowness of vision. Nor do literary critics, especially those who restrict their field of inquiry to one writer or even to the literature of one nation, always recognize the richest emanations of a masterpiece.

Melville grasped a truth we may pursue—that modern novelistic complexity results in an overly reactive and negative series of private formulations. Although his self-awareness is insufficient to repel the influence of the declining culture in which he is steeped, it enables him to call for a renewal of the old alliance of artistry with just action. For whatever has furthered the preoccupation of the narrative mode with ressentiment can yet be altered. Social institu-

tions wax and wane, and romanticisms of various sorts yield eventually to the ebullient creativity of self-willed people with a firm sense
of communal ethics. Literary art, ever the reflection of a culture's
sense of itself, may again join with a positive system of law to generate admirable language.

Afterword

We have now traversed the exceedingly intricate worlds of four major writers and have emerged with refreshed sensitivities and new insights about the novel in its modern form. I hope that we have opened new avenues of comparison here, not only by emphasizing legalistic themes, but also by adding Flaubert to a triad of novelists hitherto more frequently analyzed together. Failure to recognize the participation of that master craftsman in the crisis of values central to his day impoverishes both his works and those of the more clearly socially oriented Dostoevski, Melville, and Camus.

I suspect that the varied depictions of lawyers, investigations, and statutes in the modern novel may now seem a bit more comprehensible. Since Balzac and Scott, Hawthorne and Cooper, the novel has resonated with the language of law. The threads we have traced through the works of four writers will, I hope, be extended to other great novelists as well. Such work is beginning to appear as critics recognize that the appearance of legality in the novels of writers as disparate as Thackeray, Trollope, Tolstoi, Dickens, Kafka, Twain, Faulkner, Doctorow, Malamud, and Barth is no coincidence. Clearly, generic rumblings are taking place, and (as in one or two other literary epochs) law has its structural place in both the self-criticism and the change.

We are now in a position to understand more clearly the "philosophy" of certain well-recognized intellectual protagonists in terms of the legal pronouncements of less extensively analyzed characters sharing the same texts. Verbalizers all, these figures exhibit the deep ambivalences of the novelists who have created them. It is astounding how violent their passive verbal medium becomes, and how small the tangible benefits to the community from their other-wise admirable eloquence.

With this is mind, I believe we may profitably ask some harder questions about modern law, religion, literature, and criticism. Time after time in these texts, narrative acts lead to passivity in the face of clear injustice or, worse still, to the creation of injustice it-self. As questioning about the act of writing as these great novelists were, might they not have been suggesting that narrative institu-tions such as their own had run upon hard times? Language cannot replace ethics and values, they seem to have been saying, but it will fill the vacuum when all else dissipates. Law seemed to these men the most significant extrinsic cultural system against which to test their doubts. As bound up in narrative form as their own enterprise, law was beginning to substitute wit for judgment, elegance for sub-stance, words for values. Not only did they fear the degradation of their own medium, but they grasped the even more cataclysmic consequences of the aestheticizing of law. Significantly, they inte-grated the puffery of the outmoded European clergy into their depic-tions of legal subjects. Ultimately, it was a bankrupt moral system which had, after nearly two millennia, brought the mainstream of Western culture to and over the brink.

We have identified the compendium of traits which these nov-elists set into clear opposition. Ressentiment, the antithesis of spon-taneous human sympathy, joins with eloquence in their texts to produce injustice, but the use of words in the service of positive val-ues remains, for these authors a magnificent possibility. No single victim of a resentful philosopher, priest, or lawyer epitomizes all those salutary traits. But it is not improbable that a bit of Meur-sault's blend of vitality and sincerity, Mitya's passionate involve-ment with others, Giscon's ethical leadership, Nelson's understand-ing in the values of his subordinates, Billy Budd's refusal to let clear wrongdoing survive—a bit of all these qualities combined in one individual or ethical system would have pleased these literary gi-ants. Judging from our structural analyses, they did not seem to worry that such traits conflicted with articulateness. On the contrary, as they occasionally remind us, in other ages political leaders combined strong-willed ethics with verbal force.

This observation brings us back to the novel itself. We have seen how richly legal structures serve modern novelistic form, with all its anti-Aristotelian digressions, delays, and authorial confessions. But since World War II, the future of the genre has been very much in doubt. The French have been unable to sustain a coherent theory of the "new novel," although they have identified atrophied aspects of the form, and few exciting novelists have come out of France since Camus, prix Goncourt notwithstanding. German literature must be admired, particularly in Grass and Böll, for its courageous (if distressingly subtle) evocation of the Nazi period. In America, the novelistic tradition of treating legal themes continues apace in the excellent early work of John Barth and E. L. Doctorow, and with some blurring of fact and fiction, in Truman Capote, Norman Mailer, and Judith Rossner, for example. There has been a flair on these shores which is lacking abroad, yet it seems to me that the seeds of a revivified genre lie in the works of less legalistically inclined writers. In Saul Bellow, particularly, a vitalism and true ethical perspective point the way to a reintegration of language and values.

The implications of my method and practice for literary criticism must depend on the success of these chapters. But Postwar literary theory has drifted so far from textuality toward verbosity that one must fear for its ultimate place in the history of ideas. (As I hope I have shown, Nietzsche, for one, would have had such fears.) Surely our generation more than previous ones should be wary of language systems bereft of ethical referents. Why our criticism has tended in that precise direction, indeed has called into question the very notion of a referent, is matter for a subsequent volume. We may discover that the relationship of aesthetics to ethics, of form to substance, and of interpretive theory to historical context is nowhere better approached than through literature's use of law.

APPENDIX   "What Means of Proof Can the Jew of
            Mixed Blood Offer to Establish His
            Nonaffiliation with the Jewish Race?"

The Commission on the Jewish Laws has been established by the head of State to give its view on the interpretation of Article 1 of the Law of 2 June 1941 concerning the subject of nonaffiliation with the Jewish race.

The Commission believes that the statute writers allowed more proof than merely that of belonging to another religion recognized by the State prior to the law of 9 December 1905. It has noted that "in each case, the adjudicator may ascertain that the claimant either has never belonged, or has ceased to belong in fact, to the Jewish community" (*Gazette du Palais* 1943, 1st sem., Doctrine, p. 14). . . .

We believe that neither good sense nor the law could lead to the view that the statute writers required of an individual having only two Jewish grandparents proof of his belonging to the Catholic or Protestant denominations in order to avoid being included on the lists of Jews. . . .

Since the courts must now decide each case on its own merits, we would do well to cite as an example German law, and thus to see how it overcomes any difficulty relating to proof of nonaffiliation with the Jewish race. This exercise reveals a largeness and objectivity of spirit. . . .

A recent case of particular note dealt with the female descendant of two Jewish grandparents, baptised as a Protestant, who, under the Article stipulating the definition of a citizen of the Reich, only would become Jewish if she adhered to the Jewish religion, the same solution incidentally as is reached under the law of 2 June 1941.

This woman of mixed Protestant and Jewish heritage had, for a period of

The material in this appendix originally appeared as an article by Joseph Haennig, a Parisian lawyer, in the edition of the *Gazette du Palais* (the traditional reporter of French statutes and cases) covering the first semester of 1943, p. 31. The translation is my own.

six months, at the express request of her Jewish father and against the wishes of her Protestant mother, attended classes at religious school to learn about the Jewish faith. Once each year until her father's death in 1931, she accompanied him to synagogue on the New Year.

On the other hand, she never contributed to the synagogue, while still retaining her name on the list kept there.

Under these circumstances and facts, the Supreme Court of Leipzig was called on to consider her case. It first noted that, as soon as she learned of the presence of her name on the Jewish lists, she requested its removal, in the spring of 1938.

The Court affirmed the lower court judge's view that she had only attended New Year's services in order to preserve family peace. The view that there was no sufficient tie to the Jewish community in this case was thus deemed correct.

[However, the defendant had called herself a Jew in order to obtain employment from a Jewish agency.] Theoretically, the Court of Leipzig refused to consider the motives leading an individual to certain specific acts apparently linking him to the Jewish community. However, where these links have been merely for pretense, the court instructed lower courts not to take them into account if it has been established, as in the instant case, that the defendant was merely using the Jewish religion as a means to acquire an advantage by that intermediary.

This analysis of the German law furnishes an interesting contribution to the study of a subject still little understood by the French courts. The analysis indicates a possible route, without risk of distorting the statute writers' intention, and in conformity with the principles which underlie the racial statutes and cases.

JOSEPH HAENNIG,
Member of the Appellate Bar
Paris

Notes

CHAPTER 1

1   On the dichotomy drawn by Nietzsche between heroic Jewish values and resentful Christian ones, see the discussion below, in this chapter. See also *The Will to Power*, aphorisms 180–82; the epilogue (and note) in *The Case of Wagner*; and the magnificent philo-Semitic aphorism 205 in *The Dawn of Day* ("The People of Israel").

   Jaspers appears to misperceive the latter point when he remarks parenthetically that Nietzsche regarded *"Socratic and Judaeo-Christian* morality . . . as identical"; Karl Jaspers, *Nietzsche*, trans. Charles Wallraff and Frederick Schmitz (Tucson: University of Arizona Press, 1965), p. 141.

2   Nietzsche's skepticism about an ethic overtly predicated on the highly personal emotion of love is brilliantly paralleled in Dostoevski's portrayal of literary ressentiment. Lofty sentiments frequently mask envy, bitterness, and violence. See the discussion of *Notes from Underground* in chapter 2.

3   *The Genealogy of Morals*, trans. Francis Golffing (New York: Doubleday, 1956), 1.16:185–86. All references to the *Genealogy* are to this edition (by book, aphorism number, and page). The original text, *Zur Genealogie der Moral*, is in Nietzsche, *Werke* (Berlin: De Gruyter, 1968), vol. 6, bk. 2, pp. 259–430. On occasion I have interjected the original German in brackets.

4   *Beyond Good and Evil*, trans. Marianne Cowan (Chicago: Regnery, 1966), aphorism 52, pp. 59–60. Unless otherwise stated, all references to *Beyond Good and Evil* are to this edition. For the original text, see Nietzsche, *Werke*, vol. 6, bk. 2, pp. 3–250.

5   Ibid., aphorism 251, p. 186. I am struck by similar sentiments expressed by an exceptionally forthright Christian theologian, Franklin H. Littell:

In stubborn fashion, and in spite of flirtations with assimilation at different seasons and in different places, the Jews have clung to history, earthiness, concrete events. And Israel, which came into being as part of a specific series of historical events, cannot properly be judged by persons whose dominant thought patterns are ruled by a flight from history.

Littell, *The Crucifixion of the Jews* (New York: Harper and Row, 1975), pp. 95–96. See also pp. 21, 39, and 57 on this theme.

6   For an example of the utilitarian approach, see Hume, "Of Justice and Injustice," in *A Treatise of Human Nature*, book 3, part 2 (Oxford: Clarendon, 1888), p. 477.

7   Nietzsche always supports the primacy of the text whenever critical evaluations of a text have widely strayed from the original source. His insights on the gap between text and reader have significance for modern theories of hermeneutics, as noted by Harold Bloom in *The Anxiety of Influence* (New York: Oxford University Press, 1973), p. 49.

    Like Heidegger, Nietzsche recognizes the importance of the interpreter's grasping his inevitable subjective biases. These include the analyst's personal biography and cultural and temporal environment— Heidegger's *Geworfenheit*—elements which, if ignored by the analyst in the name of a supposed "objective" approach to his materials, will actually impede his ultimate goal of insight and appreciation. Only when the interpreter consciously admits the difference between himself and the text may he enter into the quest for the inherent truth of that text. See Hans Georg Gadamer, *Truth and Method*, trans. Borden and Cumming (New York: Seabury, 1975); on the relationship between literary and legal hermeneutics in this regard, see pp. 232–38 of that text, and Gadamer, *Kleine Schriften* 1 (Tubingen: Mohr, 1967).

    In a number of aphorisms I have quoted, Nietzsche asks us to "discern what has been written," reminding us, too, of the "literary sophistry" which occasionally has taken readers quite far from literary meanings. We will pay heed to Nietzsche's advice as we strive to understand a body of works whose contextual significance does not necessarily exhaust textual meanings.

8   The myth of Nietzsche's anti-Semitism persists, despite the undeniable effusiveness of his admiration for virtually all of Judaism except its priestly and Hellenic strains. Two factors explain this misreading of Nietzsche: the actual perversion of some of his texts by his viciously anti-Semitic sister, and the almost predictable exaggeration of certain language in Nietzsche which only superficially merges with Nazi rhetoric and racial theory.

    Once clarified, the power of Nietzsche's thought will be considered in its own right. My sense is that his influence on Western ideas will survive even that of the currently more palatable Freud and Heidegger.

9   The neologism "ressentient" is borrowed from Carl Nordstrom, Edgar Z.

Friedenberg, and Hilary A. Gold, *Society's Children: A Study of Ressenti-ment in the Secondary School* (New York: Random House, 1967).

Scheler discusses Nietzsche's thought on this topic in his essay "Das Ressentiment im Aufbau der Moralen," which appears in vol. 3 of his *Gesammelte Werke* (Bern: Francke Verlag, 1955), pp. 33–147. The excel-lent translation, used throughout this book, *Ressentiment*, is by William W. Holdheim (New York: Free Press, 1961; paper, New York: Schocken, 1973).

10 Richard Weisberg, "Hamlet and Ressentiment," *American Imago* 29 (1972): 328.

11 Thersites, in book 2 of the *Iliad*, wordily advises the Greek heroes to give up the wars and return home. Odysseus responds:

Fluent orator though you be, Thersites, your words are ill-considered. Stop, nor stand up alone against princes. Out of all those who came be-neath Ilion with Atreides I assert there is no worse man than you are. Therefore you shall not lift up your mouth to argue with princes, cast re-proaches in their teeth, nor sustain the homegoing. (Richmond Lattimore translation [Chicago: University of Chicago Press, 1961], 2.246–51)

12 Nietzsche had a strong distaste for German nationalism, based in part upon his view of the ressentient types who dominated the movement even then. The nationalist and his anti-Semitism were one (*Genealogy* 2.11; *Beyond Good and Evil*, aphorism 251). He also embodied the utter decline of what had once been a noble race (*Genealogy* 1.11; *Beyond Good and Evil*, aphorisms 244–51). See also Nietzsche's letter to Franz Overbeck in 1885, in *Selected Letters*, trans. and ed. Christopher Middleton (Chicago: University of Chicago Press, 1969), p. 146: "There are certainly good enough reasons for not generally trusting the anti-Semites any further than one can see them." One might easily speculate that Nietzsche's reac-tion to the Nazis would have been one of energetic abhorrence. Ironically, the philosopher who intended to counter Nietzsche's inherent vitalism, Martin Heidegger, became an apologist for the Fascists in the early period of the regime. Implicitly, as certain literary texts also indicate, the ab-sence of vitalism all too frequently leads to the acceptance, rather than the rejection, of palpable injustice.

13 *Der Fall Wagner*, aphorism 5; Nietzsche, *Werke* 6:16–17, my translation.

14 Nietzsche first made a dichotomy between "Apollonian" and "Dionysian" art in *The Birth of Tragedy*. The Dionysian suggests a measure of instinctive awareness which Nietzsche deemed essential to integrated art. For him, the cerebral, "Apollonian" element dominated modern art. See Nietz-sche's "Dionysian" poetry, "Dionysos-Dithyramben," in *Werke* 6:373–408. See also Charles M. Barrack, "Nietzsche's Dionysus and Apollo, Gods in Transition," *Nietzsche Studien* 3 (1974):115–30. For an elabora-tion of the dialectic in terms of ressentiment, see my "Literature as Nega-

tivity: Ressentiment in Dostoyevski and Flaubert" (Ph.D. diss., Cornell University, 1970), pp. 6–12.

15   Götzen-Dämmerung, Werke 6:109–10. In contrast, see Nietzsche's view of the "heroic" Jewish influence on art ("der jüdisch-heroische Zug"), in Werke 6:421.

16   Der Fall Wagner, aphorism 7; Werke 6:21. See also p. 22, and aphorism 11, p. 31.

17   Jean-Paul Sartre, What Is Literature?, trans. Bernard Frechtman (New York: Harper and Row, 1965), pp. 115–25. See also Sartre, L'Idiot de la famille (Paris: Gallimard, 1971), 1:20–24 (for an exemplary argument) and 2:1107–1287 (for an association of Flaubert's sense of craft with his biographical obsessions).

18   "Wir Antipoden," in Nietzsche contra Wagner, Werke 6:24–25. Sartre considers Flaubert's stance toward his female characters specifically as one of ressentiment. See L'Idiot de la famille 2:1287; his point there is elaborated below, in chapter 5.

19   Epilogue to Der Fall Wagner, Werke 6:44–45. For Nietzsche's positive appraisal of Dostoevski, see, of course, Götzen-Dämmerung, aphorism 45: "Dostoevski, the only psychologist from whom I have ever learned anything."

20   The present study of the relationship between law and literature in the modern novel begins after Balzac (and Dickens) less because earlier nineteenth-century writers do not deal with the law than because their narrative stance toward the subject renders their work less relevant to this book. Balzac has been identified by theorists of the novel in France as a dividing line in the development of narrative. His omniscience, his control over objects, his confident assumption of a unified world view—these elements quickly fade into the narrative subtleties and ambiguities of Flaubert, more reflective of a disintegrating society. See especially Nathalie Sarraute, L'Ere du soupçon (Paris: Gallimard, 1956), pp. 69–94.

CHAPTER 2

1   See chapter 1, note 9. The work was first published in 1912. I use here the Holdheim translation, Ressentiment. For works analyzing Scheler's concept of ressentiment, see Maurice Dupuy, La Philosophie de Max Scheler (Paris: Presses Universitaires de France, 1959); Martin Buber, "Scheler's Philosophical Anthropology," Philosophy and Phenomenological Research 6 (1946): 307–21; Maurice Merleau-Ponty, "Christianisme et ressentiment," La Vie intellectuelle 7 (June 1935): 278–306; and J. R. Staude, Max Scheler (New York: Free Press, 1967).

2   See Lewis Coser's introduction to Ressentiment (Holdheim translation), pp. 5–36; Nordstrom, Friedenberg, and Gold, Society's Children; and, for

a brilliant work of journalistic sociopathology, Gary Wills, *Nixon Agonistes* (Boston: Houghton Mifflin, 1970).

3 The work of René Girard, in particular, effectively expands upon Scheler's central theories; Girard's notion of "désir triangulaire," for example, can be creatively juxtaposed, as Girard himself recognizes, to Scheler's phenomenology of sympathy. See René Girard, *Mensonge romantique et vérité romanesque* (Paris: Grasset, 1961); I use here the fine translation by Yvonne Freccero, *Deceit, Desire, and the Novel* (Baltimore: Johns Hopkins University Press, 1965). For a quite recent use of ressentiment theory in a stimulating essay on the novelist V. S. Naipaul, see Roger Sandall, "'Colonia' According to Naipaul," *Commentary*, December 1983, pp. 77–81.

4 See Paterculus, *Compendium of Roman History*, trans. Frederic Shipley (Cambridge: Harvard University Press, 1967), pp. 45–46; John Sandys, ed., *The Rhetoric of Aristotle* (Cambridge: Cambridge University Press, 1877), p. 23; Thomas Aquinas, *The "Summa Theologica,"* trans. English Dominicans (London: Washbourne, 1917), p. 475; and Plutarch, *Moralia*, trans. Philemon Holland (London: Dent, 1937), p. 324 (Holland's 1603 translation was well known to writers from Elizabethan times on and provides an interesting slant on Hamlet, among other cerebral characters).

5 Not all words, of course, represent failures to resolve negative impressions. Scheler points to the embittered servant's "venting his spleen in the antechamber" after closing the door between his master and himself as a possible resolution to his resentful feelings. It is noteworthy, however, that literary characters from Hamlet on rarely effectuate even a salutary *verbal* response to deeply felt insults. The indirect irony and wit of Hamlet's "asides" about Claudius (whom he never chastises to his face) are insufficient to allay his resentment and negativity.

6 *Götzen-Dämmerung*, aphorism 45.

7 *Ressentiment*, p. 64. The political critic (or journalist) might, at the most complex extreme of those who would engage in those professions, suffer from ressentiment because his life is spent as a constant reaction to those in power. The phenomenon of "investigative journalism" still needs to be studied for its occasional extremes of reactionary thrashing about.

8 Whether one perceives the movement toward irony as a rhetorical advance over earlier modes or as a temporary degradation outside the major progress of Western art (Paul de Man, for one, hints at both possibilities), one probably must see irony as the dominating narrative feature in the literature of the period from 1862 to 1956. In this study, I explore the thesis that the novelist, while employing irony constantly, strives to undermine its power in his works. See especially chapter 9.

9 The title in Russian is *Zapiski iz podpol'ja*. I have followed the Constance Garnett translation in *Three Short Novels of Dostoyevsky*, ed. Avrahm Yarmolinsky (Garden City, N.Y.: Anchor, 1960), pp. 127–222, including at

some points the original Russian in brackets. Page references are to this edition.

10   *Notes from Underground* was first published in two separate numbers of the journal *Epokha.*

11   See especially Lev Shestov, *Na vsakh Iova* (Paris, 1929), pp. 27–94; and *Athens and Jerusalem* (1938), ed. Bernard Martin (Athens: Ohio University Press, 1966). For a recent apology, see Reed Merrill, "The Mistaken Endeavor: Dostoevski's *Notes From Underground,*" *Modern Fiction Studies* 18 (1972–73), 505–16. See also my riposte to Mr. Merrill: Richard Weisberg, "An Example Not to Follow: *Ressentiment* and the Underground Man," *Modern Fiction Studies* 21 (1975–76), 553–63.

12   People occasionally express the ephemeral desire to have been born in earlier or later periods. But the narratively resentient type exacerbates this "untimeliness" into a personal, enduring insult. See especially chapter 5, below, on Flaubert.

13   See Shestov, *Athens and Jerusalem,* p. 371. For an excellent skeptical view of the Underground philosophy, see Viktor Shklovski, *Za i protiv; Zametki o Dostoevskom* (Moscow, 1957), 154–64; and A. Skaftimov, "*Zapiski iz podpolja* sredi publitsistiki Dostoevskovo," *Slavia* 8 (1929–30): 101–17, 312–39. For American views of the protagonist's philosophy closer to my own, see Joseph Frank, "Nihilism and *Notes From Underground,*" *Sewanee Review* 69 (1961): 1–33; and Robert L. Jackson, "Aristotelian Movement and Design in Part Two of *Notes from the Underground,*" in *Twentieth-Century Views on Dostoyevski,* ed. Robert L. Jackson (Englewood Cliffs, N.J.: Prentice Hall, 1984), pp. 66–81.

  The Russian verb *pasovat'* in this passage is often mistranslated. Garnett, for example, translates as follows: "By the way: facing the wall, such gentlemen—that is, the 'direct' persons and men of action—are genuinely *nonplussed*" (p. 134). David Magarshack, on the other hand, may render it too strongly: "Incidentally, before such a stone wall such people . . . as a rule *capitulate* at once"; *The Best Short Stories of Dostoevski,* ed. Ralph Matlaw (New York: Modern Librar/, 1955), p. 114. Active, ongoing consternation about the wall is absent in the original; since one usage of *pasovat'* is as a card-playing term meaning "to pass," it would seem that the "natural man" does no more than to *defer* to the wall.

14   See Shestov, *Na vsakh Iova,* p. 35. See also his *Dostojevski i Nitzsche: Philosophija tragedii* (St. Petersburg: 1903); and *Dostoevski, Tolstoi and Nietzsche,* trans. Bernard Martin (Athens: Ohio University Press, 1969).

15   The term "satisfying determinism" is Reed Merrill's; see his "Mistaken Endeavor," p. 513n17. But rejecting certain absolutes as much as accepting them may lead to determinism!

  Placing the case for a moment in an altered setting, assume that I decide one morning to paint the sky black. I make this decision because it occurred to me the night before (perhaps during a dream) that all "givens" of human experience are personally affronting to me. I call on my neighbor, Fred, to help me out. Fred, less intelligent than I, loves action. While I watch from my sheltered vantage point, Fred rents a plane, buys some paint, and tries to effectuate my scheme. He quickly discovers the impossibility of the task, and, deferring to forces beyond himself, lands the plane and heads off to work. Meanwhile, I sit at home, having attempted far less than Fred, but still doggedly unwilling to accept the material veracity of the sky's unalterably blue appearance. Who is the "freer" man, really —Fred, who goes on acting (however banally), or I, who sit at home railing against the laws of nature? More vital still, which of the two of us will be more likely to take steps against *actual* injustice—I, who do nothing but hypothesize such enemies as time, space, and matter, or Fred, who defers to external forces only after having tried his utmost to exert his free will?

16   Victor Shklovski, *Za i protiv*, pp. 154–56. In later pages of this perceptive analysis, Shklovski emphasizes the Underground Man's debilitating sense of being out of joint with his time (p. 159) and his constant reliance on "the muse of vengeance and sadness [*mesti i pevčali*]." Shklovski associates these traits with Dostoevski himself (p. 159), seeing the work as a vengeful attack by the author upon the writers Chernyshevski and Belinski.

17   Several excellent psychoanalytic approaches to the Underground Man have been written in recent decades. See, for example, Dr. Herbert Walker, "Observations on Fyodor Dostoevski's *Notes from the Underground*," *American Imago* 19 (1962): 195–210; Barbara Smalley, "The Compulsive Patterns of Dostoyevski's *Underground Man*," *Studies in Short Fiction* 10 (1973): 389–96; and Bernard J. Paris, *A Psychological Approach to Fiction* (Bloomington: Indiana University Press, 1974), pp. 190–214.

18   The root *zlo*, not by coincidence, frequently appears in words describing all of Dostoevski's tortured intellectual philosophers and lawyers. Other examples of the use of this root (which always carries with it connotations of ressentient behavior) are noted in brackets, below.

19   "Now might I do it pat, now he is praying / And now I'll do't. And so he goes to heaven, / And so am I reveng'd. That would be scann'd. . . . Up, sword, and know thou a more horrid hent" (III.iii. 72–75, 87).

20   Girard calls the Underground Man's attraction to Zverkov the finest literary example of the "imitation of Christ [becoming] the imitation of one's neighbor" (p. 59).

21   *Genealogy* 2.8.203. Reading Nietzsche on justice together with Rawls' widely discussed *A Theory of Justice* (Cambridge: Harvard University Press, 1971) raises interesting problems better handled in a different forum. Suffice it here to observe that both thinkers grapple with the triad of justice, equality, and resentment. For Nietzsche justice cannot emerge from a resentful community but rather controls the inevitable forces of ressenti-

ment through the positive actions of well-motivated individuals. Nietzsche's principal aim is to locate the cultural norms which tend to produce a nonresentful (and hence just) community. Since Nietzsche believes in the inevitability of struggle, yet also proposes a notion of absolute justice, he clearly believes that justice and inequality can coexist. Equality for Nietzsche means equality of *strength*. For Rawls, equality of *opportunity* must be sought: justice arises when the potential for equality in a group is maximized. He assumes away from his original position emotions such as envy and even moral approaches such as ressentiment until quite late in his book, when (in sections 80 and 81) he tries to deal briefly (citing Nietzsche and Scheler) with the implication that equality of opportunity, unmatched by equality of strength, is likely to increase resentment and hence to decrease the potential for justice.

While I treat here the relationship between justice and ressentiment, I do not pretend to analyze that between justice and equality. But even in the present context it is possible to argue that justice will not arise until members of a group *feel* both equal to one another and also good about themselves and each other. I do not think we can effectively discuss justice (except theoretically) without grappling with the forces in our culture which tend to eliminate such feelings. See on this point Helmut Schoeck, *Envy: A Theory of Social Behavior* (London: Secker and Warburg, 1969).

CHAPTER 3

1   *Juge d'instruction*, *Untersuchungsrichter*, and *sudebni sledovatel'* in French, German, and Russian, respectively.
2   See O. J. Rogge, *Why Men Confess* (New York: Da Capo, 1975), pp. 23–48.
3   The Code of 17 November 1808 establishes the institution and function of the juge d'instruction, making reference to similar provisions in the Revolutionary codes of four years earlier.
4   See *Code d'instruction criminelle* (Paris: Dalloz, 1942), supplement for Algeria, pp. 361–64.
5   Both *Crime and Punishment* and *The Brothers Karamazov* make extensive use of the examining magistrate. Their technical references to this figure demonstrate Dostoevski's grasp of the subtle developments within the codes dating from the reforms of Alexander II.
6   Balzac, Hugo, Tolstoi, Kafka, and, of course, Camus all provocatively incorporated the inquisitor into their narratives as well. Nor should European novelists' attraction to this figure be dissociated from English and American writers' fascination with the complexities of legal ratiocination. Three fine recent comparative studies are David I. Grossvogel, *Mystery and Its Fictions: From Oedipus to Agatha Christie* (Baltimore: Johns Hopkins University Press, 1979); Michael Porter, *The Pursuit of Crime* (New Ha-

ven: Yale University Press, 1981); Peter J. Rabinowitz, "The Click of the Spring: The Detective Story as Parallel Structure in Dostoevski and Faulkner," *Modern Philology* 79 (1979): 355–69.

7 The European procurator, like the inquisitor who is one step beneath him in the hierarchy, theoretically serves not "the people" or any political party, but only the interests of truth. He does argue in open court (unlike the inquisitor), but even at that late stage he has no vested interest in having the defendant convicted. For the inquisitorial, as opposed to the adversarial, nature of the procurator, see Charles Szladits, ed., "European Legal Systems" (Unpublished materials, 1972, available at Parker School of Foreign and Comparative Law, Columbia University, New York), pp. 353–65; and Judah Zelitch, *Soviet Administration of Criminal Law* (Philadelphia: University of Pennsylvania Press, 1931), pp. 381–404. Contrast one American district attorney's conception of his role: "I've always thought of myself as a cop," *New York Times*, 7 May 1976, p. B5, col. 3.

8 See, for example, the Russian lawyers N. Rozin, *Ugolovnoe sudoproizvodstvo* (St. Petersburg, 1914), pp. 194–97; and G. B. Slyuzberg, *Dorevolutsionni stroj Rossii* (Paris, 1933), pp. 153–54. For a comparative analysis of the German and Russian examining magistrates in Dostoevski's time, see Leuthold, *Russische Rechtskunde* (Leipzig: Duncker and Humblot, 1889), pp. 331–35.

9 See Szladits, ed., "European Legal Systems," pp. 353–57.

10 See Rogge, *Why Men Confess*, pp. 33–39.

11 See Szladits, ed., "European Legal Systems," pp. 355–56.

12 On the function of Continental police inquiry into serious crimes (which until quite recently rarely extended beyond the first twenty-four hours, after which an inquisitor was called in), see, for example, V. Slučevski, *Učebnik Russkovo ugolovnovo protsessa* (St. Petersburg: 1885), pp. 625–32. For the French equivalents, see *Code de procédure pénale* (Paris: Dalloz, 1968), articles 63 and 125–26.

13 My text for *Prestuplenie i nakazanie* is *Crime and Punishment*, trans. Jessie Coulson, ed. George Gibian (New York: Norton, 1964). I have made some alterations in the translation to suit the information provided here about technical legal terms. All page references are to this excellent edition.

On the subject of public ignorance of, and displeasure with, prereform czarist legal procedures, see Samuel Kucherov, *Courts, Lawyers and Trials under the Last Three Tsars* (New York: Praeger, 1953), especially p. 38n54. For Dostoevski's specific association of Porfiry with the reformers, see also *The Notebooks for "Crime and Punishment,"* trans. and ed. Edward Wasiolek (Chicago: University of Chicago Press, 1967), p. 167.

14 Articles 261 and 270 of the Code of Criminal Procedure of 1864. Compare Slučevski, *Učebnik Russkovo*, p. 630.

15 For the parallel French provisions dealing with the relationship between

inquisitor and procurator, see *Code de procédure pénale* (1968), articles 72, 82, and 120.

16   The interviewing of persons who might shed light on the general personalities of all possible suspects was considered the most important function of the inquisitor. See the czarist code, Articles 265, 269, 377; see the French code, articles 101–21.

17   Slučevski, *Učebnik Russkovo*, p. 635; translation my own.

18   Raskolnikov only seems to react this way to *lawyers*, however, unlike the universal resentments (indicated by the same Russian word) of the Underground Man and Ivan Karamozov. In his earlier scenes with Dounia's suitor (the lawyer Luzhin), Raskolnikov also experiences resentful rage, but largely for different reasons. See the discussion of *zlost'* and its Nietzschean analogue, ressentiment, in chapter 1, above.

19   For the finest integration of Dostoevski's fascination with the law and his use of legal details in the novels, see Sven Linner, *Doestoevski on Realism* (Stockholm: Almquist, 1967), especially pp. 136–44.

20   See Kucherov, *Courts, Lawyers and Trials*, pp. 168–70.

21   My text for *Brat'ja Karamazovi* is the Garnett translation (New York: Signet, 1957). Book 9 encompasses pages 408–68; book 12 includes pages 594–682. Parenthetical page references are to this edition.

22   Dostoevski again displays his precise knowledge of czarist criminal procedure by employing "deputy procurator" as Ippolit's title (p. 414). Indeed, in the real system, these deputies were usually the ones to go out to the local courthouses to plead cases. See Kucherov, *Courts, Lawyers and Trials*, p. 95.

23   See Rozin, *Ugolovnoe Sudoproizvodstvo*, p. 422. See also the French code, Articles 72, 82, and 129.

24   The czarist preliminary investigation characteristically commenced with a search and seizure of the victim's *and suspect's* persons and surroundings. See N. Rozin, *Ugolovnoe Sudoproizvodsto*, p. 420. As with many other such inquisitorial powers, the Continental system thus allows actions which in America would be unconstitutional.

25   The law allows an immediate interrogation (without the presence of an attorney) if the inquisitor deems the situation pressing enough. See the French code, Article 115. Generally, the first interrogation takes place without benefit of counsel (Article 116); see Szladits, "European Legal Systems," p. 355.

26   Recall Porfiry's three interviews with Raskolnikov; compare Smerdyakov's three discussions with the increasingly tortured Ivan Karamazov.

27   Perhaps understandably, the translator made the decision not to follow too carefully Dostoevski's generally precise use of legal terms; hence the word *lawyer* appears in places where the original has *sledovatel'*, *prokurator*, or *sudebni sledovatel'*. The Russian words for a simple lawyer (e.g., "iurist") are rarely used here by Dostoevski.

28 In Robert Belknap's enlightening structural study, *The Structure of "The Brothers Karamazov"* (The Hague: Mouton, 1967), the association of "lechery with feet" is seen as a constant aspect of sensual "Karamazovism" (p. 27), but he appears not to include this telling moment in the preliminary investigation.

29 See W. Wolfgang Holdheim, *Der Justizirrtum als literarische Problematik* (Berlin: De Gruyter, 1969), pp. 17–30, for a fine analysis of Fetyukovich's "artistic" role at the trial. For Professor Holdheim, the defense counsel's long summation to the jury affords a focal point for a theory of interpretation; I have been greatly influenced by his cogent arguments. My own emphasis here, of course, is on the evocation of novelistic ressentiment in the *procurator*.

30 Ibid., p. 13. Professor Holdheim speaks of Smerdyakov in the same terms (p. 33), but does not choose to elaborate upon the net of resentments, deriving from those of Ivan and culminating at the trial, which produces, more than does mere "contingency," the judicial error. Dostoevski perceives here not a world without meaning, but one in which *willed*, reactive, negative values have overturned positive ones.

31 For a lesser-known example of prosecutorial artistry in the service of vindictive motives, see Jakob Wassermann, *The Maurizius Case*, trans. C. Newton (New York: Liveright, 1929), a novel brought to my attention by the revered, late Professor Max Rheinstein of the University of Chicago.
    For an analysis of Mitya's trial in the context of the comparative theory of law and literature, see R. Weisberg and J. P. Barricelli, "Literature and the Law," in *The Interrelations of Literature* (New York: Modern Language Association, 1982), pp. 150–75.

32 Grigori, after all, has twice been assaulted grievously by Mitya, blows which deeply insult him (p. 136) and irrevocably prejudice his testimony against the defendant. (Incredibly, Fetyukovich fails to establish these earlier incidents, and the narrator, like the jury, deems Grigori's damaging testimony "impartial.") Katerina, a woman scorned for Grushenka, vents her accumulated spleen against Mitya at the trial. Her testimony is selective and hence inaccurate. These two ressentient witnesses gain their revenge against Mitya through the indirect medium of a theoretically objective legal procedure.

CHAPTER 4

1 The Russian title, "Veliki Inkvizitor," permits the pun (in English only) upon the word *inquisitor* as applied also to the examining magistrate.

2 No wonder comprehensive critics such as Jean Drouilly have found a basically non-Christian epistemology hidden in Dostoevski's treatment of human evil, misery, and injustice. See his *La Pensée politique et religieuse de Dostoïevski* (Paris: Librairie des cinq continents, 1971), pp. 439–40.

3   Camus, "L'Homme révolté," in *Essais* (Paris: Gallimard, 1965), pp. 465–71.

4   See Littell, *Crucifixion of the Jews.*

5   For another such devil, created by the fictional composer Adrian Leverkühn, see Thomas Mann's brilliant variation on the theme of Goethe and Dostoevski, *Doktor Faustus.*

6   Ivan, unlike his two brothers, does not usually permit others to address him as "ti" or by the diminutive of his name (Vanya).

7   A nonnarrative example of the modern artist's sense of alienation from others is to be found in Mallarmé's early poem "Le Guignon."

8   In this respect Ivan imitates Dostoevski, whose inspiration for *Crime and Punishment, The Possessed,* and "The Gentle Spirit," among other works, came from the *faits divers* sections of newspapers.

9   *Dostoyevski, The Making of a Novelist* (New York: Vintage, 1962), pp. 348–63. I might disagree by suggesting that *Mitya* is finally the best example among the brothers of the "seekers of life." Compare Belknap's excellent study, *The Structure of "The Brothers Karamazov,"* pp. 26–31. Belknap's discussion of "Karamazovism" links all three brothers to the quest for life.

10 "The Dream of a Ridiculous Man," in *The Best Short Stories of Dostoevski,* ed. and trans. David Magarshack, pp. 318, 322.

11 For a similar thesis, couched in very different terms, see Kleist, "Über das Marionettentheater" (c. 1805).

12 Dostoevski's view of the criminal not only inspired Nietzsche (see part 1, above), but also presaged modern literature's frequent equation of criminality with freedom, as in Sartre's *Saint Genet* (1952). But in my analysis, even if such an equation reflects a necessary development in Western culture, it indicates a basic flaw in the ethical framework of formal institutions created during the Christian era.

13 See Magarshack's fine biography, *Dostoevski,* p. 253, where Dostoevski's fear of the overly verbose and "theoretical" nature of his enterprise is discussed.

14 *Dostoïevski: Du double à l'unité,* (Paris: Plon, 1963), p. 158 (translations are my own).

15 *Dostoïevski: Du double à l'unité,* pp. 165, 12.

16 My text for Dostoevski's letters is *Pis'ma,* ed. A. S. Dolinin (Moscow, 1928–59; reprint, Ann Arbor, Mich.: University Microfilms International, 1983), here 2:261–65. All translations are my own. This letter appears to establish the religious conflict in *The Brothers Karamazov.*

17 Letter to Nikolai Lyubimov, 10 May 1879, ibid. 4: 52–54.

18 Letter to Anna, 18 November 1867, ibid. 2: 55.

19 Cited in Magarshack, *Dostoevski,* pp. 317–18.

20 Dostoevski uses this significant word or its variants three times in this letter to describe his state of mind about the act of writing; it literally means "without peace."

21   Letter to Konstantin Pobedonostsev of late August 1879, *Pis'ma* 4: 108–10. Magarshack cites this letter in *Dostoevski*, pp. 372–73.

22   The same dilemma may inhere in *The Divine Comedy*. The poet, by the very act of writing, appears to distort God's command to "spend your vision" exclusively upon Him. The poem, necessarily subsequent to the epiphanal vision itself, paradoxically represents a regression into self-observation, into the very egocentricity which the poetic traveler sought to overcome at the beginning of his journey. Literary structures impede the vision of the Christian religious poet; they insist on separating his spiritual "essence" from his earthly concerns, but ironically always depend on the latter.

23   Letter to Sonya in 1870; *Pis'ma* 2:272–75.

24   Holdheim, *Justizirrtum*, p. 13, translation my own. See also, more generally, pp. 10–42.

25   There is no absolute assurance that Dostoevski definitely intended Alyosha to become "The Great Sinner" of a sequel to *The Brothers Karamazov*. Dostoevski died too quickly (1881) to commence a new project. But friends and family report his plan to have Alyosha go through a stage of criminality (see Magarshack, *Dostoevski*, p. 377), and such a development would have been fully consistent with Dostoevski's view of the progression into spirituality.

CHAPTER 5

1   See Lukacs, *Der Historische Roman* (Berlin: Aufbau-Verlag, 1955), pp. 194–219; Brombert, *The Novels of Flaubert* (Princeton: Princeton University Press, 1966), especially pp. 120–24 (on *Salammbô*); and Culler, *Flaubert* (Ithaca, N.Y.: Cornell University Press, 1974). See also Weisberg, "Literature as Negativity."

2   The flow of comparative scholarship seems not yet to have commingled these two giants. Rather, Dostoevski has been readily compared to Dickens (for their social realism and their clear mutual fascination for law and other institutions), and Flaubert to Henry James (for their obsession with craft) or Tolstoi (for their historical subjects and brilliant depictions of women). The present study may encourage recognition of the structural element linking the narratives of Dostoevski and Flaubert: authorial uncertainty about the verbal act.

3   Levin, "Flaubert, Portrait of the Artist as a Saint," *Kenyon Review* 10 (1948): 32.

4   Oscar Cargill, in his introduction to James, *The Ambassadors* (New York: Washington Square Press, 1967), p. vii.

5   See, for example, J. Killa Williams, "The Ecstasy of Gustave Flaubert," *French Quarterly*, 1931: 53–61.

6   Auerbach, *Mimesis*, trans. Willard Trask (Garden City, N.Y.: Doubleday Anchor, 1957), pp. 429–30.

7   For Flaubert's letters, I have used his nine-volume *Correspondance*, ed. Louis Conard (Paris: Conard, 1926). (Hereafter, *Correspondance*.) All translations are my own. The reader lacking French is now, of course, immensely aided by the recent translations of Flaubert's letters by Francis Steegmuller: *The Letters of Gustave Flaubert*, 2 vols. (Cambridge: Harvard University Press, Belknap, 1980–82). Here, letter of 18 March 1857 to Mlle. Leroyer de Chantepie, *Correspondance* 4:164, emphasis Flaubert's.

8   Letter of 6 July 1852 to Louise Colet, *Correspondance* 2:461.

9   Letter of 1861 to Mme. Roger des Genettes, *Correspondance* 4:463–64, emphasis mine.

10 Letter of 4 September 1852 to Louise Colet, *Correspondance* 3:17–18, emphasis mine.

    Sartre observes that Flaubert's distaste for his time and place was odd in a period in which there *was* a great deal to be done, politically and socially. Flaubert criticized from the safety of his study. See, for example, Sartre's interview, in the *New York Review of Books*, 26 March 1970; and his *What Is Literature?*

11 See letter of 30 March 1857 to Leroyer de Chantepie, *Correspondance* 4:170–71, in which, after labeling all contemporary political activity "false," he states, "I have attended, as a spectator, almost all the rallies of my day." We will recall this letter in analyzing *L'Education sentimentale*.

12 Letter of 23 January 1858 to Leroyer de Chantepie, *Correspondance* 4:247, emphasis Flaubert's.

13 Interestingly, Flaubert sees his social isolation ("le silence du cabine") as a kind of spiritual masturbation, as does the Underground Man in part 2 of Dostoevski's tale (see above, chapter 2). See Flaubert's letter to Ernest Feydeau of April 1857, *Correspondance* 4:175.

14 Flaubert describes his view of life in bovine terms elsewhere as well. He writes to Leroyer de Chantepie, 18 March 1857, "j'ai peu mangé, mais considérablement ruminé" (*Correspondance* 4:165). Such verbs cannot help but evoke that ultimate listless protagonist, Charles Bovary, whose last name and such descriptions as the following link him to Flaubert's pattern of passive existence: "ruminant son bonheur, comme ceux qui mâchent encore, après dîner, le goût des truffes qu'ils digèrent." My text for *Madame Bovary* is *Oeuvres complètes* 1: 575–692; here, p. 585. Where translations appear, they are my own. For a comparison of Charles and Flaubert, see Sartre, *L'Idiot de la famille* 2: 1202.

15 *Correspondance* 2:6–7. See Benjamin F. Bart, *Flaubert* (Syracuse, N.Y.: Syracuse University Press, 1967), pp. 47, 416.

16 Bart, *Flaubert*, p. 635. See also Bart, p. 225, in which he speaks of Flaubert's being "quite content to adopt from Theophile Gautier the notion of wishing to be a woman."

17 Flaubert, *Intimate Notebook*, trans. Francis Steegmuller (Garden City, N.Y.: Doubleday, 1967), pp. 26, 47.

18 Canaris, a Greek hero of Flaubert's time, fascinated the writer, who met him in 1850. Flaubert was greatly struck by the fact that "he can neither read nor write; when [Canaris] was naval minister, he couldn't even sign his name. He doesn't know any of what has been written about him in Europe" (*Correspondance* 2:283). The letters of 1850 especially, describing Flaubert's travels through the Middle East, convey his sensuous, violent attraction to feminine and heroic modes, and his concomitant despair at never being able to attain them.

19 To Flaubert, woman was at once life itself and utter mendacity, a part of the animal world but therefore also vicious beyond the capacities of intellectual man (see *Correspondance* 2:257, 440). For a fascinating insight into Flaubert's education in things exotic, see Jean Seznec, *Flaubert à l'exposition de 1851* (Oxford: Clarendon, 1951).

20 Letter of 18 May 1857 to Mlle. Leroyer de Chantepie, *Correspondance* 4: 182.

21 Letter of 15 December 1850 to his mother, *Correspondance* 2: 268–69.

22 The Marquis de Sade was a lifelong hero for Flaubert, who called him "cet honnête écrivain." Writing to Ernest Chevalier on 15 July 1839, he says, "I love to see men like that, like Nero and de Sade"; *Correspondance* 1: 51. See Bart, *Flaubert*, e.g., p. 379.

23 Letter of 11 January 1859 to Ernest Feydeau, *Correspondance* 4: 304.

24 See introduction to *Madame Bovary*, p. 573.

25 Emma Bovary progresses toward a stance of ressentiment, inspired first by her husband's ineptitude (which she takes as a personal insult), then extended to encompass all men because of their theoretically freer condition. But Flaubert's women never fully succumb to ressentiment; instead they surmount it through their will to act, to improve their condition at all costs. For Emma, a character too frequently slighted by male critics, this drive to escape mediocrity finds expression in her seeking of lovers. No matter how unfortunate her choice of alternatives to Charles, Emma's ability to act, to rebel, and to avoid stagnation places her head and shoulders above her creator, in whom ressentiment reaches full fruition.

Emma's most negative side comes to the fore in her relationship with her daughter, an innocent victim of Emma's ressentient rage against Charles. Like Hamilcar Barca's stance toward Salammbô, Emma's distaste for her offspring evolves from the desire to have had a child of the opposite sex. But apart from this failing, Emma's main errors in the novel are excusable as the weaknesses of an individual actively seeking to rise above a situation which she feels is, *although it may not be,* unworthy of her.

26 Sainte-Beuve's remarks appeared in *Le Constitutionnel*, in December 1862. These translations by F. C. Green appear in the appendix to *Salammbô* (London: Everyman's Library, 1948), pp. 309–10, 302. (For Nietzsche's unfriendly view of Sainte-Beuve, see *Twilight of the Gods*.) For James' comments, see *The Art of Fiction* (New York: Oxford University Press,

1948), pp. 130, 145. See also Brombert, *The Novels of Flaubert*, for a sample of the more enlightened recent view on *Salammbô*: "Were the thought not so heretical, one might even venture to say that in many ways *Salammbô* is more truly representative of the patterns of Flaubert's imagination than *Madame Bovary*" (p. 123).

27   Hannibal, the most colorful and famous of Carthaginians, appears here only briefly, as a young son of the central figure Hamilcar.

28   Lukacs, *Der Historische Roman*, pp. 196–97, my translation.

29   Flaubert typically imposes destructive coincidences upon his sensuous female protagonists. In Emma's case, there are the coincidences first of meeting, then of marrying, the ponderous Charles (a decision so incredible for a girl of Emma's incessantly romantic drives that the narrator avoids explaining it by not entering Emma's thoughts until the morning after the wedding); next, of giving birth to a daughter, having just been portrayed as craving a son; and finally, of having her chance for religious ecstasy foiled by the fluke appearance outside her deathbed window of a blind beggar she had seen elsewhere. What was he doing there? Why does Salammbô die? Realism flees before the casual cruelty of an author who deeply envies his protagonists. (See note 41, below.)

30   Lukacs, *Der Historische Roman*, p. 201. Brombert, who notes Lukacs' assessment of the "dehumanizing monumentality" of the work, appears to agree that there is a "gap between the human action and the political tragedy" (*The Novels of Flaubert*, p. 93). My thesis here, however, emphasizes the intricate interdependence of the personal and the civilizational elements in *Salammbô*.

31   The text for *Salammbô* is Flaubert, *Oeuvres complètes* (Paris: Seuil, 1964), 1:693–797. Translations are my own, but I have referred to that of B. R. Redman (New York: Tudor, 1931). Page references are to the Seuil edition.

32   Lukacs speaks of Matho's possessing "an animally wild character," and we know that Flaubert equated such traits with heroism.

33   Sainte-Beuve's analysis of the Matho-Spendius relationship, emphasizing the latter's verbal abilities, is a brief but perceptive section of his accompanying essay on *Salammbô*.

34   See Homer, *Iliad*, trans. Lattimore, 2.211–77 (see also chapter 1, n. 11, above). Kenneth Burke offers a poetic apology for Thersites' wordy mode (now that of almost every respectable novelistic protagonist) in *Language as Symbolic Action* (Berkeley and Los Angeles: University of California Press, 1966), pp. 100–01. For Flaubert's familiarity with the *Iliad*, see, for example, his letter of 15 January 1850 to Louis Bouilhet: "Je m'en vais relire l'*Iliade*"; *Correspondance* 2:155.

35   Letter of 23–24 December 1862 to Sainte-Beuve, *Correspondance* 5:66. The Aratus reference may be to Aratus of Sicyon, a statesman who left

memoirs, or to Aratus of Soloe, a poet. See Albin Lensky, *A History of Greek Literature*, trans. Willis and de Heer (New York: Cromwell, 1966), pp. 750, 770.

36 For a full discussion, see Arthur Hamilton, *Sources of the Religious Element in Flaubert's "Salammbô,"* Eliot Monographs no. 4 (Baltimore, 1917).

37 For Flaubert, a certain order of animals is equated with active, spontaneous heroism. Examples are numerous, from the earliest to the last of the tales. See the equation of leopards with sultans in "Novembre" (*Oeuvres complètes* 1:267), of horses with the Vaubyessard ball and then Rodolphe, in Emma's fantasies and in actuality (pp. 593, 627–28); of butterflies and lions with Hérodias' dance of death (2:197–98). Relatively placid barnyard animals (e.g., cows) are associated throughout his works with static, mediocre men; Charles Bovary's condition, noted above, is more broadly that of the provincial milieu Emma hopes to escape as she speaks to Rodolphe during the sale of cows at the *Comices agricoles* (p. 621). Elsewhere, the cows and donkeys of the common person are contrasted with Hérodias (2:189).

38 Again, a detailed look at the novel reveals subtle distinctions between types of people, even between the qualities of the rival camps. Lukacs' generalization that "the soldiers in this novel are as wild, chaotic and poorly directed a group as the citizens of Carthage" may miss the specific narrational imputation of negativity to the city-dwellers. Compare Brombert, *The Novels of Flaubert*, p. 111.

39 Compare Brombert's brief description of Schahabarim's "sterility," *The Novels of Flaubert*, p. 119.

40 On Flaubert's sense of unmanliness, see, for example, Sartre, *L'Idiot de la famille* 2:1279, n. 1. Sartre equates Flaubert's sexual ambivalence with his stance toward his female protagonists; see, for example, 2:1286–87.

41 The heroic mode survives only through Hamilcar, who shares the priest's (and author's) ambivalence toward Salammbô, since "the birth of a daughter was viewed as a calamity by the sun-religions." The parallel disappointment of Emma, when she gives birth to a daughter instead of a son, finds expression in the powerful "accouchement" paragraph, in part 2, chapter 3 of *Madame Bovary*. The novelist, having quite suddenly invested his protagonist with a virtually existential need to have a son, just as suddenly denies Emma its fulfillment: "She gave birth on a Sunday, around six, as the sun rose. 'It's a girl!' said Charles. She turned the other way and fainted" (p. 604). The last sentence might remind us of the cold brevity with which Flaubert disposes of Salammbô in the final words of the later novel. Surviving the females are only males (including the novelist) who have participated in their formation and their destruction. "[Hamilcar] still retained his sense of shattered hopes, and the force of the curse which he had pronounced against her."

CHAPTER 6

1   See chapter 5, n. 26, above.

2   Lukacs' brilliant chapter, "The Romanticism of Disillusionment," in his *The Theory of the Novel* (*Théorie des romans*, 1916), trans. Anna Bostock (Cambridge: MIT Press, 1971), situates *L'Education sentimentale* at the precise point in the development of the novel in which all tension between protagonist and external world ceases; Don Quixote's "abstract idealism" has become Frédéric Moreau's "romantic disillusionment":

> Life becomes a work of literature; but, as a result, man becomes the author of his own life and at the same time the observer of that life as a created work of art. Such duality can only be given form by lyrical means. As soon as it is fitted into a coherent totality, the certainty of failure becomes manifest; the romanticism becomes sceptical, disappointed and cruel towards itself and the world; the novel of the Romantic sense of life is the novel of disillusionment. (p. 118)

3   See chapter 5, n. 6, above.

4   Lukacs, "Romanticism of Disillusionment":

> Yet this novel, of all novels of the nineteenth century, is one of the most typical of the problematic of the novel form; in the unmitigated desolation of its matter it is the only novel that attains true epic objectivity and, through it, the positiveness and affirmative energy of an accomplished form.
>
> This victory is rendered possible by time. The unrestricted, uninterrupted flow of time is the unifying principle of the homogeneity that rubs the sharp edges off each heterogeneous fragment and establishes a relationship—albeit an irrational and inexpressible one—between them. (p. 125)

5   My text for *L'Education sentimentale* is *Oeuvres complètes* 2:8–163 (Paris: Seuil, 1964), here p. 26; where translations appear, they are my own, unless otherwise indicated.

6   The Russian noun *pošlost'*, which Gogol uses about his characters, perfectly captures Frédéric's brand of glib ambition.

7   The letter appears in *Oeuvres complètes* (Paris: Conard, 1910), 5:47.

8   The two novels make a neat contrast, since both are largely set in Paris and involve a verbally inclined protagonist's education into romantic love.

9   Lukacs erred in failing to see the importance of Frédéric's profession:

> This problematic is further intensified by the fact that, given the relationship between the two, the outside world which comes into contact with such an interiority has to be completely atomised or amorphous, and in

any case must be entirely devoid of meaning. It is a world entirely dominated by convention, the full realisation of the concept of a "second nature"; a quintessence of meaningless laws in which no relation to the soul can be found. And this means that all formal objectivations of social life lose all significance for the soul. They do not retain even their paradoxical significance as being the necessary arena and vehicle of events whilst having no essence at the core. Thus, a character's profession loses all importance from the point of view of his inner destiny, just as marriage, family and class become immaterial to the relationships between characters.

Lukacs, "Romanticism of Disillusionment," p. 113.

10 Frédéric finally succumbs to what he calls "la mode" at the very end of part 2. As for his earlier procrastinations, we must recall that Flaubert thought of a career in law as somehow dissociated from sexual activity: "I didn't make love . . . because I had promised myself not to," he declared of his own years in law school (M. Nadeau, *The Greatness of Flaubert*, trans. B. Bray [New York: Library Press, 1972], p. 51). His fictional lawyer, Frédéric, apparently abstains until eight years of frustrated desire for Mme Arnoux lead him at last to Rosanette's bed.

11 *Oeuvres complètes* 2:15. This translation is by Robert Baldick (New York: Penguin, 1964).

12 Virtually compelled by his father to study law, Flaubert, like Frédéric, failed his second-year examinations. He finally quit, ostensibly for health reasons; see, for example, Bart, *Flaubert*, p. 87. Sartre's interpretation of Flaubert's failure at law is worth noting: Flaubert "est incapable de se déterminer en fonction d'une fin transcendante—même s'il s'agit de passer un examen de droit. . . . Il condamne l'action au nom du quiétisme" (*L'Idiot de la famille* 2: 1690). Although Sartre agrees that not everyone is cut out for "l'étrange combinaison d'empirisme et d'*a priori* q'on trouve dans les raisonnements des juristes" (p. 1686), he feels that Flaubert would have succeeded at law were it not for his chronic *passivity*, which Sartre often places under the sign of ressentiment.

13 Frédéric's classmate Martinon, who passes his exams brilliantly and goes on to success with the Dambreuse family and election as a senator, stays mum during all political confrontations. Early in the book, he advises Frédéric to keep his voice low as they watch Dussardier being seized by the police.

14 Deslauriers' ambitions far exceed Frédéric's, and he seems brighter and more likely to achieve them. His hopes extend to reforming the laws of inheritance as to collateral heirs; it is no coincidence that this reform would have prevented Frédéric from inheriting through his uncle by intestate succession. Deslauriers, the quintessential lawyer in this text, frequently speaks and acts for Flaubert. Anticipating Faulkner's use of Gavin Stevens in novels such as *Intruder in the Dust*, Flaubert has a lawyer figure verbalize

approaches to many social problems. One of Deslauriers' ambitions is to write a book called *The History of the Idea of Justice* (p. 72). Eventually, his resentment makes him the factor most responsible for the downfall of Mme Arnoux (whom he tries to seduce), and he ultimately surrenders himself to the economic and political power of the Dambreuses.

15 Frédéric's scorn for "the mob" arises when he and Rosanette share a romantic escape to Versailles from the Paris street-fighting. He refuses the general call to arms, while at the same time he longs for the past, heroic generations whose images he sees portrayed in the castle and museums. No wonder Sartre, in his discussion of Flaubert's years in law school, refers to Frédéric as the writer's "doublet affadi"; Sartre, *L'Idiot*, p. 1688.

16 *Oeuvres complètes* 2: 39; Baldick translation.

CHAPTER 7

1 Camus' *L'Etranger* was published by Gallimard in 1942. For insights into the politics of publishing during the Occupation, see Herbert R. Lottman, *The Left Bank* (Boston: Houghton Mifflin, 1982); on Camus, see, for example, p. 148.

2 The standard French reporter of laws, cases, and jurisprudence, the *Gazette du Palais*, simply added a new category during the Occupation: "Juifs." Laws imported from Germany and formulated locally were easily cast in the legalistic jargon usually applied to wills, real estate, or contracts. In the same years that *The Stranger* was being read for the first time, the *Gazette* printed its compendium of laws dealing with Jews in "Algérie-Tunisie-Maroc." A series of laws, modifications, and casuistic arguments about who is or is not a Jew pervades the law books of the period. See, for example, "Loi du 17 Novembre 1941: Statut des juifs," *Gazette* 1941 (2ᵉ sem.), "Lois et décrets," pp. 945–46; and "Doctrine," pp. 122–24 (an article applying legal logic and rhetoric to the Nuremberg laws). See, in general, Michael R. Marrus and Robert O. Paxton, *Vichy France and the Jews* (New York: Basic, 1981), particularly pp. 106 and 127 (Camus' Algeria) and pp. 138–44 (laws and courts in World War II France). For the best compilation of French racial statutes and ordinances, see R. Sarraute and P. Tager, *Les Juifs sous l'occupation* (Paris: Centre de documentation juive contemporaine, 1982). See Richard Weisberg, "Narrative Terror: The Failure of French Culture under the Occupation," *Human Rights Quarterly* 5 (1983): 151–70; here, pp. 161–70.

3 Camus' thematic debt to Dostoevski has been widely recognized. On the similarities between the two authors' structuring of their legal novels, see Holdheim, *Justizirrtum*, pp. 43–80; and Richard Weisberg, "Comparative Law in Comparative Literature: The Figure of the 'Examining Magistrate' in Dostoevski and Camus," *Rutgers Law Review* 29 (1976): 237–58, reprinted as *Cornell Soviet Studies* 33 (1976).

4   There is a similar critique of Soviet society under totalitarianism present, of course, in Solzhenitsyn's *The First Circle* and *The Gulag Archipelago*, works which can be effectively compared and contrasted with Gunter Grass' novels set in Nazi Europe (just as these authors' brilliant novellas *One Day in the Life of Ivan Denisovich* and *Cat and Mouse* have much in common).

5   My text here is *L'Etranger* (Paris: Gallimard, [1942] 1957). All translations are my own.

6   See current French *Code de procédure pénale*, Articles 81 and 331, for example. Compare Szladits, ed., "European Legal Systems," p. 353: "On juge l'homme, pas les faits."

7   Most modern novelists who treat criminal procedure at one point or another associate theology with legal persecution. For Camus in 1942, the link must have been graphically clear. Religious figures managed to conform, and even to thrive, as their civilization's values crumbled around them. Or was it that their civilization's values had implicitly *led* to what was happening, and that therefore conformity was perfectly natural? The latter thought is the more troubling, but it is supported by the increasing amount of data emerging about those horrible years. One example is a Roman Catholic scholar's convincing data that a Jesuit academician from Paderborn wrote a report for Hitler stating that the Church would have no fundamental objection to forced euthanasia; see Rev. Robert A. Grahamm, "The 'Right to Kill' in the Third Reich — Prelude to Genocide," *La Civiltà Cattolica* 126 (15 March 1975): 557–76. See also Littell, *Crucifixion of the Jews*, pp. 104–08. For a discussion of the legal-religious approach in Vichy France, see Marrus and Paxton, *Vichy France and the Jews*, pp. 139 and 277, for example.

8   The inquisitor must turn over the full record to the accused man's counsel at least twenty-four hours before each new interrogation (Article 118).

9   Szladits, ed., "European Legal Systems," p. 356: "A very fascinating element in the investigatory stage is the reenactment of the crime, where the *inculpé* is asked to reenact what happened. It is apparently felt that, during the process of reenactment, facts not previously disclosed will emerge; even an accomplished liar may encounter difficulty in portraying a false account."

10 The presence at the session of the inquisitor's clerk (*greffier*) again exemplifies Camus' detailed knowledge of the procedural code (Article 119); the inquisitor is legally required to hire such an assistant.

11 Conor Cruise O'Brien sees an element of anti-Arab feeling in Meursault's fairly casual acceptance of having killed only "an Arab"; see his *Albert Camus of Europe and Africa*, (New York: Viking, 1970), p. 25. However, had Camus wished to emphasize the "racial" nature of the crime, he might well have integrated into the technically accurate trial scene the French law, then in effect, which allowed only Europeans to sit on a jury trying a

European yet demanded that a certain number of Frenchmen sit when the defendant was an Arab (Dalloz, *Code d'instruction criminelle*, [Paris: Dalloz, 1951], pp. 361–62); this point is never raised at the trial. What is more, the European jury condemns Meursault to death for his crime.

12   After the first interview, the accused must be interrogated in the presence of counsel, unless he waives that right (Article 118).

13   During the eleven-month period (not unusually long for serious crimes), Meursault is held in "preventive detention." The length of such pretrial incarceration has been the subject of some criticism in France. (See Szladits, ed., "European Legal Systems," p. 357.)

14   Neither Dostoevski nor Camus enters the minds of any of the jurors, but in all their trial scenes the jury system is an implied subject of interest. Can twelve people be counted on to deal impartially with evidence? More pressing still, can they see through the grandiloquence of the procurator and the bias of the witnesses to find the "true" defendant? There is an equation here of jury with reader; together they are the audience whom the narrative speaker seeks to convince of his own vision of reality. See my discussion of Captain Vere's handpicked jury in *Billy Budd, Sailor*, below in part 4.

15   The word *bizarre* is used at least eight times in this short novel, a fact which is lost when translators mysteriously decide to render the word differently each time. As employed by Camus, *bizarre* becomes a leitmotif for the inalterable differences between Meursault and any person or institution which smacks of formalistic (usually linguistic) artificiality.

16   Camus has Meursault recall the concierge's remark only after he refuses to see his mother's body; but chronologically, the distasteful impression of decomposition precedes the decision to leave the coffin closed.

17   This testimony would be excluded as hearsay or irrelevant under American rules of evidence. The more narrative French system allows a witness to quote words which he himself did not originally hear uttered. Camus' treatment stands as a good argument for the hearsay restrictions.

18   See Szladits, ed., "European Legal Systems," especially pp. 351–61. The "polished literary style" of the lawyers (p. 260) and the staginess of the proceedings are facilitated on many occasions by the virtual certainty that the accused is guilty, often because he has actually confessed, but always because of the thoroughness of the preliminary investigation. The lawyers and parties may sometimes appear to be "reading their lines," which have already been written by the inquisitor in his dossier.

19   See my discussion of the ending of *The Brothers Karamazov* in chapter 4, above; as my analyses of each of these legalistic novels makes clear, in each case the conclusion is structurally vital.

20   As Brian Masters puts it in his fine *Camus: A Study* (London: Heinemann, 1974), "The startling difference in [Meursault's] language at the close of the book is sufficient indication of a profound change in his attitude (p.

32). True. But Masters concludes that this change is necessarily a laudable one, despite his earlier assertion that the Meursault of part 1 excels only in "his absolute and unshakeable refusal to lie about his own feelings" (see pp. 26, 126). Why would Meursault's last-minute attainment of narrative ability, which Camus everywhere else associates with falsehood, represent a salutary advance?

Masters seems to lose the thread of an otherwise fine analysis here. He goes on to agree with Robert Champigny's depiction of Meursault as "an epicurean hero of pagan stock, a man who seeks harmony with the natural world in opposition to the Christian, . . . [who] avoids abstractions, . . . adapts himself to what he has and makes the most of it" (p. 34). This describes the Billy Budd type, whose honesty lies in his nonverbality. Meursault's uncharacteristic closing diatribe, conversely, leagues him with the lawyers, the priest, the "bizarre" lady at Céleste's, and those other regimented approaches to existence to which he was never forced to conform prior to his crime and trial.

21 My text is *La Chute* (Paris: Gallimard, 1956). Page references are to this edition. All translations are my own.

22 The text is called a "récit" (not a "roman") by Camus. Its monologic quality and its implied single listener deliberately evoke Dostoevski's *Notes from Underground*, the diary and confessional of another "juge-pénitent." Both stories have their roots in Rousseau.

23 Clamence's self-conscious laugh marks him as perhaps the archetypical lawyer-intellectual in the modern novel. And that same grotesque laugh that has surrounded so many of fiction's tortured verbalizers and philosophers has been dear to French poets and essayists as well. Baudelaire's famous passage on laughter from "Rire et Caricature" best defines such figures as Clamence, Raskolnikov, Ivan, Barth's Todd Andrews (*The Floating Opera*), and Mann's Adrian Leverkühn (*Doktor Faustus*): "Il est certain que le rire humain est intimément lié à l'accident d'une chute ancienne, d'une dégradation physique et morale. Le rire et la douleur s'expriment par les organes où résident le commandement et la science du bien et du mal: les yeux et la bouche. . . . La joie n'était pas dans le rire."

24 Camus subtly makes us aware of modern man's tragic susceptibility to glib, clever speech, but the recognition first requires us to resist Clamence's turns of phrase. Since these, of course, originate in Camus himself, the task is both ironic and difficult. A comparison of two recent critical treatments of this theme makes the complexity of the author's stance evident. Brian Masters in *Camus: A Study* (Totowa, N.J.: Rowman & Littlefield, 1974), notes: "I do not think it has been sufficiently noticed that *La Chute* is a protest against the misuse of language. Throughout his career, Camus was consistent in his demand that language should serve as an instrument of clarification" (p. 126); while Jean Orimus, in *Albert Camus and Christianity*, trans. E. Parker (University: University of Alabama

Press, 1970), observes: "The author inserted himself into his character" (p. 93). The flights of falsifying language must ultimately come home to roost upon the desk of the modern novelist himself.

25   See Rolf Hochhuth's play *The Deputy* for one of the earliest literary treatments of the touchy subject of religious sanctioning of the Nazi regime. Emerging documents have revealed, for example, that Marshal Pétain received great solace from a response by his Vatican ambassador Léon Bérard to a question about papal views on the Vichy racial statutes. "I can affirm," wrote Bérard in 1941, "that no pontifical authority has been concerned or preoccupied in any way with this part of French politics." See also Georges Wellers, André Kaspi, and Serge Klarsfeld, eds., *La France et la question juive, 1940–44* (Paris: Sylvie Messenger, 1981), pp. 154–55; Marrus and Paxton, *Vichy France and the Jews*, pp. 200–01; and Weisberg, "Narrative Terror," p. 160n49.

CHAPTER 8

1   Indeed, the text has perhaps too often served as a vehicle for critics anxious to leap into metaphysical speculation. I give in to the same temptation, but only after exploring the less-travelled path of material textuality.

2   *Billy Budd, Sailor*, ed. Harrison Hayford and Merton Sealts (Chicago: University of Chicago Press, 1962), pp. 1–39. I have used this fine text throughout, noting its differences from earlier versions and from Milton Stern's 1975 edition (Indianapolis: Bobbs-Merrill). All page references are to the Hayford and Sealts edition as well.

3   A distinguished Melville scholar tells how in his early days in the field (in the mid 1950s), he took the then "radical" stand that Captain Vere was not an unambiguously good character, but instead shared some of Claggart's circumspect evil. His professional audiences would grow restive; some turned beet-red. A very private chord had been struck.

4   See Robert Cover, "Prelude: Of Creon and Captain Vere," in *Justice Accused: Antislavery and the Judicial Process* (New Haven: Yale University Press, 1975), pp. 1–7.

As chief justice of this court (famous for such seminal torts opinions as *Brown v. Kendall*, 60 Mass. (6 Cush.) 292 (1850), Shaw felt he had to apply the Fugitive Slave Act, ch. 60, 9 Stat. 462 (1850) (repealed 1865), against the dictates of his private conscience, as he did in the case of Thomas Sims, 61 Mass. (7 Cush.) 285 (1851).

5   Melville cites the history and text of the Articles at some length in *White Jacket* (chapters 71–72). As shall be shown shortly, he knew the British and American statutes almost verbatim (see below, n. 34).

6   See, for example, Charles R. Anderson, "The Genesis of *Billy Budd*," *American Literature* 12 (1940): 329–46; Gansevoort, a lieutenant on the *Somers*, joined with Captain Mackenzie in recommending that the three

sailors be summarily hanged for conspiracy to mutiny. Once on shore, Mackenzie, Gansevoort, and another officer were court-martialed for their action on board and finally acquitted. The relationships between Vere, Billy, and Claggart were paralleled on the *Somers* by those between Mackenzie and the sailors Spencer and Wales: Wales succeeded in ingratiating himself with Captain Mackenzie (who had an antipathy to Spencer) by reporting Spencer's plot to mutiny. Melville had earlier criticized Mackenzie's actions on the *Somers* in chapter 72 of *White Jacket* (1850).

7 See *Billy Budd, Sailor*, ed. Hayford and Sealts, pp. 29–31. But contrast Michael Rogin, "The *Somers* Mutiny and *Billy Budd*: Melville in the Penal Colony," *Criminal Justice History* 1 (1980): 187.

8 Cooper was another novelist fascinated by the *Somers* case, so much so that he edited a full transcript of the proceedings with an analysis of the matter to which I shall refer below. See Cooper, *Review of the Proceedings of the Naval Court Martial in the Case of Alexander Slidell Mackenzie* (New York: Langley, 1844). Cooper's view of Mackenzie's actions, as detailed in the transcript of the trial, is highly critical.

9 See Robert K. Wallace, "*Billy Budd* and the Haymarket Hangings," *American Literature* 47 (1975): 108–13.

10 Shklovski, "Sterne's *Tristram Shandy* and the Theory of the Novel," included in Lemon and Reis, eds., *Russian Formalist Criticism: Four Essays* (Lincoln: University of Nebraska Press, 1965), p. 57.

11 The best-known cinematic recreation of the story is the version directed by Peter Ustinov, with Ustinov as Vere and Terrence Stamp as Billy.

In the libretto for Benjamin Britten's striking opera, the "plot" is virtually reduced to a bald confrontation between Claggart's unambiguous evil and Billy's lyrical innocence, which produces Vere's tragic dilemma. See E. M. Forster and E. Crozier, *Libretto for "Billy Budd"* (1961). Melville's narrative, as we shall see, evokes meanings that cannot be reproduced by other media.

As for literary criticism, whatever we may think of Vere, he is not a "tragic" hero. Critics who limit the plot to the interaction of the three most prominent characters tend to miss the narrative (not tragic) quality that is central to the tale. As we shall see, the story is at least as much about Nelson, the "Handsome Sailor" type, "a certain X," or the narrator himself as it is about Vere.

12 Vere is so described on pages 62 and 96. Like Claggart's, Vere's "exceptional" quality lies in his keen intelligence and complex morality. The narrative also suggests that these two are the only figures "intellectually capable of adequately appreciating the moral phenomenon presented in Billy Budd" (p. 78).

13 Melville specifically mitigates the "goodness" of Billy and the "evil" of Claggart through his use of narrative epithet and detail. Billy is "a sound human creature" (p. 52), not a saint: he is organically (if justifiably) vio-

lent, (see, for example, p. 47), and, on shore leave, as prone to "fun" as the next sailor (see p. 49). He is far more the "barbarian," the Old Testament hero, or the classical pagan than a Christian innocent. As for Claggart, he is a man of advanced intelligence, education, reasonable good looks, and pragmatic diligence (see pp. 64–65). These characterizations hardly make for straightforward allegory.

14   The remark introduces the chapters about Nelson, "bypaths" which contribute (more than many main roads) to the story's meaning.

15   See Richard Chase's excellent analysis of this incident in *Herman Melville: A Critical Study* (New York: Macmillan, 1949), pp. 271–72; and Martin Leonard Pops, *The Melville Archetype* (Kent, Ohio: Kent State University Press, 1970), p. 240.

16   As we shall see, the whole of chapter 20 concerns the skepticism of Vere's fellow officers about his procedural approach to the case.

17   Vere admits the inappropriateness of combining these roles in his famous speech to the court (pp. 109–10). This procedural lapse is analyzed more fully below.

18   Other trial scenes bearing a similar structural importance are legion. See, e.g., act 4 of *The Merchant of Venice*.

19   I have noted a persuasive opposing line of analysis. Perhaps the most influential and representative of the early pro-Vere approaches was E. L. Grant-Watson's "Melville's Testament of Acceptance" *New England Quarterly* 6 (1933): 319–37, answered by Phil Withim, "*Billy Budd*: Testament of Resistance," *Modern Language Quarterly* 20 (1959): 115–27. Analyses of the legal dimension of the tale (that of C. B. Ives excepted; see note 26, below) have generally reflected a pro-Vere stance. The 1970s and early 1980s have seen a marked reversal in both regards, as younger scholars take a fresh look at the uses of authority and law. A leading critic among those inclined to condemn Vere is Kingsley Widmer, *The Ways of Nihilism* (Los Angeles: California State Colleges, 1970).

20   Chase, Simon Lesser, and other Freudians began to see the narrative complexities that rendered Vere an equivocal figure at best.

21   Reich, "The Tragedy of Justice in *Billy Budd*," *Yale Review* 56 (1967): 368.

22   See Cover, pp. 4–6 and 249–52; see also note 4, above.

23   In *Perspective* 5 (1952): 146–52.

24   Melville, *White Jacket* (1850), vol. 5 of *Writings of Herman Melville*, ed. H. Hayford, H. Parker, and G. Tanselle (Evanston, Ill.: Northwestern University Press, 1968–71).

25   Merlin Bowen, *The Long Encounter* (Chicago: University of Chicago Press, 1960), pp. 217–18.

26   C. B. Ives, "*Billy Budd* and the Articles of War," *American Literature* 34 (1962): 31–38; here, p. 32. The Hayford and Sealts edition, published in the same year as the Ives article, also notes a few of Vere's legal errors, but

comes to the remarkable conclusion (when Melville's close knowledge of the law is considered) that "Melville simply had not familiarized himself with the statutes of the period" (p. 176). All the evidence, within and without the text, points to a rigorously well-informed novelist whose use of legal errors is deliberate and meant to reflect upon Vere.

27   See, e.g., p. 34, n. 14, on the custom of "leniency in cases involving the death penalty . . . in the early days of the Articles."

28   Edgar A. Dryden, *Melville's Thematics of Form* (Baltimore: Johns Hopkins University Press, 1968), especially p. 213.

29   The word *innocent* has become a critical epithet for Billy. Actually, the text shows Billy to be a happy-go-lucky, fun-loving sailor, given to the usual adventures while on shore leave and thoroughly unwilling to accept unjust incursions on his well-being (see the Red Whiskers incident, p. 47). I would suggest the adjective *overt*, a term which only becomes synonymous with *naiveté* in an age of undue irony, complexity, and dissemblance.

For an analysis in terms of absolutism versus relativism, see Wendell Glick, "Expediency and Absolute Morality in *Billy Budd*," PMLA 68 (1953): 103–10, which contains a fine perspective on Vere's type of "pragmatism." The Grant-Watson and Withim dialogue treats the conflict in terms of individual versus communal needs; see above, n. 19. And for discussions of good versus evil, see, e.g., Ursula Brumm, "The Figure of Christ in American Literature," *Partisan Review* 24 (1957): 403–13; and R. E. Walters, "Melville's Metaphysics of Evil," *University of Toronto Quarterly* 9 (1940): 170–82.

30   See, e.g., Reich, "Tragedy of Justice," p. 378.

31   Mackenzie was questioned on board about the justification for his summary action in hanging defendants without right of appeal; he, like Vere, went on to receive the blessing of a man he had condemned. Newspaper accounts also distorted the *Somers* situation by falsifying facts and praising the executioners. See Cooper, *Review of the Proceedings*, pp. 205, 206, and 264–65.

32   For a fine, detailed analysis of Melville's lifelong inquiry into the use and abuse of the American Articles of War (including a source guide to Melville's wide reading on the subject), see Herbert Vincent, *The Tailoring of Melville's White-Jacket* (Evanston, Ill.: Northwestern University Press, 1970), pp. 103–06.

33   22 Geo. 2 ch. 33 (1749, repealed 1860). James Snedeker, an authority on the British naval law, reports that "it was ordered that the articles be read openly twice each week"; *A Brief History of Courts Martial* (Annapolis: U.S. Naval Institute, 1954), p. 44.

34   Melville knew British and American naval customs well, not only because of his lifelong fascination with sailors, but also as a result of having served

in 1843 and 1844 on a ship upon which the equivalent American statute was read in full at frequent intervals. See Newton Arvin, *Herman Melville* (New York: Sloane, 1950), p. 72:

> Then, on the first Sunday of every month he would take part with the rest of the crew in the "muster round the capstan"; passing in review before the officers, being inspected by them, and listening—Melville, with angry rebellion in his heart—to a reading of the grim Articles of War.

In *White Jacket*, Melville carefully recites and criticizes specific provisions of the statute governing the American navy (see pp. 292–304). In a historical note to this portion of the story, Melville observes that these Articles "may be found in the second volume of the United States Statutes at Large, under chapter xxxiii" (p. 298). There he refers also to the British Articles enacted "in the twenty-second year of the reign of George the Second." Although less overt, the older Melville was no less knowledgeable.

35 See Snedeker, *A Brief History*, p. 45.

36 See John McArthur, *Principles and Practices of Naval and Military Courts Martial*, 4th ed., vol. 1 (London: Strahan, 1813), pp. 67–68.

37 See section 19 of the Articles, cited in text, below. For a typical American colonial equivalent of this law, see U.S. Continental Congress, 1775, *Rules for the Regulation of the Navy of the United Colonies of North America* (Washington, D.C.: Naval Historical Foundation, 1944).

38 The Articles retained the customary minimum of five, but apparently altered the maximum from the traditional nine to thirteen, occasioning some debate. See *The Parliamentary History of England*, 36 vols. (London: T. C. Hansard, 1806–20); here, 14: 416–17. The higher number seemed easier to achieve than it might appear, for naval custom "obliges every captain who comes in sight of the [court-martial] flag to go on board and take his place in the court" (p. 416). In America, the numbers five and thirteen were the clear tradition; any captain operating under naval law would have known them. See, e.g., *Act for the Better Government of the Navy*, chap. 33, art. 35, 2 Stat. 45, 50 (1800, repealed 1950).

39 Marines were only to serve when a marine was being court-martialed; Vere seems more comfortable in minimizing the numbers of sailors on the court.

40 Articles of War, section 7; see *Parliamentary History of England* 14:411. Apparently, opponents of the Articles felt that "[t]o pretend that the chief commander, by being president, may influence the court to do as he pleases, is contrary to experience." As, presumably, did the proponents of the statute, Melville strongly disagreed; Vere's control—even when he is not speaking—is felt throughout the trial. As sole witness, and as the unrivaled authority figure on the ship, he should surely have withdrawn after offering his testimony, as the law required.

41   In Parliament, opponents of the section's mandatory death penalty spoke
     as follows:

> But when we consider the infirmities inseparable from human nature,
> which abound even in the most upright hearts—the unguarded moments
> of passion, which at times no prudence of circumspection can govern, and
> the numberless unforeseen causes which may suddenly arise amidst the
> fluctuating humours and caprices of mankind, it is devoutly to be wished,
> that on a legislative revision of this article, a discretionary power may be
> vested in a court martial to inflict death, or such other punishment as the
> crime, from the palliating circumstances attending it, shall merit.
>   Indeed this is so essentially requisite towards the administration of
> justice, that the omission of this discretionary power must have proceeded
> from oversight and not from intention; for, it is to be observed, that the
> original article on this subject introduced by the statute 13 Charles II, c.9.
> contains the discretionary alternative alluded to, and is distinguished by
> its conciseness and simplicity. The words are, "none shall presume to
> quarrel with any superior officer upon pain of severe punishment, nor to
> strike any such person upon pain of death, or otherwise as a court martial
> shall find the matter to deserve."

     After a seaman (Admiral Byng) was actually executed under this provision
     (in 1757), the controversy heightened and, according to Snedeker, the
     capital sentence again became discretionary. Snedeker, A Brief History, p.
     47.
42   See McArthur, Principles and Practices, p. 164 (quoting the "New Regula-
     tions and Instructions for the Navy" of 1806); see also Snedeker, A Brief
     History, p. 46.
43   McArthur, Principles and Practices, p. 163.
44   Ives, "Billy Budd and the Articles of War," p. 36, n. 22.
45   Naval Courts and Boards (Annapolis: U.S. Naval Institute, 1917), section
     217. The 1917 handbook is a compilation of the late nineteenth-century
     naval laws with which Melville was familiar.
46   W. E. Birkheimer, Military Government and Martial Law (London: Paul,
     Trench, Trubner, 1914), p. 375. For Melville's knowledge of this meaning
     of "martial law," see Bowen, The Long Encounter, p. 91.
47   Charles Fairman, The Law of Martial Rule (Chicago: Callaghan, 1943), p.
     19.
48   Birkheimer, Military Government and Martial Law, pp. 404, 416.
49   Fairman's summary of British historical situations necessitating the fre-
     quent use of martial law contains no mention of the last decade of the
     eighteenth century; see The Law of Martial Rule, pp. 50–63.
50   The phrase is from a purported preface to the story found in many earlier
     versions of Billy Budd, Sailor. Hayford and Sealts' research indicated that

the preface did not belong in Melville's final version; see their edition, pp. 18–19. Yet the phrase lends insight into the larger meanings of the story we are exploring.

51   F. B. Wiener, *A Practical Manual of Martial Law* (Harrisburg, Pa.: Military Service Publishing Co., 1940), p. 16.

52   See Ives, "*Billy Budd* and the Articles of War," p. 32; and Hayford and Sealts, notes and commentary to their edition of *Billy Budd*, p. 181. The statute controls "every person being in their Majestye's Service in the Army . . . who shall . . . excite, cause or joyne in any mutiny or sedition in the Army"; William Winthrop, *Military Law and Precedents* (Washington, 1896), vol. 2, p. 1446.

53   See Articles, section 2, paragraph 28: "All murders committed by any person in the fleet, shall be punished with death by sentence of a court martial."

CHAPTER 9

1   Cooper, *A Record of the Proceedings*, p. 344.

2   Critics who overly emphasize Billy's "simplicity" appear to disregard Vere's evident respect for his responsible seamanship.

3   As with Melville's other invocations of Nelson, this one is historically accurate. See A. T. Mahan, *The Life of Nelson: The Embodiment of the Sea Power of Great Britain* (Boston: Little, Brown, 1897), vol. 1, pp. 289ff.

4   Recall our discussion of the examining magistrate's approach to such figures as Mitya Karamazov and Meursault.

5   See the Hayford and Sealts edition at pp. 175–76.

6   We learn early that Billy was "by no means of a satirical turn. . . . To deal in double meanings and insinuations of any sort was quite foreign to his nature" (p. 49).

7   For the reader interested in looking further into the notion of considerate communication, a requisite first text is Leo Strauss' brilliant and still controversial *Persecution and the Art of Writing* (Chicago: University of Chicago Press, 1952). Strauss feels that many great writers and philosophers, to avoid persecution of various sorts, masked their "heterodox" sentiments with a kind of coded speech intelligible only to select readers in every generation. Although he is not one of Strauss' examples, Melville surely perceived that great truths were too threatening to be declared overtly. See Melville's description of truth as "a scared white doe" (see epigraph to part 4, above).

8   From *The English Myrror*, 1585, as quoted in Mira Brenner, "Shakespeare and the Elizabethan Concepts of Envy" (Ph.D. diss., Brandeis University, 1968).

9   "Nelson and Vere: Hero and Victim in *Billy Budd, Sailor*," PMLA 82 (1967): 372.

10 Marvell's *Upon Appleton House* refers to the Fairfax offspring who fought in "France, Poland, either Germany" and to General Sir Francis Vere (ll. 241–45 and 36–37). Melville evidently knew the entire poem quite well (see the Hayford and Sealts edition, pp. 152–53).

11 "Melville's Concern with the Arts in *Billy Budd*," *Arizona Quarterly* 28 (1972): 79.

12 With the exception of Vere's tête-à-tête with Billy, no distinction regarding "considerate" communication is made between Melville and the narrator. Their interests merge in the service of the "inside" message of the text. Like Robert Merrill ("The Narrative Voice in *Billy Budd*," *Modern Language Quarterly* 34 [1973]: 283), I thoroughly reject Lawrance Thompson's unsupported earlier claim that the narrator is either unreliable or "stupid" (*Melville's Quarrel with God* [Princeton: Princeton University Press, 1952], p. 377). Edward A. Kearns' formulation of "omniscient ambiguity" offers a more helpful approach to this chapter; see his "Omniscient Ambiguity: The Narrators of *Moby Dick* and *Billy Budd*," *Emerson Society Quarterly* 58 (1970): 117–20.

13 The words "closeted" and "interview" appear on earlier occasions when Billy's well-being is threatened. The first is the "interview" in the ship's "shrouds," in which Billy is offered a bribe (described as "screened," "refined," and "obscured") to mutiny (pp. 81–82); the second is the "closeted" meeting on the "decks below" between Vere, Claggart and Billy (p. 97).

14 *Madame Bovary* is not Emma's "tragedy." It begins with Charles' lengthy history; it ends not with Emma, but again with Charles and, finally, Homais, the male survivor of the piece. As Aristotle himself might well advise, a novel is not a tragedy.

15 Compare the versions of this paragraph in Chase, *Herman Melville*, p. 276; and Turnage, "Melville's Concern with the Arts," p. 81.

16 See Henry F. Pommer, *Milton and Melville* (Pittsburgh: University of Pittsburgh Press, 1970), especially p. 60, on Melville's use of Homer.

17 As Lukacs says of the modern short story, "meaninglessness as meaninglessness becomes form"; *The Theory of the Novel*, trans. Anna Bostock (Cambridge: MIT Press, 1971), p. 51.

18 This is Lawrance Thompson's famous titular phrase. Among the many authors who discuss Melville's conflict with Christianity and his tendency toward pagan, classical, and Jewish modes, see Braswell, *Melville's Religious Thought*; Widmer, *Ways of Nihilism*; Bowen, *Long Encounter*, pp. 128–197.

19 Braswell's observation in 1957 that the "good-hearted Billy Budd and the evil Claggart have inspired relatively little dissent among the critics" still holds true; see his "Melville's *Billy Budd* as an 'Inside Narrative,'" *American Literature* 29 (1957): 138.

20 I include as "pagan" here the many epithets about Billy's barbaric ("an up-

right barbarian," p. 52) and animal ("a young horse fresh from the pasture," p. 84) nature; as "classical," the allusions to his heroic form ("Billy's youth and athletic frame," p. 70) and similarity to epic heroes ("Apollo with his portmanteau," p. 48); and as "Judaic," references to the Old Testament ("Adam . . . ere the urbane serpent wriggled himself into his company," p. 52). "Christian" epithets include the rare New Testament references and such ironic formulations as "the fighting peacemaker" (p. 48) and a "Catholic priest striking peace in an Irish shindy" (p. 47).

21 William H. Shurr, *The Mystery of Iniquity* (Lexington: University Press of Kentucky, 1972), pp. 259–60; Ursula Brumm, "The Figure of Christ in American Literature," *Partisan Review* 24 (1957): 403–13; and Nathalia Wright, "Biblical Allusion in Melville's Prose," *American Literature* 12 (1940): 185–99.

22 Melville's choice as between the Judaic "shekinah" and the classical "rose of dawn" (see Homer, *Iliad* 1:477, 6:175, 11:1) exemplifies his consistently non-Christian approach to Billy's final moments. (See the Hayford and Sealts edition, pp. 191–92.)

23 To my knowledge, the only critic to mention the association of Claggart and Christ, via their initials and the "man of sorrows" epithet, is Martin Leonard Pops, *The Melville Archetype* (Kent, Ohio: Kent State University Press, 1970), p. 241; but he concludes that Claggart is a kind of antichrist who shares some of Billy's qualities. With this conclusion, compare Leslie Fiedler, *Love and Death in the American Novel* (New York: Criterion Press, 1960), p. 435. "Man of sorrows" is an epithet from Isaiah 53, which is adopted in the New Testament to apply to Christ.

The symbol X has stood for Christ's name since at least the time of Constantine and is modern American parlance. The symbol derives from the appearance of the first two letters of the name in Greek, *chi* and *rho*. (See H. Leclerc, *Dictionnaire d'archéologie chrétienne et de liturgie* (Paris: Letougey et Ané, 1913), pp. 1481–1534; *New Catholic Encyclopedia* (New York: McGraw Hill, 1967–79), 4:473–79.)

24 See *Paradise Lost* 7:112–14, and *The Divine Comedy, Paradiso*, canto 33. In his edition, John D. Sinclair observes that, unlike the staggering vision of the Divinity, "the extremes of human degradation are within the competence of imagination and literature."

25 Oddly, this observation seems never to have been made. Hayford and Sealts, for example, observe that "Melville dropped his direct reference to the gospel story, perhaps after his prose elaboration . . . of the encounter between Billy and the chaplain," but they reveal that the "garbled news account" stood for a long time as the final chapter in the work (pp. 5–6).

26 I believe this sense of the captain's name to be more central to the story than its Latin meanings.

27 *Moby Dick*, ed. Harrison Hayford and Hershel Parker (New York: Norton, 1967), p. 542.

Index